Sustainability and Interprofessional Collaboration

Dawn Forman · Marion Jones ·
Jill Thistlethwaite
Editors

Sustainability and Interprofessional Collaboration

Ensuring Leadership Resilience in Collaborative Health Care

palgrave
macmillan

Editors
Dawn Forman
University of Derby
Derby, UK

Marion Jones
Auckland University of Technology
Auckland, New Zealand

Jill Thistlethwaite
University of Technology Sydney
Ultimo, NSW, Australia

ISBN 978-3-030-40280-8 ISBN 978-3-030-40281-5 (eBook)
https://doi.org/10.1007/978-3-030-40281-5

This Palgrave Macmillan imprint is published by the registered company Springer Nature Switzerland AG
The registered company address is: Gewerbestrasse 11, 6330 Cham, Switzerland

Foreword

On Sustainability in Interprofessional Education and Practice (IPEP)

We have long been rather opportunistic consumers of the resources, funding and opportunities available to us; lacking a long-term view, we focus on the next step, the next patient, the next grant and the next cohort of students. The pressures of health care and of academia are such that we often feel we are left with little choice but to do so. On a personal level however, as the editor-in-chief of the international *Journal of Interprofessional Care*, seeing through over a thousand submissions from over 50 countries every year, sustainability is never far from my thoughts.

Sustainability is a challenge for any field, but especially for our own. IPEP is a field often led by local champions, by people who see the opportunity and potential of the collaborative project. We rely on colleagues who are brave enough to put their head above the parapet and skilfully negotiate for a change to the status quo. Inspirational leaders are plenty in our field, but what happens once they move on? How do we avoid sliding back into old habits? How do we maintain, if not accelerate the interprofessional momentum we inherit?

This timely collection of chapters from across the world reflects on these and many more issues, encouraging us to think beyond the present and plan into the future. Plan not for our current clinics, programmes, our students or research groups, but rather plan for the next generation of interprofessional change agents. The honest and personal accounts in this book, skilfully pieced together by the editors, invite us to consider the kind of interprofessional future we want for our colleagues, students and patients—and start planning for this now. The case studies and narratives in this book are unique in their own right, tackling diverse but real issues faced in the process of initiating and maintaining local and international initiatives. Looking at these collectively one thing becomes clear: sustainability does not just happen—it takes energy, careful planning and, of course, leadership.

Structured in four parts, each helps tell a story; a story of good people and wicked problems. Through the words of enthusiasts and visionaries, we follow them on a journey of tenacity, hardship and small victories. In Part I, the combination of contributions from established and new IPEP networks is to be commended. The Centre for the Advancement of Interprofessional Education (CAIPE) in the UK is a prime example of what to do well but its history has not been plain sailing and its future not guaranteed. The African IPE Network (AfrIPEN) is a promising and ambitious endeavour with a mountainous challenge ahead, tasked with building and sustaining developments across a beautiful but very diverse continent. In a world of limited funds for interprofessional research it is encouraging to witness the rebirth of the Interprofessional Research Global Network (IPR.global) and its addition here is notable.

The key drivers in Part II remind to us to consider our own push and pull factors. The international contributions here demonstrate that movements such as IPEP happen within a wider sociocultural and organisational context, having a clear understanding of which allows us to craft a narrative for what drives us forward. The specific examples shared in Part III are for me the heart of this book. Practical applications of IPEP are to be celebrated, and each being unique in the challenges it has faced and overcome, these accounts provide many real-life lessons on actually implementing initiatives on the front line. The range of examples here is rather impressive.

Sustainability is not just about the future but also about the past. And, it is often less about innovation as it is about succession. The last Part (IV) of the book is a clear reminder of this, as it revisits earlier initiatives and gives updates on their development. From Canada to Qatar, Malaysia and South Africa these reflections are evidence of the global reach of the IPEP movement.

The chapters in this collection are inspiring to be sure, but sustainability is not easy to achieve, and it certainly does not just happen. There are plenty of pitfalls and challenges on the path to sustainability, and this book makes a start in helping us understand how to prepare, plan for and overcome these. So, what lessons does the book provide and what does the future of sustainability in IPEP hold? I suspect every reader will focus on different take home messages, influenced by their individual circumstances and the stage they find themselves on their IPEP journey.

This book is both a celebration and a call to action. A timely and strong contribution in the field, the volume offers something for everyone. Whether an IPEP neophyte or a veteran, the stories here will appeal to many.

Andreas Xyrichis
Editor-in-Chief, Journal of
Interprofessional Care
King's College London
London, UK

Acknowledgments

The editors and authors of this book would like to thank their institutions, colleagues, students and clients for their cooperation in the production of this book and their commitment and resilience towards sustaining an interprofessional ethos.

The editors would particularly like to thank Jeanne Clark for her patient editing and administrative assistance, and Sneha Sivakumar for all the guidance through the publishing process.

Praise for *Sustainability and Interprofessional Collaboration*

"This book provides a true international perspective on interprofessional education and practice (IPEP). It makes a timely and important contribution to the field. As an academic and registered Social Worker with a belief in IPEP I feel this book will support students, academics and practitioners to develop a depth of understanding of IPEP as well as the challenges and progressive ways of working."

—Dr. Mohammed Jakhara, *Executive Dean of Faculty—Newman University Birmingham. Prof. Doc. Health and Social Care, MBA, FHEA, PQSW, CQSW, BA (Hons) Applied Social Studies, HCPC Registered*

"As an educator of students and practitioners and as an interprofessional placement coordinator, this book contributes another valuable resource encompassing rural and global perspectives and the strategies necessary to grow interprofessional practice in fieldwork. These authors are IP pioneers with a significant body of published work as evidence of their expertise, but also their professional and clinical experience means they are able to translate theory to practice with authenticity using 'real world' illustrations. I will be recommending this text as the next iteration in their series to students and practitioners alike."

—Keryn Bolte RN/RM, *PG Cert Critical Care, Master of Clinical Education, Student Placement Manager, Going Rural Health Program, Department of Rural Health, Faculty of Medicine, Dental & Health Sciences, The University of Melbourne*

"This book is a concise guide to effective leadership in interprofessional education. It clearly defines the three aspects critical to the success of interprofessional education in interprofessional programmes which are; patient-provider interaction, professional teams in the community and supporting organisations. The book systematically builds a framework for solving the real challenge which is building health systems that are centered around relevance, equity, people, quality and cost-effectiveness."

—Simeon K. Mining, DVM, M.Sc., Ph.D., *Doctor of Medicine (h.c), Professor of Immunology and Director of Research–Moi University, Kenya, additionally senior advisor Moi–Linkoping Universities Thirty Year collaboration*

"In a fast moving international area of research and practice this edited book provides a very timely contribution from many contributors working in several countries, The well chosen chapters are short, readable and all provide an important contribution. The chapters tend to compliment and contrast each other very effectively. Interesting to have the opportunity to have an insight into cross cultural practice.

The book is makes an important contribution and is published at a time as the demand for collaborative practice increases."

—Emeritus Professor Chris Brannigan, *University of Derby*

"In my former role coordinating interprofessional student placements, liaising with multiple stakeholders, and establishing collaborative partnerships in health and education settings, I would have appreciated being able to dip into this book.

The book continues the authors highly valued series on leadership in interprofessional education and collaborative practice, and moves the work along to the next level by introducing sustainability. The timing is perfect. As many of the well-known IPEP initiatives are maturing, the energy to continue could easily be lost. Readers will be inspired by chapters on sustaining leadership, resilience, cultural changes, partnerships and networks, and of course research. The challenges of implementing IPEP are not avoided or sugar coated but sensitively explored, and insights offered with thoughtful consideration and real-world examples. The book provides an opportunity to review what has been accomplished by looking at the drivers and successes of IPEP in previous developments, and an update on these is a welcome addition to the topic of sustainability.

This book will be valuable for all practitioners of IPEP to draw on for support and guidance. The lasting impression on the future of IPEP is optimistic, and that planning for sustainability is both essential and possible."

—Robynne Snell, *AdvAPD, Advanced Accredited Practising Dietitian, Ph.D. Candidate, Curtin University*

"This book will be a valuable asset for all those concerned with the outcomes of interprofessional education and collaborative practice regardless of discipline. It provides key insights from a global conversation about future directions in promoting sustained cultural change for interprofessional collaboration. Real case studies from around the world address a diverse range of issues, faced in planning and maintaining local and international initiatives. There is much to commend in chapters including leadership, interprofessional networks, exemplar educational initiatives, patient partnerships, indigenous health, rural health, and measuring change."

—Chris Roberts | *Associate Professor, Northern Clinical and Sydney Medical School, Faculty of Medicine and Health, The University of Sydney*

"As we strive in the NHS to continuously improve our services and to innovate and transform we need to make time to read and reflect on what others are achieving and how they identify and negotiate challenges and constraints. This book is a shining example of how that time can be very well spent. It is supportive, realistic and grounded. We all face local demands and priorities, the here and now of delivering services in an increasingly complex social, economic and political landscape. We know that the recruitment and retention of colleagues is key to our success and that how we support and develop them is fundamentally important. We also know, to varying degrees, that interprofessional and collaborative working are critically important to achieving this and to serving the needs of those who use our services. What this book skilfully provides is an articulation of some of the universal challenges of an interprofessional approach and some of the creative and dynamic activity being taken to address them.

A key strength of the book is that it is truly international, drawing in experience and expertise from a diverse group of contributors across continents. It is broad in scope, but also focused on detail. The big issues are here: resilience, sustainability and significant cultural change. So too are individual case studies, updates on established projects and reflections on some very practical issues in implementation. I particularly like the openness and the spirit of enquiry that run through these contributions. They will engage and sustain the reader of this very timely and thought-provoking text."

—Professor Sandra Jowett, *Non-executive Director and Senior Independent Director, Pennine Care NHS Foundation Trust, Ashton-under-Lyne, England, UK*

"This is an impressive textbook offering detailed information on the aspect of sustainability of interprofessional education and practice. As such, the textbook advances the knowledge in this field and focuses on a much needed information gap. I thoroughly recommend this book for a number of reasons and relevant chapters it encapsulates. Specifically, I think this textbook is unique in that rather than focusing on one particular geographical area, it offers insights from practices in very various settings such as Sweden, Qatar, Malaysian, Brazil, New Zealand contexts, which helpful for global readers to get a better understanding of the topic. Additionally, the textbook touches base on specific population groups such as indigenous health as well populations living in rural and remote areas. I think this offers practical insights for readers to gain a wider understanding of how to ensure that both interprofessional education and interprofessional practice should be implemented."

—A/Prof. Kreshnik Hoti, *Associate Professor, Faculty of Medicine, Division of Pharmacy, University of Prishtina, Kosova. Head of Pharmacy Practice and Pharmaceutical Care Department*

Contents

Notes on Contributors

Elizabeth Anderson is Professor of Interprofessional Education at the University of Leicester, Medical School. Working in Medical Education she is lead for patient safety and patient involvement for the Faculty of Life Sciences. Elizabeth was awarded a National Teaching Fellowship by the Higher Education Academy for outstanding contributions to education in 2007. She served on the Board for the Disability Partnership, 'The Prince of Wales Advisory Group on Disability' while supporting education on disability awareness. She has also served on the Board for the UK Centre for the Advancement of Interprofessional Education UK (CAIPE) and on the Health Advisory Board for the Higher Education Academy. In 2016 she was awarded a CAIPE Fellowship for her contributions to interprofessional learning. She is widely published in the area of IPL in practice. She has previously worked as a nurse, midwife and health visitor.

Mahisa Arain obtained her Bachelor of Dental Surgery from the University of Birmingham in 2019 and is now a year 1 Foundation Dentist in Derbyshire, UK. From 2016 to her graduation, Mahisa was the Knowledge and Skills Exchange Events Coordinator. In 2018,

Mahisa jointly presented the work of KASE at All Together Better Health IX, international IPE conference in Auckland, New Zealand.

Emily Audet is a Junior Doctor at Shrewsbury and Telford Hospitals NHS Trust, UK. Emily entered medicine having previously obtained a B.Sc. Hons. in Medical Microbiology and Immunology from Newcastle University. As an undergraduate, she co-founded the Knowledge and Skills Exchange IPE society; and was its first President from 2015 to her graduation in 2017. In 2018, Emily won her Trust Foundation Year 1 Doctor of the Year award; and in 2019 the West Midlands Regional Foundation Audit Poster Competition. Emily is Chair of the Patient Voices Programme Advisory Board, which works interprofessionally to bring the patient experience to the forefront of health care improvement.

Mehmuna Ayub obtained her Bachelor of Dental Surgery from the University of Birmingham in 2019 and is now a year 1 Foundation Dentist in Buckinghamshire. From 2017, Mehmuna was the KASE committee lead for volunteering and communications, arranging for KASE members to work with the Birmingham Langar Seva charity in helping the homeless in the city. Mehmuna was also president of the University UN Sustainable Goals Society and an enthusiastic member of the university Taekwando club where she served as social media officer. In 2018, Mehmuna jointly presented the work of KASE at All Together Better Health IX, international IPE conference in Auckland, New Zealand.

Hugh Barr is Emeritus Professor of Interprofessional Education and Honorary Fellow at the University of Westminster. He has held visiting chairs in interprofessional education at various times during the past 25 years at the following universities: Curtin (Australia), Kings College London, Kingston with St George's London, Nottingham, Otago (New Zealand), Suffolk and Tokyo Metropolitan (Japan). Concurrently, he has offered long-standing faculty development in the Nordic countries especially Finland with Oulu University of Applied Sciences. He is President of the UK Centre for the Advancement of Interprofessional Education (CAIPE) and Emeritus Editor for the *Journal of Interprofessional Care.* He served on the WHO study group on interprofessional education and collaborative practice and was the first convenor for the coordinating committee now Interprofessional.Global. He has been awarded honorary doctorates by East Anglia, Southampton and Kingston Universities for his role in promoting interprofessional education nationally and internationally. He was previously an Assistant Director of the then Central Council for Education and Training in Social Work (CCETSW) following social studies at the University of Nottingham and ten years in probation, prison aftercare and criminology.

Sharon Buckley is a UK National Teaching Fellow and Senior Lecturer in Medical Education at the University of Birmingham. A microbiologist by background, Sharon is an experienced educator with a strong record in expanding IPE. She established and now leads the Birmingham IPE steering group, is a Board member for the UK Centre for the Advancement of Interprofessional Education (CAIPE) and Associate Editor (IPE) for the journal *The Clinical Teacher*. Since 2005, Sharon has led four major regional IPE projects, including the 2015 West Midlands Health Care Team Challenge, the first held in England. Since 2015, she has worked with Birmingham students to establish the Knowledge and Skills Exchange IPE Society.

Professor Wanicha Chuenkongkaew qualified in Medicine in 1986. She was appointed as Professor of Ophthalmology at Mahidol University in 2005 and is internationally recognised in her field and widely published and is a member of the Royal College of Ophthalmologists of Thailand. Dr. Wanicha has been Regional Coordinator for AsiaPacific Network on Health Professional Education Reforms (ANHER) since 2011, and a coordinator in organising the annual Prince Mahidol Award International Conference (PMAC) since 2007 aiming at being a global policy forum to discuss and recommend policies and social commitments towards public health development and improvement.

Dr. Wanicha is also secretary on the commission for strategic movement on the development of Health Workforce Education in the twenty-first century and a member of the Technical Working Group on Health Workforce Education Assessment Tools, World Health Organization as well as TWG 2: Transformative education, Global Health Workforce Alliance.

Johanna Dahlberg is a biomedical laboratory scientist, Ph.D. and Senior lecturer in Clinical Chemistry at the Faculty of Medicine and Health Sciences, Linköping University, Sweden. Her research interest started in cellular signalling but has shifted into pedagogical processes in health care and education of health care workers, specifically interprofessional education and practice in simulation-based settings. Johanna has more than 10 years' experience of managing interprofessional education. Over the years, Johanna has been engaged in NIPNET, the regional network of IPECP in the Scandinavian countries and the global confederation for IPECP Interprofessional.Global, which Johanna has been chair of since 2018. Closely related is Johanna's work in the Swedish network of Quality Improvement. Johanna was responsible for introducing quality improvement knowledge in the IPE curriculum at the Faculty of Medicine and Health Sciences in 2011.

Madeleine Abrandt Dahlgren is a Professor in Medical Education at the Faculty of Medical and Health Sciences (FMHS) in Linköping. Her professional background is as a physiotherapist and she holds a Ph.D. in Education. Her research interests include professional learning and pedagogical processes within the socio-material practices of health care and medical education, such as interprofessional learning, simulation-based medical education and patient learning. She has published widely within the field of higher education and professional learning and led the group of faculty members involved in the revision of the existing interprofessional curriculum at the FMHS. She has recently also completed a four-year research project on simulation-based interprofessional education in health care.

Associate Professor Roger Dunston joined the Faculty of Arts and Social Sciences, University of Technology Sydney (UTS) in 2007. He is located as part of the School of Communication and is a member of the International Research Centre for Communication in Healthcare (IRCCH). Roger's research and development interests are diverse—the nature of professional practice, making change and service redesign, 'patient' participation and co-production and professional learning—learning of all kinds. Roger has a long-standing engagement with interprofessional and collaborative practice, education and learning. He has lead a number of large national development and research projects in these areas. The current SIF project being a large scale development form earlier work. Roger has a strong interest in socio-material approaches to making sense of and intervening in the complex world of practice and change.

Prior to joining UTS, Roger worked as a senior health services manager, educator across a range of professions, health policy analyst and organisational consultant. He has over 30 years' experience within the health sector. During the past six years, he has led and/or participated in a number of Australian Research Council, Office for Learning and Teaching, UTS and other government funded studies, primarily in the areas of interprofessional education and learning, handover practices in health, and service redesign in primary health care and child and family health.

Mattias Ekstedt, M.D., Ph.D. is a senior lecturer at the Faculty of Medicine and Health Sciences at Linköping University, and a consultant hepatologist at the University Hospital in Linköping. He has been active at the medical programme for many years with a special interest in student-centred learning and problem-based learning. He is passionate about interprofessional collaboration working clinically in an interprofessional team caring for patients with severe liver disease. In June 2019 he stepped down as head of the interprofessional curriculum at Linköping University after implementing the latest major revision.

Dr. Alla El-Awaisi, MPharm, MRPharmS, M.Sc., PgCert, Ph.D. received her Master of Pharmacy degree from Strathclyde University in Glasgow (UK), and M.Sc. in Prescribing Science and Ph.D. in Interprofessional Education and Collaborative Practice from the Robert Gordon University (UK). She is an experienced academic administrator possessing creativity, innovation and dedication to her field. Prior to her academic career, she was a pharmacist in Scotland for more than nine years. She is the assistant dean for student affairs at Qatar University College of Pharmacy and QU Health chair of the interprofessional education (IPE) committee. Dr. El-Awaisi has led successful IPE initiatives locally and internationally including leading the first Middle Eastern conference in interprofessional education and collaborative practice in December 2015 and is leading the organisation of the tenth All Together Better Health (ATBH) conference to be held in Qatar in 2020. Her research expertise lies in the area of interprofessional education and collaborative practice, patient safety, pharmacy education and pharmacy practice and she has published numerous articles in peer-reviewed journals.

Annika Lindh Falk, Ph.D., MScOT is a senior lecturer at the Faculty of Medicine and Health Sciences at Linköping University. She has been actively engaged in the Occupational Therapy programme for many years as a teacher and has been Programme director at the Occupational Therapy programme (2004–2010). She was the first occupational therapy supervisor at the interprofessional training ward (IPTW) when started 1996 in Linköping and has continuing the work about problem-based learning (PBL) and interprofessional education (IPE) during the years. She was involved in the latest revision of the interprofessional curriculum at Linköping University and since June 2019 she is the head of interprofessional curriculum programme at the Faculty of Medicine and Health Sciences at Linköping University. Her research area is regarding interprofessional education and collaboration in health care.

Brenda Flood, Ph.D. is a senior lecturer at the Auckland University of Technology (AUT), where she is an interprofessional education and practice development leader within the Faculty of Health and Environmental Sciences. Brenda chairs the Interprofessional Steering Committee who have been tasked with the development, implementation and evaluation of an embedded and sustainable interprofessional education pathway across the Faculty and is also the Clinical Manager for AUT Integrated Health. AUT Integrated Health is an interprofessional, health centre where students from a range of professions work collaboratively to provide person/whānau-centred services to the public. Brenda's doctoral research explored health professionals' experiences of interprofessional practice, the insights from which are informing interprofessional education development.

Professor Dawn Forman, Ph.D., MBA, PG Dip Research, PG Dip Executive Coaching, TDCR MDCR over the last thirteen years, has been privileged to have worked as a consultant with universities and health services internationally. Her main areas of work include leadership development, governance, executive coaching, research development and interprofessional education. She has worked on the past five Australia wide interprofessional curriculum renewal projects including the latest which is included in this book, *Securing an Interprofessional Future.*

Dawn is an Associate for the Higher Education Academy and the Leadership Foundation for Higher Education, and a Senior Associate of Ranmore Consulting. Dawn was a Dean the Faculty of Education Health and Sciences at the University of Derby where she now works part of her time as a Professor of Academic Leadership. She is also an Adjunct Professor at Auckland University of Technology (New Zealand) and Curtin University, (Australia). Dawn is widely published, including eight previous books and over 120 peer-reviewed articles, she has been a keynote speaker at numerous national and international conferences.

Aldaísa Cassanho Forster is an Associate Professor at the Department of Social Medicine in the Ribeirão Preto Medical School of the University of São Paulo (FMRP-USP), Brazil. She develops and guides research on Primary health care, health policies and administration and education of health professionals. Aldaísa is the coordinator of the Education Programme for Health Care Work/Interprofessionality (PET-Saúde/Interprofissionalidade) of the University of São Paulo/Ribeirão Preto Campus. She is a doctor with a Ph.D. in preventive medicine and a Postdoctoral in public health.

José Rodrigues Freire Filho is an International Consultant on Interprofessional Education and Collaborative Practice in the Department of Health Systems and Services (HSS) at the Pan American Health Organization/World Health Organization (PAHO/WHO). He is responsible for the implementation of interprofessional education and collaborative practice in health and provides technical assistance to countries in the Region of the Americas, as well as supporting the process of establishing the Regional Network for Interprofessional Education in the Americas (REIP) in 2017. Currently José assists with interprofessional education implementation processes in 19 Latin American and Caribbean countries. His experience incorporates leadership and management of human resources for health policies, as well as strategic activities such as interprofessional education faculty development, researches in this theme, among others. He is a pharmacist with a Ph.D. in interprofessional education.

Professor Sue Fyfe is an epidemiologist, anatomist, speech pathologist and teacher with educational research interests in interprofessional education, collaborative practice and innovative approaches to teaching and learning. She has held senior leadership and management roles at Curtin University as inaugural Dean of Teaching and Learning in the Faculty of Health Sciences, Head of School of Public Health and Professor of Medical Education. She has taught both anatomy and physiology to students in Nursing and was instrumental in developing interprofessional units for all first year degree courses in health sciences. She has published and presented widely on learning innovation and change.

Dr. John H. V. Gilbert has been a seminal leader in the education of health professionals in British Columbia, Canada and internationally. His vision and leadership led to the concept of interprofessional education being developed as a central tenet of collaborative person-centred practice and care.

Dr. John Gilbert is founding Principal and Professor Emeritus, College of Health Disciplines, University of British Columbia, and Founding Director, School of Audiology and Speech Sciences. He is a Senior Scholar, WHO Collaborating Centre on Health Workforce Planning and Research, Dalhousie University; Adjunct Professor, School of Nursing, Dalhousie University. He holds the DR. TMA Pai Endowment Chair in Interprofessional Education and Practice, Manipal Academy of Higher Education, India, and is an Adjunct Professor, University of Technology, Sydney. He is Founding Chair, The Canadian Interprofessional Health Collaborative.

He has been an Adjunct Professor, University of Pittsburgh, and at the National University of Malaysia. He was Co-Chair of the WHO Study Group on Interprofessional Education and Collaborative Practice.

He was elected a Fellow, Canadian Academy of Health Sciences, in 2008. He was awarded the Queen's Diamond Jubilee Medal in April

2012, and in October 2013 received the Outstanding Lifetime Contribution to International Allied Health Development Award from the International Chief Health Professions Officers Organisation.

Dr. Gilbert was appointed a Member of the Order of Canada, Canada's highest civilian award, in July 2011. He received the degree Doctor of Laws, Honoris Causa from Dalhousie University in June 2016. He was the recipient of the Pioneer Award, National Centre for Interprofessional Practice and Education, USA, 2017 for his ground-breaking work in advancing the field of interprofessional practice and education. He was named Foundation Fellow of Green College, UBC in 2018.

William Godolphin is Professor Emeritus in the Department of Pathology and Laboratory Medicine and Co-director of Patient and Community Partnership for Education, Office of UBC Health, previously the Division of Health Care Communication in the College of Health Disciplines at the University of British Columbia, Vancouver, Canada. Dr. Godolphin has been a teacher and researcher for many years, with projects and publications ranging across lipoproteins, breast cancer prognostic factors, clinical laboratory toxicology, laboratory automation & robotics and medical education. For over two decades he has, in collaboration with Angela Towle, developed and studied educational interventions that aim to help health professionals engage patients/clients in informed and shared decision-making. The most promising of these has been bringing the authentic and autonomous voices of patients and community into health professional education.

Mats Hammar is MD and professor emeritus in obstetrics and gynaecology at Linköping University practising at the University hospital of Linköping. His area of research is reproductive medicine, where he has supervised a number of Ph.D. students. Mats was the director of the medical programme between 1992 and 1996. During that time he suggested and took active part in the development and implementation of the interprofessional student ward. Later, as the Dean of the Faculty of Medicine and Health Sciences at Linköping University (2006–2011), he initiated inclusion of Quality Improvement knowledge as an interprofessional learning module. Mats has been co-supervisor of one Ph.D. student researching interprofessional learning and collaborative practice.

He has published a number of papers within education, for instance based on the implementation of the interprofessional student ward.

Christine Hirsch is Senior Lecturer in Clinical Pharmacy and Director of Clinical Learning (MPharm) at the University of Birmingham. Christine's experience as a pharmacist in oncology, neurology and surgery has made her passionate about enabling future health professionals to learn and work interprofessionally. As Deputy Chair of the Birmingham IPE Steering Group, she works to bring the patient and public voice to IPE developments and expand interprofessional clinical skills learning. Since 2015, Christine has worked with Birmingham students to establish the Knowledge and Skills Exchange IPE Society. Her research interests include medicines management in palliative care.

Professor Marion Jones, Ph.D., RGON, M.Ed. (Admin) (Hons), BA, M.Ed. Admin. (Hons) is Dean of the University Graduate Research School at Auckland University of Technology, a director of the National Centre for Interprofessional Education and Collaborative Practice in New Zealand and Professor of Interprofessional Education at the University of Derby in the United Kingdom. A significant focus of her academic career has been the development of postgraduate study. For ten years she provided her expertise as Associate Dean Postgraduate to the Faculty of Health and Environmental Sciences. Her area of research expertise and publication is interprofessional practice and education, postgraduate supervision and perioperative nursing. Her latest publications include co-editing three books, with one in process, on interprofessional leadership, author or co-author of more than 30 journal articles, multiple book chapters and presentations at more than 70 national and international conferences on these topics. Her Ph.D. examined the shaping of interprofessional practice in the context of health reform. Some of her national and international activities include being the Representative for the Australasian Interprofessional Practice and Education Network (AIPPEN) on the Confederation of Interprofessional Education and Collaborative Practice, Member of the Professional Education Committee for the Perioperative College of the New Zealand Nurses Organisation and Member of the New Zealand Deans and Directors of Graduate Research group.

Dr. Hossein Khalili, RN, BScN, MScN, Ph.D. is an internationally recognised scholar, expert and leader in the field of interprofessional education and collaborative practice (IPECP) and serves as the director of the University of Wisconsin Centre of Interprofessional Practice and Education (UW CIPE) at the University of Wisconsin-Madison and an adjunct research professor at Western University. He is the co-founding lead of the Global Network for Interprofessional Education and Collaborative Practice Research (InterprofessionalResearch.Global), serves as a member of the leadership team with the Global Confederation for Interprofessional Education & Collaborative Practice (Interprofessional.Global), and is a board member of the Canadian Interprofessional Health Collaborative (CIHC) and CASN Accreditation Bureau. Dr. Khalili is on the editorial boards of the *Journal of Interprofessional Care*, *Journal of Geriatric Medicine*, and *Journal of Clinical and Nursing Research.*

His primary research focuses on interprofessional education and socialisation, team-based care, patient engagement and partnership and interprofessional simulation.

Cathy Kline is the Research Coordinator, Patient & Community Partnership for Education, University of British Columbia (UBC), Vancouver, Canada. Cathy joined UBC in 2003. She manages research and development initiatives that promote patient and public involvement in health professional education and has helped to build a network of over 150 patient educators and 80 community organisations at UBC. Her work involves collaborations between the university and community to integrate patient expertise and experience into mainstream educational practice. Her research interests are in the outcomes of patient engagement, particularly the impacts on professional identity, health care communication and decision-making. Her background is in qualitative research, programme planning and evaluation. She has a Masters of Arts (Health Education) from Dalhousie University and a Bachelor of Arts (Psychology) from Simon Fraser University.

Darren Lauscher is a patient/advocate from the HIV Community. As a person living with HIV since 1985 I bring to the classroom those many years involved with the health care system and the many years spent engaged within the HIV community. I'd like to acknowledge the role that community has played in my own growth and exposure to learn from many different people from all walks of life, which has ultimately lead to my involvement in the health care classroom. It is important to hear from the 'Patients' not just as story tellers but as holders of knowledge to be learned from. It's about creating that collaborative learning opportunity across the disciplines to facilitate conversation brought about by a patient in the room.

Dr. Loo Jiann Lin is a psychiatrist and the Head of Department of Medical Education, Faculty of Medicine and Health Sciences in Universiti Malaysia Sabah (UMS). He is active in academic teaching, research, clinical practice and community services. He is the founding president of the Young Asia Pacific Psychiatrists Network since 2018, which is a chapter under Pacific Rim College of Psychiatrists. His interest is to improve the mental health literacy, through empowerment of health care professionals and the community. He believes strongly that mental wellness of the community drives the advancement of the society.

Monica Moran is a registered occupational therapist and associate professor of rural health with the Western Australian Centre for Rural Health. She supports the development of rural health workforce through the creation of authentic student learning experiences, the development of support strategies for rural health teams and research and evaluation of integrated team programmes in some of Australia's most remote communities. She holds adjunct professorial appointments at Queensland University of Technology, Central Queensland University and the University of Derby in the United Kingdom. She was a contributor to the WHO Framework for Interprofessional Education and Collaborative Practice (WHO, 2010) and participates in interprofessional research projects at local, national and international levels. She is a member of the nationally funded project team tasked with developing a national governance structure to secure the development and sustainability of interprofessional education and collaborative practice across Australia (SIF project). Over the past 10 years she has been a director of the Health Fusion Team Challenge growing the project from a local event involving one university to an international event involving students and staff across Australia and internationally.

C. Jane Morgan is a Senior Lecturer in the Auckland University of Technology, teaching and researching in the Faculty of Health and Environmental Sciences. Dr. Morgan teaches in both undergraduate and postgraduate health science papers, specifically in the area of interprofessional practice innovation. She also develops and co-facilitates interprofessional learning activities for staff and students across the faculty along with practice-based programmes for students in the final year of their undergraduate study. Dr. Morgan's research focus is on the development, implementation and evaluation of interprofessional education and practice initiatives for developing interprofessional teamwork capability in students, academic and clinical education staff.

Simon Munro joined Tamworth University of Newcastle Department of Rural Health (UONDRH) in 2015. Simon previously held numerous positions in New South Wales (NSW) government and non-government social welfare, education and corrective service sectors working primarily with his own and extended Aboriginal and Torres Strait Islander communities.

Being of Aboriginal heritage (Gomeroi and Anaiwan of North West NSW) paternally, he has brought a collective of cultural, educational and community Aboriginal knowledge which he applies in research practice.

Methodologies for Simon sit soundly in qualitative (critical paradigm) drawing on a background in visual arts, Aboriginal metaphysical ways of knowing and learning as well as the lived experiences of growing up Aboriginal in Australia.

Academically he has attained undergraduate (Visual Arts) and postgraduate (Master Training and Development/Adult Education) awards through University of Newcastle NSW and Griffith University QLD, respectively.

Travis Norton is a registered nurse at the University Hospitals NHS Foundation Trust, Birmingham, having obtained his BNurs from the Birmingham School of Nursing in 2018. He was the Nursing Times Adult Student Nurse of the Year, 2018, an achievement he attributes in part to his contribution to KASE, first as treasurer and, subsequently, as president. Travis has a part-time educational role at the University and plans to combine clinical work with academia, specialising in critical care nursing or infection control. In 2018, Travis jointly presented the work of KASE at All Together Better Health IX, international IPE conference in Auckland, New Zealand.

Professor Maree O'Keefe a Principal Fellow of the Higher Education Academy (UK) is an expert in academic governance and health curriculum development. She is the Deputy Chair of the University of Adelaide Academic Board and Director Curriculum. She continues her clinical practice as a paediatrician and has over 30 years' experience of teaching and major curriculum innovation in health. She has held a number of appointments to national committees and councils as an expert in health profession education and accreditation standards development. Her research interests include interdisciplinary collaboration, interprofessional learning and developing quality clinical experiential learning environments. Professor O'Keefe has won a number of institutional and national grants fellowships and awards for her teaching and health education research. She continues her work to realise a 'whole of system' approach to interprofessional learning including the establishment of a national governance framework to ensure leadership and promotion of interprofessional learning as a central component of all Australian health professional practice.

Carole Orchard is professor emerita in the Arthur Labatt Family School of Nursing and the former Coordinator of Interprofessional Health Education and Research at the University of Western Ontario. Her research focuses on interprofessional patient-centred collaborative practice. Dr. Orchard and her colleagues have developed several measurement instruments: Interprofessional Socialisation and Valuing Scale (ISVS) and the Assessment of Interprofessional Team Collaboration Scale-II (AITCS-II), Interprofessional Collaborative Leadership Scale (ICLS) and Patients with Diabetes Self-Care Ownership Scale (PD-SCOS). She has recently published revisions to the AITCS with a new instrument specifically for assessing collaboration in IP students during group learning. Dr. Orchard co-chaired the Canadian Interprofessional Health Collaborative's IP Competency Working Group who developed the CIHC National IP Competency Framework and an international working group is now working on audit tools to measure the process of collaboration in teams. In 2015 she published a book with colleagues on Interprofessional Client-Centred Collaborative Practice: What does it look like? How can it be achieved? Dr. Orchard has also published articles on the role of nurses within collaborative teams. Her research currently focuses on the role of patients both in their own self-care and in collaborative teams. Her work is frequently cited in the field of IPC.

Richard Pitt is the current Chair of the Centre for the Advancement of Interprofessional Education in the UK (CAIPE, www.caipe.org). An active CAIPE member since 1997 and having served six years as Board member and three years as Vice Chair. As CAIPE Chair Richard engages in promoting interprofessional education and collaborative practice with the UK health and social care regulatory and professional bodies, Higher Education Institutions and National Health Service practice Trusts and educational bodies. Richard previously was Associate Professor and Director of the Centre for Interprofessional Education and Learning at the Faculty of Medicine and Health Sciences, University of Nottingham (UK). Following a varied and distinctive 41 year career expanding both adult and mental health nursing practice and latterly higher education he has had extensive experience in curriculum design and development in undergraduate health and social care programmes. Richard is experienced in: leadership; facilitation of learning; group work; workshops; interprofessional education & learning; collaborative practice; team building and working; interviewing; teaching and managing meetings. He has attended many national and international conferences presenting on IPE and has a number of publications.

Professor Gary D. Rogers is a health professions educational leader, public health researcher and medical doctor with a focus on HIV medicine. He hails from Adelaide, South Australia, where he pioneered the development of interprofessional community-based care for people living with HIV in the 1990s. His Ph.D. research at the University of Adelaide focused on interprofessional Primary Health Care for people of sexual diversity utilising a health inequity framework. Before moving to Queensland, Australia in 2008, he worked for two years for the Secretariat of the Pacific Community, based in Nouméa, New Caledonia, where he coordinated HIV care training and mentorship across 22 Pacific Island countries and territories.

Gary is currently Professor of Medical Education and Deputy Head of School (Learning and Teaching) at the Griffith University School of Medicine, in addition to roles as Programme Lead in Interprofessional and Simulation-Based Learning for the Griffith Health Institute for the Development of Education and Scholarship (Health IDEAS), Chair of the Health Chapter of the Griffith Learning and Teaching Academy and clinical work at Gold Coast University Hospital. He is a former President of the Australian and New Zealand Association for Health Professional Educators (ANZAHPE) and chairs the Association's Fellowship Committee. Gary was a member of the Executive Committee of AMEE, the international association for health professional education, from 2013 to 2019 and currently serves on the association's Fellowship and Faculty Development committees. In 2017, he was recognised as a Principal Fellow of the Higher Education Academy. Gary's educational research focuses particularly on the affective learning associated with the acquisition of professional and interprofessional values among health professional students, as well as the education and professional development of simulated patients.

John Rogers currently serves as an independent consultant and trainer on leadership, adult learning and consensus-based partnership development. With postgraduate qualifications in adult learning, and experience of developing partnerships internationally, he spent eleven years as international training director for Interdev, an organisation dedicated to building consensus-based partnerships between 1992 and 2003. Subsequently, he joined Development Associates International (DAI) as Senor Consultant, where he created curriculum for a number of academic and non-formal workshop programmes, including Servant Leadership, Facilitating Learning, Partnerships, Fundraising and Conflict Management and Transformation. Although now retired, he continues to be involved with DAI and provides training and consultation to a number of other organisations. He lives in Oxford (UK), is married to Kathryn and has two daughters and three grandchildren.

Margot Rykhoff is a faculty member in the University of New Brunswick/Humber College ITAL Collaborative Nursing Programme within the Faculty of Health Sciences and Wellness at Humber. She has 37 years' experience in education and health care. While working within education she has worked several roles as faculty and a coordinator including teaching in the classroom and maintaining her clinical practice working with students in surgical, medicine and rehabilitation settings. She has been involved in a number of IPE initiatives at Humber. Her research interest is in collaborative leadership within health care teams.

Dr. Wendy Diana Shoesmith is an Associate Professor of Psychiatry at Universiti Malaysia Sabah, who has been teaching psychiatry and communication skills to medical and nursing students for the last 12 years, as well as practising clinically. She trained in Cambridge and London before coming to Malaysia. Her research interests are in reducing alcohol related harm, mental health literacy, improving access to psychological interventions and collaborative practice. She is currently completing her Ph.D. in health care systems, conducting an action research project to improve collaboration in the mental health system in Sabah, Malaysia.

Erin Sinclair is a practising Emergency Department Registered Nurse at Guelph General Hospital in Southwestern Ontario, Canada. She obtained her BScN at Memorial University of Newfoundland and Labrador in 2010 and later completed her Master Degree in Nursing Education and Leadership at Western University in 2019. She became involved in research for Collaborative leadership in the winter of 2018 and has since been actively involved in collaborations which explore and expand upon the current knowledge base of said concept. Her research interests include team-based clinical environment education, and interprofessional collaboration and leadership dynamics.

Tony Smith is an Associate Professor and Academic Lead for Research in the University of Newcastle, Department of Rural Health (UONDRH), in Australia. He is radiographer by health profession, with decades of clinical experience in both the public and private health systems. Dr. Smith has also been an academic for many years, teaching medical imaging at undergraduate and postgraduate level. His position with the UONDRH took him inland to Tamworth in New South Wales for ten years before he returned to the coast at Taree on the rural Mid-North Coast. Dr. Smith's research interests are in rural allied health workforce and interprofessional education and collaborative practice. He has had a long-term interest in educating and supporting rural doctors and nurses who perform limited-licence radiography in rural and remote locations where no radiographers are available.

Stefanus Snyman is an occupational medicine practitioner and health professions educationist. He is a research associate at the Centre for Community Technologies at Nelson Mandela University (South Africa) and project manager of the WHO-FIC Collaborating Centre for the Africa Region. He also serves as facilitator of the International ICan-Function (*m*ICF) Partnership: an initiative to develop a state-of-the-art mobile solution to facilitate interprofessional collaborative practice. He is member of the Advisory Board of the Journal of Interprofessional Care and of Interprofessional.Global's Facilitation Team. He also served as the first partnership facilitator of the Africa Interprofessional Education Network (AfrIPEN). He lives in Cape Town (South Africa), is married to Helena and has a son and daughter in primary school.

Carole Steketee is the Director of the National Learning and Teaching Office at the University of Notre Dame Australia, as well as the Associate Head of the Fremantle campus. As Office Director she provides strategic leadership for and oversees the implementation of many of the academic priority areas for the University. She is also Chair of the Academic Council. Between 2007 and 2015, Carole was the Associate Dean Teaching and Learning in the School of Medicine Fremantle where she was Director of the Medical Education Support Unit. Carole has participated in a number of national Office Learning and Teaching (OLT)-funded projects, including Curriculum Renewal Studies in Interprofessional Health Education.

Professor Jill Thistlethwaite, B.Sc., MBBS, Ph.D., MMEd, FRCGP, FRACGP, DRCOG is an adjunct professor in the Faculty of Health at the University of Technology Sydney (UTS), clinical chair of the hospital non-specialist programme at HETI (Health Education and Training Institute) in New South Wales, Australia, a general practitioner and a health professional education consultant. In 2014 she spent four months at the National Center for Interprofessional Practice and Education in Minneapolis, USA, as a Fulbright senior scholar. She has written and edited many books and book chapters, particularly on medical education, professionalism and interprofessional education, and published over 90 peer-reviewed papers. Jill is the editor-in-chief of *The Clinical Teacher* and an associate editor of the *Journal of Interprofessional Care*, and has been an invited keynote speaker and workshop facilitator at conferences and institutions around the globe.

Angela Towle is Co-director of Patient and Community Partnership for Education (PCPE) in the Office of UBC Health at the University of British Columbia (UBC), Vancouver, Canada. PCPE has a research and development focus on patient involvement in health care decision-making and in health professional education. It has developed, implemented and evaluated innovative educational programmes that involve patients and community members as educators for health professional students. Angela's commitment to university-community engagement led to her appointment in 2013 as Academic Director of the UBC Learning Exchange with a responsibility to strengthen engagement between the university and Vancouver's inner city (Downtown Eastside) communities. Angela is also an Associate Professor in the Department of Medicine and Senior Scholar in the Centre for Health Education Scholarship at UBC.

Kalyaani Vickneswaran is a Year 1 Foundation Doctor at the Royal Wolverhampton NHS Trust (is it a Foundation Trust?), having obtained her MBChB from the University of Birmingham in July 2019. Her ambition is to specialise in care of the elderly, a field that Kalyaani recognises requires a high standard of collaboration and she is committed to furthering interprofessional learning and working in the clinical context. As committee secretary, Kalyaani was instrumental in integrating the Knowledge and Skills Exchange into the University Student Guild. In

2018, Kalyaani was awarded a Centre for the Advancement of Interprofessional Education (CAIPE) travel award to present her work with KASE at All Together Better Health IX international IPE conference.

Professor Denise Wilson (Ngāti Tahinga, Tainui) is a Co-Director of Taupua Waiora Centre for Māori Health Research, and the Associate Dean Māori Advancement at the Auckland University of Technology University. Denise is a registered nurse undertakes research and publication activities focusing on Māori/indigenous health and health service engagement, family violence, cultural responsiveness and nursing and health workforce development. She has chaired the Family Violence Prevention Investment Advisory Board (Ministry of Social Development), and is a member of the MSD's Family Violence Prevention Expert Advisory Group, the Ministry of Justice's Integrated Safety Response Research and Evaluation Expert Advisory Group, HQSC's Roopū Māori, and the Chair of the Mortality Review Committee's Māori Caucus. Denise served six years on the Family Violence Death Review Committee and contributed to the development of the Ministry of Health's Violence Intervention Programme. Denise is a co-author of The People's Report and The People's Blueprint for the Glenn Inquiry into child abuse and domestic violence. She was appointed to the Advisory Council for the Center for Indigenous Nursing Research for Health Equity (INRHE) at Florida State University, and she holds a visiting professor position with Oxford Brookes University in the UK and has other international collaborations.

List of Figures

List of Tables

Part I

An Introduction to This Book and an Overview of the Situation

1

Developing and Maintaining Leadership, Resilience and Sustainability in Interprofessional Collaboration

Dawn Forman

Introduction

Interprofessional collaboration has grown significantly in health care organisations, becoming a critical part of the way in which health and social care is delivered. It is now seen as an essential part of effective health care delivery. Health professionals can be assigned to designated teams due to the increasing complexity of health care delivery, or more commonly a number of professionals with different expertise work together in collaborations which can be configured over some distance (Thistlethwaite, Dunston, & Yassine, 2019).

Since our last book we have also seen a growth in the amount of interprofessional research taking place (M. A. Girard, 2019; Wooding, Gale, & Maynard, 2019).

In spite of the growth in research and the increase in interprofessional education, practice and collaboration internationally, there seems to be

D. Forman (✉)
University of Derby, Derby, UK
e-mail: dawn@ilmd.biz

D. Forman et al. (eds.), *Sustainability and Interprofessional Collaboration*,
https://doi.org/10.1007/978-3-030-40281-5_1

a difficultly both in sustaining good practice when there is a change in leadership and ensuring both individual practitioners (Dunston et al., 2018) and interprofessional teams have the resilience to cope with education and health care changes (McCann et al., 2013).

This chapter proves a taster for these terms and introduces the key themes of this book.

Sustainability

To ensure the sustained development of interprofessional skills and thereby the continuity of effective health care teams we need to ensure the philosophy, policies and procedures are so embedded that these will exist, continue and develop even if there is a change of leadership. In research in this area Micklan and Rodger (2005) undertook a study involving 202 health care professionals; participants identified leadership as the most significant factor in maintaining interprofessional teamwork effectiveness. Sharing leadership functions was critical to the teams' performance.

Leadership commitment is therefore not only necessary from the top but from the team itself. For example if one professional is absent in a multidisciplinary team, a key leadership role would be to ensure resources are in place to provide the professional specific support required. In practice this may need political knowledge and strategies to fight for resources and lobby key players in economically tough times.

But, what happens when the top leader changes and the new leader does not see interprofessional collaboration as a priority? To ensure the sustainability of interprofessional collaboration we need to ensure the policies and procedures are reinforced with regulations and good governance systems.

M. A. Girard (2019) following research into regulations in interprofessional collaboration concluded that to strengthen interprofessional collaboration, there must be more socio-legal research to properly address and inform policymakers.

As you will read (Chapter 8) one of the countries leading in creating a sustainable governance system is Australia where the recent research undertaken there aimed to:

> Implement an innovative, consensus-based and sustainable approach to the governance and further development of interprofessional education across Australian health professional education. (Dunston et al. 2019)

Resilience

Until this book the only article that seems to address resilience in health professionals was a review of the resilience literature by McAllister and McKinnon (2009). They confirm that resilience in the health professions involves a combination of individual and contextual factors. They make three recommendations for building resilience in health professionals:

1. that the concept of resilience is introduced in all training programmes—including both individual and team resilience
2. that practitioners are given opportunities to reflect and learn from experience and other practitioners and
3. that experienced health professionals share lessons from experiences and encourage mentoring, leading, coaching and motivating others.

Earlier research seemed to indicate that team resilience also correlated positively with team optimism and satisfaction (Delarue, Van Hootegem, Procter, & Burridge, 2008; Tugade & Fredrickson, 2004) suggest resilience is the ability to bounce back from negative emotional experiences, and flexible adaptation to the changing demands of stressful experiences.

We have taken the term resilience to mean the intrinsic ability of a health care system to adjust its functioning prior to, during, or following changes and disturbances so that it can sustain required operations, even after a major mishap or in the presence of continuous stress (Nemeth, Nunnally, & O'Connor, 2007), and there are many examples in this book of how interprofessional resilience is being developed and sustained.

The terms 'resilience' and 'sustainability' therefore seem to go together; as Meads, Jones, Harrison, Forman, and Turner (2009) found in their research 10 aspects are necessary for sustainable change:

1. Individual policies and projects
2. New organisational relationships and structures
3. Regulatory requirements
4. Multidisciplinary (interprofessional) research agendas
5. Initiatives to promote participation
6. Financial reforms
7. New operational procedures
8. Professional bodies
9. Skills mix and skills substitution
10. Personal leadership.

Many of these themes will be found recurring in this book along with examples as to how different organisations have developed resilient and sustainable interprofessional collaboration.

How to Use This Book

As with our previous books we hope this guide will help you dip in and out of the book and find what you are looking for within easy reach. We have separated the book into five parts.

Part 1—An Introduction to This Book and an Overview of the Situation

In addition to this chapter there is an overview of the interprofessional situation internationally by the esteemed Professor John Gilbert.

Part 2—Interprofessional Centres and Networks

This section will outline their experiences (some over many years) of how they have tried to bring together those involved in interprofessional education practice and research. The aim of these groups is usually to share good practice, but this demands a huge commitment on the part of the organisers and often this is difficult to sustain.

Part 3—Key Drivers

Different policies, practices, community needs, changes in funding or leadership, often impact on the development and sustainability of interprofessional practice and collaborative care. This section will outline the experiences of different organisations in different countries.

Part 4—Specific Examples

This section provides an array of different examples of practice in different countries. Each outlines how they have developed, and sustained their practice, the difficulties they have experienced and the resilience they have developed.

Part 5—Updates on Previous Developments

As readers will be aware this is the fourth book which we have edited and we thought our regular readers may like an update on some of the developments which have taken place since colleagues outlined their experiences in previous books.

Table 1.1 Useful definitions

Term	Definition or Interpretation
Adaptive leadership	This is a practical leadership framework that helps individuals and organisations adapt and thrive in challenging environments. It is being able, both individually and collectively, to take on the gradual but meaningful process of change
Canadian Interprofessional Health Collaborative's Interprofessional Collaborative Competency Framework (CIHC)	In 2010 CIHC identified collaborative leadership as a competency domain for health providers who share the leader role as collaborators within their teams. Collaborative leadership is described as: 'learners/practitioners work[ing] together with all participants including patients/clients/families, to formulate, implementation and evaluate care/services to enhance health outcomes' (CIHC, 2010, p. 15)
*Collaboration	This is an active and ongoing partnership, often involving people from diverse backgrounds who work together to solve problems or provide services
*Collaborative patient-centred practice	This is a type of arrangement designed to promote the participation of patients and their families within a context of collaborative practice
Collaborative/shared leadership	Collaborative leadership is an influence relationship, which engenders safety, trust and commitment among leaders and their partners who intend to make substantive or transforming change that reflects their mutual purpose, shared vision and common goals

Term	Definition or Interpretation
Communication	This 'is the activity of conveying information through the exchange of thoughts, messages, or information, as by speech, visuals, signals, writing, or behaviour. It is the meaningful exchange of information between two or a group of persons'
Community engagement	This is the process of working collaboratively with and through groups of people
Community immersion (or field practicum) programmes	These are embedded in the pre-licensure curricula of many of the health professional disciplines. Students, usually in their final year, are required to immerse in communities to practise the skills they have acquired under the supervision of discipline-specific university faculty preceptors
Competency and capability	Bainbridge, Nasmith, Orchard, and Wood (2010) define competency as 'identify specific knowledge, skills, attitudes, values and judgments that are dynamic, developmental and evolutionary'
*Continuing education	This encompasses all learning (e.g. formal, informal, workplace, serendipitous) that enhances understanding and improves patient care
*Continuing professional development (CPD)	This is the process of working collaboratively with and through groups of people

(continued)

Table 1.1 (continued)

Term	Definition or Interpretation
Culture	The main definition of culture we use in this book is: 'Culture is all aspects of life, the totality of meanings, ideas and beliefs shared by individuals within a group of people. Culture is learned, it includes language, values, norms, customs. Art has played a central, integral role in most cultures' (www.design.iastate.edu/NAB/about/thinkingskills/cultural_context/cultural.html)
Distributed leadership	Distributed leadership is primarily concerned with mobilising leadership at all levels in the organisation, not just relying on leadership from the top. It is about engaging the many rather than the few in leadership activity and actively distributing leadership practice. The emphasis here is about leadership practice and not leadership functions. 'A distributed model of leadership, is one premised upon the interactions between many leaders rather than the actions of an individual leader' Harris and Spillane (2008)
Effective inter-professional education	According to Reeves et al. (2011), 'the effectiveness of IPE interventions *compared* to *education interventions* in which the *same health* and *social care professionals learn separately* from *one another*; and to *assess* the *effectiveness* of *IPE interventions*'
*Entrustable professional activities	This is a concept that allows faculty to make competency-based decisions on the level of supervision required by trainees

Term	Definition or Interpretation
*Ethnography	This approach entails studying the nature of social interactions, behaviours, and perceptions that occur within teams, organisations, networks and communities. The central aim of ethnography is to provide rich, holistic insights into people's views and actions, as well as the nature of the location they inhabit, through the collection of detailed observations and interviews
*Evaluation	This refers to the systematic gathering and interpretation of evidence enabling judgment of effectiveness and value and promoting improvement. Evaluations can have either formative or summative elements or both
Interdisciplinary approach (IDA)	Frequently used synonymously with interprofessional education; that is, it occurs when 'students from two or more professions learn with, from and about each other' (CAIPE, 2002). It is also used to mean different disciplines within the same profession, for example surgery, paediatrics, gynaecology and so on
*Interprofessional collaboration (IPC)	This is a type of interprofessional work involving various health and social care professionals who come together regularly to solve problems or provide services

(continued)

Table 1.1 (continued)

Term	Definition or Interpretation
Interprofessional competencies in health care	This is the integrated enactment of knowledge, skills and values/attitudes that define working together across the professions, with other health care workers and with patients, along with families and communities, as appropriate to improve health outcomes in specific care contexts
Interprofessional competency domain	A generally identified cluster of more specific interprofessional competencies that are conceptually linked, and serve as theoretical constructs (Cate & Scheele, 2007). 'Interprofessional Education occurs when two or more professions learn with, from and about each other to improve collaboration and the quality of care' (CAIPE, 2002)
Interprofessional education (IPE)	When students from two or more professions learn about, from and with each other to enable effective collaboration and improve health outcomes (WHO, 2010)
Interprofessional Global	As a consensus-based partnership, it functioned as the World Coordinating Committee (WCC) at All Together Better Health
*Interprofessional learning (IPL)	This is learning arising from interaction involving members or students of two or more professions. It may be a product of *interprofessional education*, or it may occur spontaneously in the workplace or in education settings and therefore be serendipitous

Term	Definition or Interpretation
*Interprofessional practice (IPP)	'Occurs when all members of the health service delivery team participate in the team's activities and rely on one another to accomplish common goals and improve health care delivery, thus improving patients' quality experience' (Australasian Interprofessional Practice and Education Network)
Interprofessional practice and collaboration (IPCP)	Two or more professions working together as a team with a common purpose, commitment and mutual respect (Freeth, Hammick, Reeves, Koppel, & Barr 2005, pp. xiv–xv)
Interprofessional team-based care	Care delivered by intentionally created, usually relatively small work groups in health care, who are recognised by others as well as by themselves as having a collective identity and shared responsibility for a patient or group of patients; for example, rapid response teams, palliative care teams, primary care teams, operating room teams

(continued)

Table 1.1 (continued)

Term	Definition or Interpretation
Interprofessional teams	A group of people from different professional backgrounds who work together to deliver services and coordinate care programmes across agencies throughout the patient pathway; goals are set collaboratively through consensual decision-making to improve practice for patient safety, which results in individualised care plans/quality services delivered by one or more team members, thereby maximising the value of shared expertise and minimising the barriers of professional autonomy
*Interprofessional teamwork	This is a type of work involving different health or social care professionals who share a team identity and work together closely in an integrated and interdependent manner to solve problems and deliver services
Interprofessionality	The development of a cohesive practice between professionals from different disciplines. It is the process by which professionals reflect on and develop ways of practising that provides an integrated and cohesive answer to the needs of the client/family population (D'Amour & Oandasan, 2005, p. 9)
Integrated care	Leutz (1999) defines integrated care as: 'The search to connect the healthcare system (acute, primary medical and skilled) with other human service systems (e.g. long-term care, education and vocational and housing services) to improve outcomes (clinical, satisfaction and efficiency)'

Term	Definition or Interpretation
Knowledge translation	This is the process of putting knowledge into practice (Straus, Tetroe, & Graham, 2009)
Leadership	This is the act of stimulating, engaging and satisfying the motives of followers that result in the followers taking a course of action towards a mutually shared vision
*One Health	This recognises that the health of humans, animals and ecosystems is interconnected
Patient focused care	This is the provision of care that is respectful of and responsive to individual patient preferences, needs, and values, and ensures that patient values guide all clinical decisions
Patient safety	'Freedom from accidental injury; ensuring patient safety involves the establishment of operational systems and processes that minimise the likelihood of errors and maximise the likelihood of intercepting them when they occur' (Kohn, Corrigan, & Donaldson, 1999)
*Profession	This refers to an occupation or career that requires considerable training and specialised study
Professional competences in health care	This is the integrated enactment of knowledge, skills, and values/attitudes that define the domains of work of a particular health profession applied in specific care contexts

(continued)

Table 1.1 (continued)

Term	Definition or Interpretation
*Quality improvement	This is defined by Batalden and Davidoff (2007, p. 2) as 'the combined and unceasing efforts of everyone – healthcare professionals, patients and their families, researchers, payers, planners and educators – to make the changes that will lead to better patient outcomes (health), better system performance (care) and better professional development'
Resilience	Resilience is described by Nemeth et al. (2007) as the intrinsic ability of a health care system to adjust its functioning prior continuous stress
*Realist evaluation	This is a method developed by Pawson and Tilley (1997) for analysing the social context in which an intervention does or does not achieve its intended outcome
*Team-based care	This is an approach to health care whereby a group of people work together to accomplish a common goal, solve a problem, or achieve a specified result
Vales-based leadership	Values-based leadership is a construct which proposes that leaders draw on their own and followers' values for direction and motivation; it asserts that people are mostly motivated by values and live according to these beliefs (Barrett, 2006)
Workplace learning	This is different from formal educational activities, and can be viewed as untapped opportunities for learning and change that are part of everyday practice and often go unrecognised as 'learning'

Notes *Cited in Institute of Medicine (2015) *Measuring the impact of interprofessional education on collaborative practice and patient outcomes.* Washington

Table 1.2 Further reading on the interprofessional, leadership sustainability and resilience

Key leadership aspect	Further reading on this leadership topic
Change management	Atter (2008) Bushe and Marshak (2014) Halvorson and Chinnes (2007) Rubin and Stone (2010)
Collaborative leadership and shared decision-making	Atter (2008) Endacott et al. (2008) Halvorson and Chinnes (2007) Kenny, Richard, Ceniceros, and Blaize (2010) Newton, Wood, and Nasmith (2012) Reeves, MacMillan, and Van Soeren (2010) Stapleton (1998) Willumsen (2006)
Communication	Atter (2008) Endacott et al. (2008) Kenny et al. (2010) Sasnett and Clay (2008) Schippers, Den Hartog, Koopman, and van Knippenberg (2008) Sinek (2010) Willumsen (2006) Wylie and Gallagher (2009)
Competency	Newton et al. (2012) Thistlethwaite et al. (2014)
Emotional intelligence	Harrison and Fopma-Lou (2010) MacDonald, Bally, Ferguson, Murray, and Fowler-Kerry (2012) Sasnett and Clay (2008) Schippers et al. (2008) Stapleton (1998)
Empowering	Sasnett and Clay (2008) Willumsen (2006)

(continued)

Table 1.2 (continued)

Key leadership aspect	Further reading on this leadership topic
Empowering leadership/transformational leadership	Abbott (2007)
	Atter (2008)
	Endacott et al. (2008)
	Metzger, Alexander, and Weiner (2005)
	Nielsen, Yarker, Randall, and Munir (2009)
	O'Brien, Martin, Heyworth, and Meyer (2008)
	Pollard, Ross, and Means (2005)
	Rubin and Stone (2010)
	Schippers et al. (2008)
	Willumsen (2006)
	Wylie and Gallagher (2009)
Evaluation	Thistlethwaite, Kumar, Moran, Saunders, and Carr (2015)
Interprofessional governance	Dunston et al. (2019)
Integrated care	Barr (2012)
	Gaboury, Lapierre, Boon, and Moher (2011)
	Leutz (1999)
	Valentijn, Schepman, Opheij, and Bruijnzeels (2012)
Mentoring and coaching	Forman, Joyce, and McMahon (2013)
	Nielsen et al. (2009)
	O'Brien et al. (2008)
Professional identity	Reeves et al. (2010)
	Willumsen (2006)
Servant-leadership	Neill, Hayward, and Peterson (2007)
	Neill and Saunders (2008)
	Willumsen (2006)
Sustainability and resilience	Endacott et al. (2008)
	Hoffman, Rosenfield, Gilbert, and Oandasan (2008)
	Harrison and Fopma-Lou (2010)
	Meads et al. (2009)
	Sasnett and Clay (2008)
	Stapleton (1998)
	Tugade and Fredrickson (2004)

Key leadership aspect	Further reading on this leadership topic
Team working	Atter (2008) Hoffman et al. (2008) O'Brien et al. (2008) Sasnett and Clay (2008) Willumsen (2006)
Transformational leadership	Bevan and Fairman (2014) Reeves, Lewin, Espin, and Zwarenstein (2013)

Reading and Using Our Book

In addition to the section outlines, as with our previous books we provide here a list of what we hope are useful definitions of the terms we use and a list of further reading in this area (Tables 1.1 and 1.2).

References

Abbott, S. (2007). Leadership across boundaries: A qualitative study of the nurse consultant role in English primary care. *Journal of Nursing Management, 15*(7), 703–710.

Atter, L. (2008). Using creative transformational leadership in shaping our hospice's journey to excellence. *Practice Development in Health Care, 7*(3), 134–142.

Bainbridge, L., Nasmith, L., Orchard, C., & Wood, V. (2010). Competencies for interprofessional collaboration. *Journal of Physiotherapy Education, 24*(1), 1–11.

Barr, H. (2012). Integrated and interprofessional care. *International Journal of Integrated Care, 12,* 1–4.

Barrett, R. (2006). *Building a values-driven organization.* Amsterdam: Butterworth-Heinemann.

Batalden, P. B., & Davidoff, F. (2007). What is "quality improvement" and how can it transform healthcare? *Quality and Safety in Health Care, 16,* 2–3.

Bevan, H., & Fairman, S. (2014). *The new era of thinking and practice in change and transformation: A call to action for leaders of health and care.* NHS Improving Quality. http://media.nhsiq.nhs.uk/whitepaper/index.html.

Bushe, G. R., & Marshak, R. J. (2014). The dialogic mindset in organisation development. *Research in Organisational Change and Development, 22,* 55–97.

CAIPE. (2002). *Interprofessional education—Today, yesterday and tomorrow (Barr, H.) higher education academy, learning & teaching support network for health sciences & practice* (Occasional Paper 1).

Cate, O., & Scheele, F. (2007). Competency-based postgraduate training: Can we bridge the gap between theory and clinical practice? *Academic Medicine, 82*, 542–547. https://doi.org/10.1097/ACM.0b013e31805559c7.

CIHC. (2010). *National Interprofessional competency framework.* Vancouver, BC: CIHC. www.cihc.ca.

D'Amour, D., & Oandasan, I. (2005). Interprofessionality as the field of interprofessional practice and interprofessional education: An emerging concept. *Journal of Interprofessional Care, 19,* 8–20. https://doi.org/10.1080/13561820500081604.

Delarue, A., Van Hootegem, G., Procter, S., & Burridge, M. (2008). Teamworking and organizational performance: A review of survey-based research. *International Journal of Management Reviews, 10,* 127–148. https://doi.org/10.1111/j.1468-2370.2007.00227.x.

Dunston, R., Canny, B., Fisher, A., Forman, D., Moran, M., Oates, M., … Steketee, C. (2019). *Securing an interprofessional future for Australian health professional education and practice.* Australian Government Department of Education.

Dunston, R., Canny, B., Fisher, A., Steketee, C., Forman, D., Rogers, G. D., … Yassine, T. (2018). *Securing an interprofessional future: Establishing an Australian interprofessional education governance and development framework—A compelling case.* Information brochure. Canberra: Australian Government Department of Education and Training.

Endacott, R., Boulanger, C., Chamberlain, W., Hendry, J., Ryan, H., & Chaboyer, W. (2008). Stability in shifting sands: Contemporary leadership roles in critical care. *Journal of Nursing Management, 16*(7), 837–845.

Forman, D., Joyce, M., & McMahon, G. (2013). *Creating a coaching culture for managers in your organisation.* Abingdon: Routledge.

Freeth, D., Hammick, M., Reeves, S., Koppel, I., & Barr, H. (2005). *Effective interprofessional education: Development, delivery and evaluation.* Oxford: Blackwell.

Gaboury, I., Lapierre, L. M., Boon, H., & Moher, D. (2011). Interprofessional collaboration within integrative healthcare clinics through the lens of the relationship-centred care model. *Journal of Interprofessional Care, 25,* 124–130.

Girard, M. A. (2019). Interprofessional collaborative practice and law: A reflective analysis of 14 regulation structures. *The Journal of Research in Interprofessional Practice and Educations, 9*(2), 1–12.

Halvorson, C. K., & Chinnes, L. F. (2007). Collaborative leadership in product evaluation. *AORN Journal, 85*(2), 334–352.

Harris, A., & Spillane, J. (2008). Distributed leadership through the looking glass. *Management in Education, 22,* 31–34. https://doi.org/10.1177/0892020607085623.

Harrison, P. A., & Fopma-Lou, J. L. (2010). Reflective journal prompts: A vehicle for stimulating emotional competence in nursing. *Journal of Nursing Education, 49*(11), 644–652.

Hoffman, S. J., Rosenfield, D., Gilbert, J. H. V., & Oandasan, I. F. (2008). Student leadership in interprofessional education; benefits, challenges and implications for educators, researchers and policymakers. *Medical Education, 42*(7), 654–661.

Kenny, D. J., Richard, M. L., Ceniceros, X., & Blaize, K. (2010). Collaborating across services to advance evidence-based nursing practice. *Nursing Research, 59*(18), S11–S21.

Kohn, L. T., Corrigan, J. M., & Donaldson, M. S. (1999). *To err is human: Building a safer heath system.* Washington, DC: National Academy Press.

Leutz, W. N. (1999). Five laws for integrating medical and social services: Lessons from the United States and the United Kingdom. *Milbank Quarterly, 77*(1), 77–110.

MacDonald, M. B., Bally, J. M., Ferguson, L. M., Murray, L. B., & Fowler-Kerry, S. E. (2012). Knowledge of the professional role of others: A key interprofessional competency. *Nurse Education in Practice, 10*(4), 238–242.

McAllister, M., & McKinnon, J. (2009). The importance of teaching and learning resilience in the health disciplines: A critical review of the literature. *Nurse Education Today, 29,* 371–379.

McCann, C. M., Beddoe, E., McCormick, K., Huggard, P., Kedge, S., Adamson, C., & Huggard, J. (2013). Resilience in the health professions: A review of recent literature. *International Journal of Wellbeing, 3*(1), 60–81. https://doi.org/10.5502/ijw.v3i1.4.

Meads, G., Jones, I., Harrison, R., Forman, D., & Turner, W. (2009). How to sustain interprofessional learning and practice: Messages for higher education and health and social care management. *Journal of Education and Work, 22*(1), 67–79.

Metzger, M., Alexander, J. A., & Weiner, B. (2005). The effects of leadership and governance processes on member participation in community health coalitions. *Health Education and Behaviour, 32*(4), 455–472.

Micklan, S. M., & Rodger, S. A. (2005). Effective health care teams: A model of six characteristics developed from shared perceptions. *Journal of Interprofessional Care, 19*(4), 358–370.

Neill, M. W., Hayward, K. S., & Peterson, T. (2007). Students' perceptions of the interprofessional team in practice through the application of servant leadership principles. *Journal of Interprofessional Care, 21*(4), 425–432.

Neill, M. W., & Saunders, N. S. (2008). Servant leadership: Enhancing quality of care and staff satisfaction. *The Journal of Nursing Administration, 18*(9), 395–400.

Nemeth, C., Nunnally, M., & O'Connor, M. (2007). Regularly irregular: How groups reconcile cross-cutting agendas in healthcare. *Cognition, Technology & Work, 9,* 139–148.

Newton, C., Wood, V., & Nasmith, L. (2012). Building capacity for interprofessional practice. *The Clinical Teacher, 9*(2), 94–98.

Nielsen, K., Yarker, J., Randall, R., & Munir, F. (2009). The mediating effects of team and self-efficacy on the relationship between transformational leadership, and job satisfaction and psychological well-being in healthcare professionals: a cross-sectional survey. *International Journal of Nursing Studies, 46*(9), 1236–1244.

O'Brien, J. L., Martin, D., Heyworth, J., & Meyer, N. R. (2008). Negotiating transformational leadership: A key to effective collaboration. *Nursing and Health Sciences, 10,* 137–143.

Pawson, R., & Tilley, N. (1997). *Realistic evaluation.* London: Sage Publications.

Pollard, C., Ross, K., & Means, R. (2005). Nurse leadership, interprofessionalism and the modernization agenda. *British Journal of Nursing, 14*(6), 32–44.

Reeves, S., Goldman, J., Gilbert, J., Tepper, J., Silver, I., Suter, E., & Zwarenstein, M. (2011). A scoping review to improve conceptual clarity of interprofessional interventions. *Journal of Interprofessional Care, 25*(3), 167–174.

Reeves, S., Lewin, S., Espin, S., & Zwarenstein, M. (2013). *Interprofessional teamwork for health and social care.* Oxford: Blackwell.

Reeves, S., MacMillan, K., & Van Soeren, M. (2010). Leadership of interprofessional health and social care teams: A sociohistorical analysis. *Journal of Nursing Management, 18*(3), 258–264.

Rubin, M. S., & Stone, R. K. (2010). Adapting the 'managing by walking around' methodology as a leadership strategy to communicate a hospital-wide strategic plan. *Journal of Public Health Management and Practice, 16*(2), 162–166.

Sasnett, B., & Clay, M. (2008). Leadership styles in interdisciplinary health science education. *Journal of Interprofessional Care, 22*(6), 630–638.

Schippers, M. C., Den Hartog, D. N., Koopman, P. L., & van Knippenberg, D. (2008). The role of transformational leadership in enhancing team reflexivity. *Human Relations, 61*(11), 1593–1616.

Sinek, S. (2010). *Start with why: How great leaders inspire everyone to take action.* London: Penguin Books.

Stapleton, S. R. (1998). Team-building: Making collaborative practice work. *Journal of Nurse-Midwifery, 43*(1), 12–18.

Straus, S. E., Tetroe, J., & Graham, I. (2009). *Knowledge translation portfolio.* Canadian Institutes of Health Research, Ottawa, ON, Canada, School of Nursing, University of Ottawa, Ottawa, ON, Canada. https://doi.org/10.1002/9781444311747.ch1.

Thistlethwaite, J. E., Dunston, R., & Yassine, T. (2019). The times are changing: Workforce planning, new health-care models and the need for interprofessional education in Australia. *Journal of Interprofessional Care, 33*(4), 361–368. https://doi.org/10.1080/13561820.2019.1612333.

Thistlethwaite, J. E., Forman, D., Matthews, L. R., Rogers, G., Steketee, C., & Yassine, T. (2014). Competences and frameworks in interprofessional education: A comparative analysis. *Academic Medicine, 89*(6), 869–875.

Thistlethwaite, J. E., Kumar, K., Moran, M., Saunders, R., & Carr, S. (2015). An exploratory review of pre-qualification interprofessional education evaluations. *Journal of Interprofessional Care, 29*(4), 292–297.

Tugade, M. M., & Fredrickson, B. L. (2004). Resilient individuals use positive emotions to bounce back from negative emotional experiences. *Journal of Personality and Social Psychology, 86*(2), 320–333.

Valentijn, P. P., Schepman, S. M., Opheij, W., & Bruijnzeels, M. A. (2012, January/March). Understanding integrated care: A comprehensive conceptual framework based on the integrative functions of primary care. *International Journal of Integrated Care, 13,* 1–12.

Willumsen, E. (2006). Leadership in interprofessional collaboration: The case of childcare in Norway. *Journal of Interprofessional Care, 20*(4), 403–413.

Wooding, E. L., Gale, T. C., & Maynard, V. (2019). Evaluation of teamwork assessment tools for interprofessional simulation: A systematic literature review. *Journal of Interprofessional Care.* https://doi.org/10.1080/13561820.2019.1650730.

World Health Organization (WHO). (2010). *Framework for action on interprofessional education and collaborative practice.* Health Professions Networks. Nursing and Midwifery. Human Resources for Health.

Wylie, D. A., & Gallagher, H. (2009). Transformational leadership behaviours in allied health professions. *Journal of Allied Health, 38*(2), 65–73.

2

Leadership Challenges When Creating and Sustaining Cultural Change for Interprofessional Collaboration

John H. V. Gilbert

Introduction

Leadership for What? Leadership by Whom?

Leadership in health care—'the action of leading a group of people or an organisation; different styles of leadership' (Oxford English Dictionary)—has been much debated, investigated and written about in thousands of publications. Apart from the most well-known texts e.g. Barr and Dowding (2019) and Lee and Cosgrove (2018) and the journal *Leadership in Health Services* (Emerald Publishing), there are literally hundreds of books which explore leadership in a broad range of industries. In this essay I shall not attempt to cover the myriad topics such publications examine but will focus particular attention on aspects

J. H. V. Gilbert (✉)
College of Health Disciplines, University of British Columbia, Vancouver, BC, Canada
e-mail: johnhvg@mail.ubc.ca

D. Forman et al. (eds.), *Sustainability and Interprofessional Collaboration*,
https://doi.org/10.1007/978-3-030-40281-5_2

of interest seen in successful attempts to create and sustain cultural change across the continuum of interprofessional education.

For the purposes of this essay I shall use the acronym IPE (interprofessional education) i.e. 'Occasions when members or students of two or more professions learn with, from and about each other, to improve collaboration and the quality of care and services' (CAIPE, 2018) to describe interprofessional education (IPE) as a continuum of collaboration that spans interprofessional learning (IPL), which is continuously and continually interwoven into interprofessional practice (IPP), and interprofessional care (IPC), beginning in the years prior to licensure/registration then further developed in post-licensure continuing professional development (CPD) and life-long learning (LLL).[1] The role of leaders in post-secondary education, and in systems of health and social care, is to create and sustain the cultural change needed to effect system change across the continuum of IPE. Leaders must be both lantern and lighthouse.

Leadership Challenges—Many Identities, Many Cultures

A major challenge confronting any leader of IPE is to understand and assess the multiplicity of identities and cultures[2] (Harper & Leicht, 2006) that are interwoven in the workforce of post-secondary education and health and social care. Each person in the workforce comes from a culture that defines her/his individual identity. Each comes gendered. Each comes as part of a community that is unrelated to her/his work site. At this time, each identifies as a member of a siloed profession, but also carries an identity as a member of a siloed professional community. Each comes with an identity as a care provider (in the sense of providing a professional service). Each carries an identity as a sometime(s) patient/client/customer/service user. Every day, the interplay of these

[1] In this essay I use the word 'professional' in its broadest sense i.e. 'a person competent or skilled in a particular activity' (Oxford English Dictionary) and not exclusively of regulated professions, in order to recognise the plethora of health and social care occupations that play important roles across the continuum of IPE.

[2] Culture encompasses shared forms of 'living and thinking' comprising 'symbols and language … knowledge … values … norms … and techniques.'

various identities contributes to the larger complex culture of her/his workplace which is, itself, most frequently siloed, and deeply rooted in personal values.

Values-based leadership (Barrett, 2006) is a construct which proposes that leaders should draw on their own and followers' values for direction and motivation; it asserts that people are mostly motivated by values and live according to these beliefs. A leader of IPE must constantly assess and evaluate how the complex of identities can be promoted to work together and understand how to manage the values of individual cultures when they come into conflict. Thus, for example, good leaders of IPE foster environments in which learners and practitioners actively engage themselves and others, including the client/patient/family, in positively and constructively addressing disagreements as they arise. But good leaders of IPE need to ensure that in a culture of collaboration there is value in learning the potential positive nature of disagreement and to ensure that all engaged in collaborative practice and care feel that in spite of disagreement, their viewpoints have been heard, and their values noted, no matter what the outcome. Culture change comes about when leaders of IPE understand these challenges, and values-based leadership assumes that an organisation based around shared values is likely to be more flexible and productive.

Creating Cultural Change for IPE—Some Challenges

Creating cultural change is defined as 'causing something to happen as a result of one's actions' (Oxford English Dictionary). In the Framework for Action on Interprofessional Education and Collaborative Practice, (WHO, 2010) three major categories of activity were identified as shaping the culture of interprofessional collaboration. These categories, which also illustrate the challenges faced by all leaders of IPE, were articulated as: (1) interprofessional education, (2) collaborative practice and (3) the systems of health and education. Since publication of the Framework, extensive research has in many senses supported these artificial categories, strengthened the concept of IPE as a continuum and heightened the need to understand, develop and integrate the three categories across the IPE continuum that might then motivate systemic cultural change. Leaders of IPE wishing to understand, develop and integrate those categories are attempting to provide cogent and coherent answers to the following questions:

First: How can universities, colleges, institutes, health and social care organisations and governments together build an interprofessional collaborative, civic community by developing a values-based organisation? A community that takes civic and social responsibility for health and social care in the broadest sense envisioned by the World Health Organization: '… there is a health baseline below which no individuals in any country should find themselves: all people in all countries should have a level of health that will permit them to work productively and to participate actively in the social life of the community in which they live' (WHO, 1981).

Second: How can universities, colleges, institutes, health and social care organisations and governments take professional education out of professional practice siloes and place it in an interprofessional matrix to ensure that graduates truly understand the effects of a broad interprofessional spectrum of health and social care practices, and how they can integrate their IPL into such practices?

Third: How can universities, colleges, institutes, health and social care organisations and governments integrate IPE policy matters—in both education and health, with evidence from scientific enquiry so that such evidence informs interprofessional collaborative practice and care in a coherent, congruent and timely fashion?

Fourth: How can universities, colleges, institutes, health and social care organisations and governments integrate interprofessional education with the health goals espoused in the large number of consultation documents produced by various levels of government in literally every country in the world, for example, the WHO Global Strategy on Human Resources for Health: Workforce 2030 (WHO, 2017a).

Creating cultural change to foster and further the continuum of IPE is the major challenge confronted by leaders of IPE, who are constantly reminded of the apt words of Machiavelli:

> It must be remembered that there is nothing more difficult to plan, more doubtful of success, or more dangerous to manage than the creation of a new system. For the initiator has the enmity of all who would profit by the preservation of the old institution and merely lukewarm defenders in those who would gain by the new one. (*The Prince*, 1513)

Recognising the aptness of this observation, how then do interprofessional education, collaborative practice and the systems of health and education, which comprise the continuum of IPE, exteriorise themselves as real life challenges in universities, colleges, institutes, and health and social care organisations and governments?

Real Life Challenges to Sustain the Continuum of IPE

Funding for the continuum of IPE is always raised as an impediment to integrating educator and practice 'mechanisms'. For example, within post-secondary institutions, funding is generally allocated to silos i.e. by faculty or department, which essentially excludes the possibility of interprofessional co-led programmes. Within health care systems, budgetary allocations tend to be driven by the 'issue of the day' e.g. access, safety, affordability. The health care system as a learning environment receives far less attention than clinical areas in terms of budget, allocation of human resources, space etc. It is clear that developing the continuum of IPE, when faced with these challenges, takes leaders who have a firm understanding of the data on efficacy of interprofessional collaborative practice, and diplomatic skills that elicit recognition and support from senior levels of administration (Gilbert, 2005) Anecdotal evidence from the practice sector shows that many managers and administrators are faced with lack of support (or lukewarm support) when attempting to introduce IPE as a new approach to learning and practice within their organisations. Sadly, despite their critical role in practice (clinical) education, community agencies (e.g. hospitals, health centres etc.) are only now being conceptualised as learning environments, but even when they are, they are almost inevitably inadequately resourced to provide exemplary teaching and learning opportunities for interprofessional person centred collaborative practice. Happily, anecdotal evidence also suggests that although members of organisations may not have money, they do have imagination, and each other, which together are slowly moving the IPE agenda forward, as will be shown later.

Traditionally, universities, colleges, institutes, health and social care organisations and governments have not imagined dedicated built environments in which the focus is on interprofessional activities It is therefore encouraging that in the past 10 years or so, the necessary interrelatedness of health and social care programmes has been developed in built environments in which the continuum of IPE is being fostered, for example at the University of Colorado in Denver, Dalhousie University in Halifax, George Brown College in Toronto and Ball State University in Indiana. Conceived by visionary leaders, these knowledge locations, along with moves to the flipped classroom, i.e. delivering instructional content online, outside the classroom, then using class time for discussion of that material, have been instrumental in developing new approaches to IPE.

IPE has frequently been misunderstood as an add-on or "non-essential" programme, rather than a new way of learning and a new way of practising. As a result of this misunderstanding it has frequently been accorded a low priority across the spectrum of learning through practice. A leader's challenge is how to correct the misunderstanding. Regulation, accreditation, legislation, the 20-year movement devoted to safety and quality care, a clearer understanding of the social determinants of health and its corollary, population health, have helped considerably in moving the thinking through requirements on curricula to address these major issues, that demonstrate the centrality of IPE, the goal of which is learning together to work together.

Sustaining the Culture of Interprofessional Collaborative Practice

By definition 'Causing to continue for an extended period or without interruption' (Oxford English Dictionary) has been and continues to be a major challenge to leaders of IPE. For example, the lack of a permanent line item in budgets for IPE related activities; changes in personnel—especially of champions for IPE; changes in the strategic plans of organisations—each confound the sustainability of system changes for IPE. The concept of IPE as a continuum can only be sustained if a leader of IPE is focused on the complex issues that cross the three broad categories—interprofessional education, collaborative practice and the systems of health and education. Those complex issues include, for example, how to share evidence based models of learning, practice and care amongst and between post-secondary institutions and health and social care agencies; how to articulate structured protocols that clearly set out the rights and responsibilities of all involved in the IPE continuum; how to negotiate agreement on a fair and equitable sharing of operating resources; how to develop clear personnel policies related to IPE across the continuum; and—perhaps most importantly—how to ensure that management practices are supported in budget and planning from the highest levels in the organisations, and championed from the front line of teachers/preceptors/mentors and practitioners.

It is now clearly recognised that because of professional silos and overlapping scopes of practice (CAHS, 2014) there is much duplication of learning and practice across health and social care programmes. Identifying this duplication and building strategies around how to minimise it is imperative. Many adverse events that occur in teams are occasioned by confusion during information transfer (communication) that occurs because of the different languages used by each profession. How to address the major problems in communication should be a top priority for every leader of IPE.

Because professional practices are tied up by scopes of practice, dictated by accreditation and sanctified by legislation, leaders of IPE are constantly confronted with the recurring theme: 'That body part (or that disease) belongs to us. Not to them'. Application of Sir William Osler's aphorism to this problem is apt 'It is much more important to know what sort of a patient has a disease, than what sort of a disease a patient has' (Bliss, 1999). A leader's imperative is to ensure that there is less time protecting turf, and more time given to how to cede pieces of scopes of practice, in order to move out of the legendary silos to better address the needs of the patient/client/customer/service user, and in general, the health and social care needs of the population. To this end, leaders of

IPE have to ensure that the large number of health and social care occupations that are not regulated (e.g. home care assistants) are viewed and accepted as an integral part of interprofessional collaborative practice and care.

As can be seen, although relatively straightforward to enumerate, the challenges facing IPE leaders are complex and legion—simplify access to other professionals; promote and enhance communication among professionals; develop strategies that recognise evidence-based practice and encourage methods that allow each profession to work interprofessionally.

Ultimately, there are personal, interpersonal and intersectoral challenges that leaders of IPE must address. Thus, all professionals, often for good reasons, dislike uncertainty and are fearful of change whether in the classroom or clinic. As professions have developed, they have built both intra- and inter-professional rivalries and misunderstanding, often because of perceived power, income and status differentials, and at the same time with little attention paid to the gendered nature of the workforce (Newman, 2014; WHO, 2018) There are, of course, differing conceptual approaches and models of 'health and care' depending on professional training, and at the same time almost all health and social care professions lack education and training about interprofessional collaborative teamwork. Finally, there are different and competing organisational priorities both within and between academic and training programmes and health care provider organisations, which can lead to a form of undesirable tribal behaviour (Burton, 2011).

It is these matters, and other related concerns not covered in this essay, which lead to a consideration of how to sustain cultural change.

Leading Sustained Cultural Change

> Our doubts are traitors and cause us to miss the good we oft might win, by fearing to attempt. (*Measure for Measure*)

Fisher and Ury (1981/2011) in their classic text *Getting to Yes*, focused on the psychology of negotiation in their method, 'principled negotiation', i.e. finding acceptable solutions by determining which needs are fixed and which are flexible for negotiators. Their method had, and continues to have, a huge impact on the development of leadership skills. The principles they set out are both simple and yet profound: listen to and focus on the problem, rather than on personalities. Explore underlying interests rather than specific positions. Consider options that may open up scope for mutual benefit. These principles can and should be applied to all situations encountered in developing interprofessional collaborative practice; they are fundamental to ensuring that cultural change is sustained. How might the principles be enacted? As may be seen from the multiplicity of monographs on leadership, although different people define leadership differently, one characteristic of leadership which remains undisputed is the rare aura of mystery and charisma which has surrounded successful leaders from almost every sphere of life (Grabo, Spisak, & van Vogt, 2017) In many ways it is this aura that allows sustainability to flourish across the continuum of IPE.

In health and social care leaders of teams have to continually and continuously focus attention on the fact that their lives are about patients and the health of the population, not about financial returns to shareholders, and that the health and social care workforce is approximately 80% female (Newman, 2014; WHO, 2018). Leadership for IPE, in the service environment, requires a grasp of an organisation's commitment to a culture of person-centred care, how collaborative practice impacts patient and worker safety, and the need for an organisation to be a focus for both service and learning. The cross-cutting themes that touch on all of these, and about which a leader must have knowledge, include operational and performance management, decision making supports, resource allocation, and the infrastructure needed to drive excellence and quality improvement in the organisation. Above all, understanding that in providing services in health and social care, much is achieved by group decision making, rather than management imperatives. People tend to confuse 'managing' for 'leading' when in fact these are two separate domains, although good leaders must be good managers in order to be good leaders (McLaughlin & Olson, 2017).

Leadership in post-secondary environments is much more closely linked to the philosophical foundations of those environments i.e. the furtherance of knowledge through research and scholarship, but senior academic leaders must also be knowledgeable about these cross-cutting themes (McCaffrey, 2010).

Good leaders are not necessarily born—by defining some of the core qualities required for leadership and with determined effort headed in the right direction anyone can, in effect, embark on the journey to become a leader. If the continuum of IPE is to be sustained, then recognising and training future leaders of IPE is imperative. How might this be imperative be approached? What are some of the key lessons that have so far been learned about leadership? 'Our doubts are traitors and cause us to miss the good we oft might win, by fearing to attempt' (*Measure for Measure*). We know that leaders need to experiment more and learn from experience, instead of being too cautious and wary of taking risks.

Leaders who take the trouble to recognise and celebrate even small steps towards a difficult goal (of which there are many in health and social care) can generate much joy. Good leaders do not regard others merely as objects which either help or hinder their path to success or realising certain goals, but instead treat them as real people who have their own hopes and aspirations. In the words of the Golden Rule 'Do unto others as you would they should do unto you.' Good leaders are not afraid to question and challenge authority, and good leaders evolve from 'leading', to helping others 'lead'. Zeiss's (2019) reflected that across the course of her professional career she learned some key lessons 'Leaders add value by serving, leadership develops daily, not in a day. Leaders know how to pursue problems and address conflicts comfortably without expressing anger, attacking, or understating the issue. Leaders need to be both nurturing and supportive persons – though, surprising as it might seem, some people who report to even the most supportive leader may be frightened of her/him. Recognising this characteristic takes a leader with special talent.'

Understanding these key lessons is fundamentally bound up with the philosophy of values-based leadership, which asserts that people are mostly motivated by deep-rooted values and live according to those values. It is values-based leadership that carries the promise that the cultural change associated with the continuum of IPE can be sustained. Values are our most natural motivators, and possibly the deepest value we hold is that of trust, and it is trust that guides behaviour. It is not surprising that leaders refer to their own values in creating a vision or making decisions (Campbell-Cree, Macdonald, & Lotten, 2018). It thus makes sense for leaders to connect with the values of those they work with since it then makes those individuals more likely to act to sustain the activities of IPE.

It then follows that, because of this value driven behaviour, people's self-expectations will influence how they behave—they want their actions to be in line with their values and their commitments. This idea of value driven self-expectations is of great importance when building a sustainable system for the continuum of IPE when trust is fundamental to best practice and care. That said, there are realities to be faced. We are all averse to loss and quite naturally tend to hang on to what we consider ours. We are not good at computing; when we make decisions we tend to put a lot of weight on recent events and too little on those that are in the future; we don't calculate probabilities well and worry too much about unlikely events; and we are strongly influenced by how the problem/information is presented to us.

What is clear from all of the work that has been put into, and is being put into building and sustaining the continuum of IPE is that everyone engaged in the process needs to feel involved in the process and know that they can effect a change—just giving people incentives and information is not enough to effect change. Other people's behaviour matters—people do many things by observing others and copying; people are encouraged to continue to do things when they feel other people approve of their behaviour. The notion 'We've always done things this way and they mostly work' is deeply bound up with habits that are hard to change. Our behaviour is probably the hardest of all human attributes to change and habits constantly compromise attempts to really move IPE forward. So how have we moved away from 'We've always done things this way.'?

Looking back across the past 10–12 years of intense work across the continuum of IPE, it is encouraging to see how good leadership has transformed the field. Looking at this interprofessional transformation, it is possible to assess the transformations that have occurred. We can get a crude but nonetheless profound sense of the difference by considering five questions: Are there signs of more learning together? Are there indications of new forms of collaboration? Are safety and quality of care being improved because of IPE? Is it possible to see how new management structures are steering change? And is the IPE transformation steering the management of change? The first three of these questions are directly linked to the CAIPE definition of IPE; the last two questions are linked to the final part of the definition '… to improve … the quality of care and services'.

The time between the National Academy of Sciences report *Educating for The Health Team* (1972) and the report of the Health Professions Accreditors Collaborative *Guidance on Developing Quality Interprofessional Education for the Health Professions* (2019) is replete with examples of the many ways in which good leadership has pushed into all of the corners of the IPE continuum. As will be seen, these examples provide a variegated set of answers to the five questions.

So, are there indications that IP transformation is leading to more learning together? It was clear from the earliest days of IPE that both academic and health care organisations would need to configure space in order that students and practitioners could learn together, i.e. a need to find ways of breaking down the physical barriers of the silos. The concept of a built environment that would provide knowledge locations in which to learn and practise was envisioned, in which there would be small spaces dedicated to interprofessional group teaching, projects, forums, seminars etc. and that would allow all parts of the continuum to be addressed in a coherent and congruent fashion (Smith & Costello, 2018). Professor Nishant Manapure, an architect, has described the built environment as 'All structures people have built when considered as separate from the natural environment. Surroundings created for humans, by humans, to be used for human activity' (Manapure, pers. com). As indicated earlier there are now a number of such spaces, developed by inspiring leaders and collaborative teams of health and social care professionals.

The movement for 'transforming education to strengthen health systems in an interdependent world' was spearheaded by *The Lancet* (Frenk et al., 2010) in its seminal study Health Professionals for a New Century, and in the same year the publication of the WHO's Framework for Action on Interprofessional Education and Collaborative Practice (WHO, 2010), then, in 2013, the WHO's publication of transforming and scaling up health professionals education and training (WHO, 2013). Health Canada made a major investment in cross country studies of IPE from 2002–2005 which motivated both academic and practice changes, many of which continue (Gilbert, 2010) Reports of study groups (Cox, Cuff, Brandt, Reeves, & Zierler, 2016), conferences, and other forums initiated by leaders in IPE have followed that have assessed the changes e.g. Measuring the impact of interprofessional education on collaborative practice and patient outcomes (IOM, 2015); Lessons from the Field: Promising Interprofessional Practices from the Robert Wood Johnson Foundation (CFAR Inc., Tomasik, & Fleming, 2015).

It was, however, the development of interprofessional competencies by an ever larger cohort of leaders (Chuenkongkaew, 2018; CIHC, 2010; IPEC, 2011) that effected profound changes in IPE curricula, which was also driven by an ever increasing number of studies published in the *Journal of Interprofessional Care*, the *Journal of Interprofessional Education and Practice*, the *Journal of Research in Interprofessional Practice and Education* and journals advancing medical and nursing education—journals with outstanding leaders as editors whose vision enabled, and continues to enable, the development of a discipline through research and scholarship.

Are we seeing transformation through new forms of collaboration? The committee for interprofessional education in health professions is an example of leadership in Germany, Austria and Switzerland coming together from medicine, nursing, and the diagnostic and therapeutic health professions (Walkenhorst et al., 2015). The Committee on Interprofessional Education and Practice of the American College of Surgeons set as its goals, to: Comprehensively address the educational needs of allied health professionals as members of surgical teams; Educate surgeons regarding the role of allied health professionals; Support and assist allied health professionals involved in the surgical care; Participate in defining duties of allied health professionals; Assist with the process of accreditation of their respective educational programmes (https://

www.facs.org/about-acts/governance/ace-committees/18). The WHO is actively facilitating new forms of collaboration through e.g. the inclusion of IPE as a framework for learning about how to address social determinants of health across a wide variety of health occupations. Remarkable leaders of student organisations, in Canada, the USA, and elsewhere have been powerful advocates of new forms of collaboration and particularly effective in carrying that message forward through the Health Care Team Challenge movement, an event started at the University of British Columbia in Canada, which now is held annually in many countries (Newton et al., 2015).

Is interprofessional transformation leading to improved safety and quality of care? There is no doubt that the Institute of Medicine's report, *To err is human* (Kohn, Corrigan, & Donaldson, 1999), was hugely important in recognising dysfunctional health and social care teams, and inherent problems of communication between health and social care professionals. It is tempting to think that this report was the stimulus for the Lancet Commission review. The downstream effects of that review, on conceptualising interprofessional teams, have been carried forward by great leaders across the spectrum of health and social care. The development of checklists, simulation, patient safety goals, quality of care can now be seen in interprofessional competencies and curricula (Kitto, Reeves, Chesters, & Thistlethwaite, 2011). Equally significant has been the development of the patient's voice in her/his own care, and in research (Thistlethwaite, 2015). Although the influence of interprofessional collaborative practice and care on improved quality of care is observed anecdotally, quantitative data are still being accumulated, an area in which the lens of implementation science would be of great value (Bauer, Damschroder, Hagedorn, Smith, & Kilbourne, 2015).

Is IP transformation leading to new management structures? What can be seen is that curricula change towards IPE has seen the appointment of managers within post-secondary institutions and health and social care organisation who now have the title, mandate and responsibility to develop IPE e.g. professorships and directorships, and frontline professionals who are charged with interprofessional collaborative team development. In Canada, the position of Vice-President, Professional Practice now more and more frequently has the additional title "and

Interprofessional Education". Transformation is also being engineered through, for example, the WHO Global strategy on human resources for health: Workforce 2030 (WHO, 2017a) and Framing the health workforce agenda for the Sustainable Development Goals (WHO, 2017b).

Finally, is IP transformation steering the management of change? Evidence for the genesis of a global movement is provided by Barr (2015) and for advances occasioned by change management in the BEME systematic review (Reeves et al., 2016). Management is also using social media, webinars, conferences, newsletters, infographics and online meetings that clearly demonstrate the ways in which IPE is steering the management of change. Over the past decade, systematic investments in developing faculty and practitioners to teach teamwork skills (Hall & Zierler, 2015); developing sound evaluation and measurement methodologies (Kitto et al., 2011) and expanding publication sources for research are demonstrating that IPE is an evidence-based discipline which covers the continuum from learning to practice and care.

Perhaps more than any other mechanism, it is the organisation of interprofessional research programmes and publication of the results of such programmes in ever increasing numbers that are pushing change. The development of Interprofessional.Global, a confederation of regional interprofessional organisations that will sustain cultural change, and Interprofessional.Global. Research, will continue to build the research base of the discipline.

As we look at the growing culture of IPE and its spreading circle of influence, the words of Bill Gates of Microsoft fame are apposite: 'We always overestimate the change that will occur in the next two years and underestimate the change that will occur in the next ten. Don't let yourself be lulled into inaction.' Early leaders of IPE across its many sectors were keenly aware that the system change they were working for would not happen in two years; they have been amazed at what has occurred in ten years—and come to realise that 'Keep track of gradual improvements. A small change every year can translate to a huge change over decades' (Rosling, 2018) as they aim for a system in which workforce planning is led by leaders in IPE, who recognise that in order to bring about system change, education and practice must be designed around patients and the health of the populations—not around the mandates of professions.

References

Barr, H. (2015). *Interprofessional education: The genesis of a global movement.* ISBN 978-0-9571382-4-7.

Barr, J., & Dowding, L. (2019). *Leadership in health care.* London, UK: Sage.

Barrett, R. (2006). *Building a values-driven organization.* Amsterdam: Butterworth-Heinemann.

Bauer, M. S., Damschroder, L., Hagedorn, H., Smith, J., & Kilbourne, A. M. (2015). An introduction to implementation science for the non-specialist. *BMC Psychology, 3,* 32. https://doi.org/10.1186/s40359-015-0089-9.

Bliss, M. (1999). *William Osler: A life in medicine.* Toronto: University of Toronto Press.

Burton, A. (2011). *The business case for the alignment of policies between the health and education sectors in interprofessional education and interprofessional collaborative practice.* (Pers. Com., unpublished MS).

CAHS. (2014). *Optimizing scopes of practice: New models of care for a new health care system.* Ottawa, ON: The Canadian Academy of Health Sciences.

CAIPE. (2018). https://www.caipe.org/about-us.

Campbell-Cree, A., Macdonald, A., & Lotten, M. (2018). *The value of trust: How trust is carried and why it matters.* London, UK: British Council.

Canadian Interprofessional Health Collaborative (CIHC). (2010). *A national interprofessional competency framework.* Vancouver, BC: The University of British Columbia.

CFAR Inc., Tomasik, J., & Fleming, C. (2015). *Lessons from the field: Promising interprofessional practices.* Washington, DC: The Robert Wood Johnson Foundation.

Chuenkongkaew, W. (Ed.). (2018). *Interprofessional education.* Thailand: The National Health Professional Education Foundation (NHPE). ISBN 978-616-8185-01-8.

Cox, M., Cuff, P., Brandt, B., Reeves, S., & Zierler, B. (2016). Measuring the impact of interprofessional education on collaborative practice and patient outcomes. *Journal of Interprofessional Care, 30*(1), 1–3. https://doi.org/10.3109/13561820.2015.1111052.

Educating for the Health Team (1972). Washington, DC: National Academy of Sciences.

Fisher, R., & Ury, W. (1981/revised 2011). *Getting to yes*. New York: Penguin Books.

Frenk, J., Chen, L., Bhutta, Z. A., Cohen, J., Crisp, N., Evans, T., ... Zurayk, H. (2010). Health professionals for a new century: Transforming education to strengthen health systems in an interdependent world. *The Lancet*. Published online November 29, 2010. https://doi.org/10.1016/s01406736(10)61854-5.

Gilbert, J. H. V. (2005). Interprofessional learning and higher education structural barriers. *Journal of Interprofessional Care, 19*(Suppl. 1), 87–106. https://doi.org/10.1080/13561820500067132.

Gilbert, J. H. V. (2010, Fall). The status of interprofessional education in Canada [Special issue]. *Journal of Allied Health, 39*(3), Pt. 2.

Grabo, A., Spisak, B., & van Vogt, M. (2017, August). Charisma as signal: An evolutionary perspective on charismatic leadership. *The Leadership Quarterly 28*(4), 473–485.

Hall, L. W., & Zierler, B. K. (2015). Interprofessional education and practice guide No. 1: Developing faculty to effectively facilitate interprofessional education. *Journal of Interprofessional Care, 29*(1), 3–7. https://doi.org/10.3109/13561820.2014.937483.

Harper, C. L., & Leicht, K. T. (2006). *Exploring social change: America and the world* (5th ed.). New York: Pearson.

Health Professions Accreditors Collaborative. (2019). *Guidance on developing quality interprofessional education for the health professions*. Chicago, IL: Health Professions Accreditors Collaborative.

Institute of Medicine (IOM). (2015). *Measuring the impact of interprofessional education on collaborative practice and patient outcomes*. Washington, DC: The National Academies Press.

Interprofessional Education Collaborative. (2011). *Core competencies for interprofessional collaborative practice: 2016 update*. Washington, DC: Interprofessional Education Collaborative.

Interprofessional Education Collaborative. (2016). *Core competencies for interprofessional collaborative practice: 2016 update* . Washington, DC: Interprofessional Education Collaborative. https://www.ipecollaborative.org

Kitto, S., Reeves, S., Chesters, J., & Thistlethwaite, J. (2011). Re-imagining Interprofessionalism: Where to from here. In S. Kitto, J. Chester, J. Thistlethwaite, & S. Reeves (Eds.), *Sociology of interprofessional health care practice: Critical reflections and concrete solutions* (pp. 207–212). New York: Nova Sciences.

Kohn, L. T., Corrigan, J. M., & Donaldson, M. S. (Eds.) (1999). *To err is human: Building a safer health system.* Institute of Medicine (US) Committee on Quality of Health Care in America.

Leadership in Health Services. 2nd ed. (Journal published by Emerald Publishing).

Lee, T. H., & Cosgrove, T. (2018). *On leadership for healthcare.* Harvard, Cambridge, MA: Harvard Business Review.

Machiavelli, N. (1513). *The Prince.* New York: Dover Publications, September 21, 1992.

McCaffrey, P. (2010). *The higher education manager's handbook: Effective leadership in universities and colleges* (2nd ed.). London, UK: Routledge.

McLaughlin, D. B., & Olson, J. R. (2017). *Healthcare operations management* (3rd ed.). Chicago, IL: Health Administration Press.

Newman, C. (2014). Time to address gender discrimination and inequality in the health workforce. *Human Resources for Health 12,* Article Number: 25.

Newton, C., Bainbridge, L., Ball, V., Baum, K. D., Bontje, P., Boyce, R. A., … Wood, V. (2015). The Health Care Team Challenge™: Developing an international interprofessional education research collaboration. *Nursing Education Today 35*(1), 4–8.

Reeves, S., Fletcher, S., Barr, H., Birch, I., Boet, S., Davies N. … Kitto, S. (2016). *A BEME systematic review of the effects of interprofessional education*: BEME Guide No. 39, Medical Teacher. https://doi.org/10.3109/0142159x.2016.1173663.

Rosling, H. (2018). *Factfulness: Ten reasons we're wrong about the world—And why things are better than you think.* New York: Flatiron Books.

Shakespeare, W. *Measure for measure.* Lucio to Isabella, Act 1, Scene 4.

Smith, B., & Costello, H. (2018, June 8). *Designing medical education space for interprofessional education.* College Planning and Management.

Thistlethwaite, J. (2015). Where's the patient's voice in health professional education? *International Journal of Practice-Based Learning in Health and Social Care, 3*(2), ii–iv.

Walkenhorst, U., Mahler, C., Aistleithner, R., Hahn, E.G., Kaap-Fröhlich, S., Karstens, S., … Sottas, B. (2015). Position statement GMA Committee—Interprofessional Education for the Health Care Professions. *GMS Zeitschrift für Medizinische Ausbildung* Vol. 32(2), ISSN 1860-3572.

WHO. (1981). *Global strategy for health for all by the year 2000.* https://iris.wpro.who.int/bitstream/handle/10665.1/6967/WPR_RC032_GlobalStrategy_1981_en.pdf.

WHO. (2010). *Framework for action on interprofessional education and collaborative practice.* http://www.who.int/hrh/nursing_midwifery/en/.

WHO. (2013). *Transforming and scaling up health professionals education and training.* https://www.who.int/hrh/resources/transf_scaling_hpet/en/.

WHO. (2017a). *Global strategy on human resources for health: Workforce 2030.* https://www.who.int/hrh/resources/globstrathrh-2030/en/.

WHO (2017b). *Framing the health workforce agenda for the sustainable development goals.* https://www.who.int/hrh/resources/bienium-report_16-17/en/.

WHO. (2018). *The Global Health 50/50 Report. How gender responsive are the world's most influential global health organizations?* https://www.who.int/pmnch/media/news/2018/gender-responsive-health-organisations/en/.

Zeiss, A (2019, January 7). A healthcare leader's view on the top 5 leadership skills. *Psychology Today.*

Part II

Interprofessional Centres and Networks

3

The CAIPE Journey—Vision, Resilience and Sustainability

Hugh Barr, Elizabeth Anderson, and Richard Pitt

The Centre for the Advancement of Interprofessional Education (CAIPE) was established in 1987 as a United Kingdom charitable trust following a series of conferences and workshops organised by the Middlesex Polytechnic (now university). John Horder who had recently retired following a distinguished career in medicine was invited to be its leader. He saw the invitation as an opportunity to promote team-based primary health care, drawing on his pioneering work as a general practitioner in North London. To imply that his vision extended no further would be to do him less than justice. CAIPE, as Horder envisaged it,

H. Barr
University of Westminster, London, UK

E. Anderson
University of Leicester, Medical School, Leicester, UK

R. Pitt (✉)
Centre for the Advancement of Interprofessional Education, Grantham, UK
e-mail: Richard.Pitt@caipe.org

D. Forman et al. (eds.), *Sustainability and Interprofessional Collaboration*,
https://doi.org/10.1007/978-3-030-40281-5_3

would be a regional network with a national council representing the professions supported by paid staff:

- to foster and improve interprofessional cooperation in the interests of a comprehensive and effective service to patients and clients;
- to promote development, practice and research in interprofessional education for practitioners associated with primary health care (CAIPE, undated).

Interprofessional education (IPE) would be the key to unlock relationships between General Practitioners (family doctors in the UK), nurses, midwives and social workers practising together in community teams. In this way it was envisaged they could resolve problems through mobilising their collective expertise and experience to improve and extend primary health care services. It would be work-based, person-centred and practice-led. These values endure in CAIPE and throughout the interprofessional movement today.

Horder eschewed the limelight. Leading by example, he set CAIPE's agenda simply and clearly, demanding impeccable standards from himself and colleagues to whom he invariably gave credit. Unwavering in commitment to his own profession, he succeeded for many in embodying the interprofessional ethos, imprinting his indelible leadership style on CAIPE during its formative years, indeed throughout his time as chair and later president (Horder, 2003).

One of us (HB) succeeded Horder as president following his own term as chair. He sought to emulate Horder's style of leadership. He welcomed opportunities to represent CAIPE, addressing conferences nationally and internationally and writing extensively for publication, concurrently editing the Journal of Interprofessional Care for much of the time.

The challenge for all who followed in Horder's footsteps was to hold fast to his vision whilst measuring up to mounting expectations within the constraints of a small charity with limited resources. Recurrent financial crises drove CAIPE on to the back foot, followed invariably by renewed pressure to do more with less. Closure loomed more than once. There were no quick fixes. Government made clear that pump priming for IPE would not be extended. Personal and charitable donations solicited by Horder were too small to retain staff and rent accommodation. For a while a business model seemed promising. Income was generated from membership subscriptions and successful bids which, however, dictated priorities and were prone to conflict with CAIPE's strategic objectives.

Escape from recurrent crises demanded a more radical solution now being put to the test. CAIPE has become a 'virtual membership organisation' no longer at the mercy of hiked office rents and no longer struggling to pay staff commensurate with their abilities. Free from these burdens CAIPE has regained its cherished independence.

Preoccupied though it often was with its survival, CAIPE remained outward looking: defining IPE; reconciling differing perceptions and expectations; delineating learning methods; enunciating principles; and weaving interprofessional perspectives into professional education (CAIPE, 2002, 2011, 2017). These tasks were hard enough to effect in primary health care, harder as CAIPE extended into other fields of practice including child protection, health promotion, acute care and patient safety.

Each of the nine chairs who followed Horder brought their distinctive personalities, preferences and priorities. All strived by one means or another to ensure CAIPE remained viable and relevant to its members, ably supported by dedicated administrative and professional staff (all but one of whom were part-time). They adopted different strategies to find common ground between stakeholders: enlist the professional associations as partners; generate income; raise CAIPE's profile; attract more members; secure the IPE evidence base, instil academic credibility; balance the books and build a viable virtual organisation, all of which became part of CAIPE's modus operandi (CAIPE, 2019; Gray, 2015).

It is difficult and arguably unhelpful to distinguish between activities instigated by CAIPE, by its individual members, its corporate members and in partnership with other organisations. Collaboration with the Learning for Partnership Network, Creating an Interprofessional Workforce, especially three of the subject centres of the Higher Education Authority and other organisations, was productive but short-lived, leaving CAIPE with the unfinished business.

In response to government (Department of Health, 2000), IPE in the UK from the turn of the century became predominantly university led, located in and integral to their professional registration programmes. Interprofessional, post-registration workshops and short courses continued but were cast in the shadows. University-led post-registration programmes were slow to take off. One priority for CAIPE was to support interprofessional activists in universities to articulate theoretical foundations, build in evaluation and secure evidence bases to win acceptance in academe (CAIPE, 2017). Another was to affirm the centrality of team-based practice learning (Brewer & Barr, 2016). Yet another was to project a continuum of interprofessional learning extending beyond qualifying courses into supervised learning in the workplace, virtual study and post-qualifying courses (CAIPE, 2017). All these outreached CAIPE's capacity alone. The solution, in part, lay in working with like-minded organisations to convene conferences, run workshops, conduct surveys, draft guidelines, and promote research with systematic reviews (Gray, 2015).

Relationships with the UK Department of Health became more tenuous as it devolved responsibility for health and social care in Scotland, Wales and Northern Ireland and entrusted professional education to the regulatory bodies. Building and sustaining relationships with a wide spectrum of organisations made heavy claims on CAIPE's resources; concurrently supporting a lengthening list of corporate members. CAIPE welcomed growing support from regulatory bodies, collaborating with them during twice-yearly group meetings that give CAIPE opportunities to influence their references to IPE standards and competencies, albeit at times reluctant to go beyond endorsing IPE outcomes, leaving CAIPE to explain the means.

Over the years, CAIPE members and staff have published seven books with Blackwell and now Routledge, been instrumental in launching and sustaining the Journal of Interprofessional Care and mounting two prestigious conferences; nationally with the St. Catherine Foundation at Cumberland Lodge and three globally in the Altogether Better Health series. Concurrently, they have advised and assisted the promotion of waves of interprofessional development in sub-Saharan Africa, Latin America, the Arab speaking countries, Australasia, Canada, Europe, the

Pacific region and Japan, establishing and supporting 'Interprofessional. Global' as the umbrella body (Box 3.1).

Box 3.1: Case Study—An Example of How CAIPE Nurtures and Develops IPE
Case study. The University of Leicester

The revelation, which would change our understanding of teaching and learning in Leicester, took place in 1995 in designing new training for medical students about patients who lived in areas of disadvantage and poverty. As the ideas permeated around the medical school a GP offered up a green leaflet entitled 'The UK Centre for the Advancement of Interprofessional Education'. Apparently in a conversation with John Horder he had shared our recent thinking for extending medical students' learning beyond primary care to the wider community and the possibility of linking up with the nursing and social work students. Did we not know that CAIPE could help, was his reply? As a team we had neither heard of CAIPE nor of interprofessional education.

CAIPE, in the late 1990s, was based in Gray's Inn Road, central London. For all who entered there was a warm welcome from Hugh Barr, Barbara Clague and Helena Low (then chair, CEO and development officer respectively). Listening, encouragement and support abounded. From hearing more about our evolving work in Leicester came an invitation to share our practice-based interprofessional learning at a CAIPE meeting. In October 1998, what was to become the Leicester model of IPE was the first to be shared; practice-learning in the inner city aligning medical students from one university with nursing and social work students from an adjacent university (Anderson, Ford, & Kinnair, 2016). CAIPE publications at that time were prolific, benefitting from active engagement in research and scholarly synthesis in the Journal of Interprofessional Care. These outputs included re-affirming the definition, guidelines and principles for IPE. An analysis of our work was summarised as one of the many IPE developments taking shape in the UK at that time (Barr, 2002).

The CAIPE Board then comprised representatives from different professional bodies plus the voluntary sector. These included education, housing and police, representatives of different subject centres of the UK Higher Education Academy, along with academics and professionals in the forefront of embedding this learning within health and social care curricula. Within this atmosphere, the tools for creating a solid sustainable interprofessional curriculum could be found. Here we absorbed the sensitivities for this learning. We were now able to share these understandings locally with academic subject leads across our two higher education institutions—Leicester and De Montfort universities—to generate a local, East Midlands, activity centre for IPE.

In 2001, we missed out on the cash injection from the Department of Health initiative—the Common Learning Bids—rejected because we could not offer common learning as we were two universities. We went on to find support from our Regional Health Authority to shape our local IPE curriculum. This injection of money could not create new academic posts but could employ help from CAIPE and a researcher. CAIPE executive members led a series of faculty development workshops. This support cannot be overstated as academics came together across two universities, bridging our differences and forming relationships with CAIPE at the helm. CAIPE as a knowledgeable external charitable organisation had ensured harmony within the leadership team across the two universities and helped to propel our strategy. This early support has led to a sustained evaluated curriculum and university alliances which have lasted for over twenty years (Anderson, Smith, & Hammick, 2015). In 2005 we launched the three-strand model curriculum for the East Midlands (Leicester and Northampton) in an informal meeting of Deans, the Regional Health Authority and local university leads with a keynote address from Hugh Barr. We have gone on to share our model widely, initially published in the CAIPE Bulletin (Anderson & Knight, 2004).

CAIPE offered constant encouragement as our teaching evolved from the medical student course (Lennox & Petersen, 1998) into an interprofessional practice-based researched model, evaluated throughout its iterative development over a further ten years (Anderson & Lennox, 2009). Hugh Barr urged us to publish our experience and Marilyn Hammick ensured the Leicester Model was ready for publication by the Higher Education Academy (Lennox & Anderson, 2007). Hammick, as a CAIPE scholar and chair, went on to become our external consultant for the evaluation of our local IPE curriculum (Anderson, Smith, & Hammick, 2015).

CAIPE support remains pivotal to our regional success so far lasting twenty years, exemplifying that which CAIPE offers to its corporate members and reflected in its publications, e.g. Barr (2007a, 2007b), Barr & Low (2013), Barr et al. (2014), and Colyer, Helme, & Jones (2005).

The depth of CAIPE, as we encounter it in Leicester, centres on its ability to listen and learn with and from the experiences of its members, putting interprofessional values into action. CAIPE remains a vibrant meeting point to debate and discuss the meaning of interprofessional learning and to share and consider the many challenges we all face. Our relationship with CAIPE is symbiotic; give and take, share and receive for constant energy and commitment to furthering IPE.

Through our alliance with CAIPE we have shared our experiences globally with other universities building collaborations which continue today, for example, with Chiba and Niigata universities in Japan in exchanging undergraduate students for placements and electives. In Leicester our two universities have helped CAIPE host international visitors supporting global alliances for the exchange of ideas with colleagues from Australia, Canada, Finland, Norway, Sweden and the USA, and many more. Remaining corporate members of CAIPE continues to sustain and re-energise our work.

Most of CAIPE's development is now assigned to working groups mobilising Board members' experience and expertise:

- to promote CAIPE and develop effective social media and communications platforms;
- to explore learning and teaching methodologies and apply technological assisted learning in IPE;
- to develop and provide workshops on IPE and collaborative working;
- to provide a platform for international liaison with IPE colleagues and share resources;
- to add publications to the collaborative practice series with Routledge;
- to enhance further CAIPE's scholarly reputation, promoting research and evaluation throughout the CAIPE membership;
- to engage students as the future workforce in the development and promotion of IPE and collaborative practice;
- to explore how scholarship awards might be made for individuals, students and service users, maintaining the John Horder Award;
- to continue to develop resources for individual members;
- to provide bi-annual forums hosted by corporate members to share innovations and good practice; and
- to engage further service users and carers.

A recurrent challenge for CAIPE is to anticipate, respond and strive to influence policy developments impacting on IPE and collaborative practice. Current moves, for example, towards integrating health and social care services, are pregnant with implications for professional and interprofessional education (Valentijn et al., 2015). Organisational solutions alone falter, as CAIPE has learnt from experience. Managing change successfully depends on enlisting the workforce in planning and implementation, resolving tensions as boundaries between professions are redrawn, duties reassigned and powers redistributed, all of which entails interprofessional learning.

Work, as we write, with the south and midlands and east regions of Higher Education England involves piloting an IPE practice workbook underpinning integrated care and with NHS Education for Scotland (NES). This work promotes CAIPE, the IPE Review and its recommendations (Barr, Helme, & D'Avray, 2011) involving the Scottish Clinical Skills Network and the Scottish Heads Association of Nurses and Allied Health Professionals.

CAIPE is being urged from within to assume an audit role to complement that of the regulatory bodies. One of its working groups is exploring in consultation with UK regulatory bodies, professional associations and universities the feasibility and desirability of developing national standards for the management and delivery of IPE to even up its quality.

CAIPE is grasping technology to promote and sustain many of its activities but remains ever mindful of the need for real time, face-to-face interprofessional communication to improve the quality of care and ensure patient safety. Its revised website launched in September 2016 provides a platform of resources, information, support and innovations in interprofessional education and collaborative practice for CAIPE members and the wider interprofessional community. Engagement with digital technology is assisting CAIPE in ensuring its sustainability and resilience as a virtual organisation through its monthly e-newsletter, virtual meetings, podcasts, digital stories and partnership with other web resources. These include Care Opinion (www.careopinion.org.uk); the (US) National Center for Interprofessional Practice and Education (https://nexusipe.org); the International Foundation for Integrated Care (https://integratedcarefoundation.org/); and Interprofessional.Global (https://interprofessional.global). CAIPE is capitalising on the popularity of Twitter and social media forums amongst students and their generation to increase participant engagement, attention and interaction (Mckay, Steiner Sanko, Shekhter, & Birnbach,

2014). Students reportedly prefer near instantaneous access to information and constant connectivity (Fox & Varadarajan, 2011). Many educators are 'digital novices' born or brought up before widespread use of digital technology and needing to learn how to be creative and innovative in their strategies to keep the attention of today's learner. Recognising this, CAIPE has engaged with a Twitter Account, @CAIPEUK, to share IPE/IPC developments. Twitter is now one of the main sources of IPE traffic to the CAIPE website. Through an initiative of the Student Working Group we engage in monthly Twitter Chats on a current IPE topic.

CAIPE as a virtual organisation is financially stable, but heavily dependent on its volunteer workforce and goodwill. This is especially true for the chair, board members and fellows, including the late Scott Reeves, appointed from the membership in recognition of their sustained and influential contributions to IPE to support its strategic thinking. To add yet more demands might call into question how long CAIPE can remain 'virtual', reactivating the case for recruiting professional and administrative staff if and when financial backing can be assured.

This unique ability to remain purposeful and relevant owes much to the commitment and dedication of its members and leaders. We might postulate that the sustainability of CAIPE comes from having been one of the earliest bodies to lead the IPE global understandings through scholarship, in shaping a definition and principles upon which others could build. Staying connected to the local, UK, policy developments and remaining faithful to its members (organisations and practitioners/academics) from which its core memberships arise, remains essential. Involving students and service users on the CAIPE Board ensures a vital litmus test of whether the aspirations for interprofessional learning have been achieved. While we see evidence of team working and collaborative practice in the UK, sadly we hear too often from the naive observers (students) and disappointingly from receivers (patients and carers) that there is still much more to be done. In this way CAIPE remains relevant, having been sustained over thirty years with resilience and hopefully for a further thirty years.

References

Anderson, E. S., Ford, J., & Kinnair, D. (2016). Interprofessional education and practice guide no. 6: Developing practice-based interprofessional learning using a short placement model. *Journal of Interprofessional Care, 30*(4), 433–440. http://www.tandfonline.com/doi/full/10.3109/13561820.2016.1160040.

Anderson, E. S., & Knight, T. (2004). *The three strand model of interprofessional education in Leicestershire, Northamptonshire and Rutland workforce development confederation.* Winter 2004/5 CAIPE Bulletin, 12.

Anderson, E. S., & Lennox, A. (2009). The Leicester model of interprofessional education: Developing, delivering and learning from student voices for 10 years. *Journal of Interprofessional Care, 23*(6), 557–573. https://doi.org/10.3109/13561820903051451.

Anderson, E. S., Smith, R., & Hammick, M. (2015). Evaluating an interprofessional education curriculum: A theory-informed approach. *Medical Teacher, 36,* 495–504. https://doi.org/10.3109/0142159X.2015.1047756.

Barr, H. (2002). *Interprofessional education, today, yesterday and tomorrow* (Occasional Paper 1). The Higher Education Academy, Health Sciences and Practice: CAIPE, HEA Kings College London.

Barr, H. (2007a). *Interprofessional education in the United Kingdom 1966 to 1997* (Occasional Paper 9). Higher Education Academy.

Barr, H. (Ed.). (2007b). *Piloting interprofessional education—Four English case studies* (Occasional Paper 8). Higher Education Academy-Health Sciences and Practice.

Barr, H., Helme, M., & D'Avray, L. (2011). *Developing interprofessional education in health and social care courses in the United Kingdom: A progress report* (Centre Occasional Paper 12). Higher Education Academy, Health Sciences and Practice Subject.

Barr, H., Helme, M., & D'Avray, L. (2014). *Review of interprofessional education in the United Kingdom 1997–2013.* CAIPE. www.caipe.org/.

Barr, H., & Low, H. (2013). *Introducing interprofessional education.* CAIPE. www.caipe.org/.

Brewer, M. L., & Barr, H. (2016). Interprofessional education and practice guide no. 8: Team-based interprofessional practice placements. *Journal of Interprofessional Care, 30,* 747–753.

CAIPE. (undated). *The centre for the advancement of inter-professional education in primary health care.* Attributable to John Horder. Circulated as a pamphlet soon after CAIPE was established in 1987.

CAIPE. (2002). *Interprofessional education—A definition.* www.caipe.org/.

CAIPE. (2011). *Principles of interprofessional education.* www.caipe.org/.

CAIPE. (2017). *Interprofessional education guidelines.* www.caipe.org/.

CAIPE. (2019). *The history of CAIPE.* www.caipe.org/.

Colyer, H., Helme, M., & Jones, I. (2005). *The theory-practice relationship in interprofessional education* (Occasional Paper 7). Higher Education Academy, Centre for Health Sciences.

Department of Health. (2000). *A health service for all the talents: Developing the NHS workforce.* London: Department of Health.

Fox, B. I., & Varadarajan, R. (2011). Use of Twitter to encourage interaction in a multi-campus pharmacy management course. *American Journal of Pharmaceutical Education, 75,* 88.

Gray, R. (2015). Changing times in the United Kingdom: The centre for the advancement of interprofessional education responds to the challenges. *Journal of Interprofessional Care, 29*(2), 93–94.

Horder, J. (2003). *A history of the Centre for the Advancement of Interprofessional Education (CAIPE) 1987–2003.* www.caipe.org/.

Lennox, A., & Anderson, E. S. (2007). *The Leicester model of interprofessional education: A practical guide for implementation in health and social care.* Higher Education Academy, subject centre. https://www.heacademy.ac.uk/knowledge-hub/leicester-model-interprofessional-education.

Lennox, A., & Petersen, S. (1998). Development and evaluation of community based, multi-agency course for medical students: Descriptive study. *British Medical Journal, 316,* 596–599.

Mckay, M., Steiner Sanko, J., Shekhter, I., & Birnbach, D. (2014). Twitter as a tool to enhance student engagement during an interprofessional patient safety course. *Journal of Interprofessional Care, 28*(6), 565–567.

Valentijin, P. M., Boesveld, I. C., van der Klauw, D. M., Ruwaard, D., Struijs, J. N., Molema, J. J. W., … Vrijhoef, H. J. M. (2015). Towards a taxonomy for integrated care: A mixed methods study. *International Journal of Integrated Care, 15,* 1–18.

4

Consensus-Based Partnerships: The Heart of Effective Interprofessional Education and Collaborative Practice

Stefanus Snyman and John Rogers

Introduction

Partnership is at the heart of interprofessional education and collaborative practice (IPECP). Whether it is in a small clinical team, at the institutional level in a clinic or hospital, in the community, or in building regional interprofessional partnerships, the principles and processes followed to develop the partnership will determine its effective functioning (Ansari & Phillips, 2001; Bleakley, 2013; Botma & Snyman, 2019; Grymonpre et al., 2016; Interprofessional.Global, 2019; McDonald, Davies, & Harris, 2009).

S. Snyman (✉)
Centre for Community Technologies, Nelson Mandela University, Port Elizabeth, South Africa
e-mail: stef@snymans.org

J. Rogers
Oxford, UK

D. Forman et al. (eds.), *Sustainability and Interprofessional Collaboration*,
https://doi.org/10.1007/978-3-030-40281-5_4

In this chapter, we examine the principles and processes involved in establishing and sustaining an effective partnership using the development and functioning of two partnerships as examples: the *Africa Interprofessional Education Network (AfrIPEN)* and *Interprofessional.Global: The Global Confederation for Interprofessional Education and Collaborative Practice.* These organisations followed a consensus-based partnership development process to gather potential stakeholders and collaborators to support their working together to achieve a common vision to see IPECP established in health and social care services to improve the health outcomes of people, to reduce the cost of care, to reduce the burden on human resources for health and to strengthen systems for health (AfrIPEN, 2016; Interprofessional.Global, 2018).

We are writing from our experience of developing and facilitating a number of different partnerships over a period of 30 years, and this chapter is based on those experiences rather than a distillation of theoretical viewpoints on partnerships. To complement the material in this chapter, we have created a number of tools to help with the development of the partnership you are looking to form. These can be found in an online *Toolkit for the development of consensus-based partnerships for interprofessional education and collaborative practice* (Rogers & Snyman, 2019). Specific tools in the toolkit are referenced as follows, *Toolkit #1, Toolkit #2*, etc.

Defining Partnership

Networks vary greatly in character and complexity, but networks tend to focus only on communication and information sharing. A network can be defined as any group of individuals and/or organisations who communicate with one another, with the sole purpose of sharing information to enhance their individual purposes; networks are usually understood *not* to include specific joint working (Taket & White, 2000, p. 25). In the IPECP context, networks have tended to suggest an informal linking of people who have a common interest. While a network is not a partnership, the relationships that are formed may lead to members of a network moving towards the idea of partnership.

A *partnership* is two or more individuals and/or organisations that collaborate (specifically and intentionally) to achieve a common purpose (Addicott, 2005, p. 20). Collaborate means not working alone, there is action and a common purpose whereas working together is intentional. Whereas the primary focus of a *network* is to share information, the primary focus of a *partnership* is to take joint action, to do something and do it better by working together. An extreme version of partnership would be a merger, where the organisations who are working together form a new legal organisation, in which they give up their individual organisational identities. However, in the type of partnership discussed in this chapter, partners need not give up their organisational identity to work together: each partner organisation retains its own identity and a clear vision for its own organisation.

Types of Partnership

Although there are various models of partnership, there are two different approaches to partnership development. The approach chosen will determine how effective you will be in working together to advocate for, collaborate on, promote, and share good practice of IPECP.

Highly Structured Partnerships

Highly structured partnerships are based on formal agreements and have a constitution and bylaws to which all potential partners must agree. There is a formal management structure, with a leadership team who make most, if not all, of the decisions. Time will be spent discussing and agreeing matters such as administration, budgets, finance, staff appointments and governance issues.

Loosely Structured (Consensus-Based) Partnerships

Loosely structured partnerships are based on relationships and informal agreements. All partner voices are represented and heard. Decisions are made by consensus (general agreement) with all partners participating in decision-making. In order to function effectively there needs to be a high degree of trust between partners and a strong element of interdependence. The main focus tends to be on the function of the partnership—the reason why the partnership exists and what it was established to achieve. In consensus-based partnerships 'function' is the priority and comes before either 'form' (the structure) or 'funds'.

This approach to cooperation resonates well with the African concept of 'ubuntu' (humanness) and ideas underlying the so-called African Renaissance (Bitzer, 2004). In the African context, a person is an embodied entity, but goes beyond the body to being embedded in family and community (similar to the interprofessional team). As the African saying puts it so well 'Umntu ngumtu ngabantu' (a person is a person by means of people). We are persons within a milieu of complex relationships with our bodies, ourselves, other persons, the rest of nature, and with our belief system and worldview (Fehrsen, 2015). AfrIPEN and Interprofessional.Global are examples of consensus-based partnerships (Box 4.1).

Box 4.1 The partnership model of AfrIPEN and Interprofessional.Global

Prior to the formation of Interprofessional.Global as a consensus-based partnership, it functioned as the World Coordinating Committee (WCC) of All Together Better Health. The WCC operated as a constitutional-based partnership, where procedures and rules took precedence over effective functioning. In 2018, a number of regional IPECP organisations agreed that this approach to governance and leadership was not sustainable. As a result, they embarked on a process to form a consensus-based partnership, modelling the ethos of interprofessionalism. This ultimately led to the formation of Interprofessional.Global.

AfrIPEN is not a network as its name suggests, but has been a functioning consensus-based partnership from its conception in 2015. During its first meeting in Port Elizabeth (AfrIPEN, 2016), all partner voices were heard, but the partners realised that it was not realistic to collaborate on each individual organisation's priorities for IPECP. The three-day consensus building process, which also focussed on building trust and mutual concern, helped everyone to feel comfortable with the priorities which were ultimately agreed upon for collaboration. When it came to the election of a new facilitator for AfrIPEN in 2019, there was initially some lobbying for the process to be open to nominations and a voting process, but ultimately, the partnership opted not to vote but to reach consensus on which candidate would serve as the best facilitator for the functioning of the partnership. This process contributed to the building of greater trust amongst the partners.

Consensus-based partnerships are not without their challenges. For example, at some stage it may be necessary to establish a formal entity with a constitution to enable the opening of a bank account and apply for grants/funding. Later we will discuss how Interprofessional.Global approached this challenge creatively. It can also be easy to revert to a default position of running a constitution-based partnership and focusing on the structure rather than the function of the partnership. This is why it is critically important to keep to the principles of a consensus-based partnership.

Principles of a Consensus-Based Partnership

Working interprofessionally in partnership reflects the unity we see in working with, for, and between service providers and service users. Partnership is one important way to demonstrate to the world the unity of a bio-psycho-social-spiritual approach to health and social care. Over a period of more than 30 years the following principles have been observed as significant in the development of effective partnerships,[1] principles which are wholly consistent with IPECP (Butler, 2006). An adherence

[1]These partnership principles are based on a set of principles which were originally articulated by Interdev, an organisation dedicated to the development of partnerships, in the mid-1990s, and which both authors were associated with at the time. These principles have subsequently been developed and promoted by other partnering organisations.

to these principles is much more likely to result in the establishment of an effective and sustainable IPECP partnership.

The principles are:

1. Effective partners share openly with one another in all they do.
   Partners are empowered and refreshed by sharing knowledge, experience, and approaches with one another; listening to and learning from one another; and supporting and caring for one another's personal needs, as well as for the work.
2. Effective partnerships have a facilitator or a facilitation team.
   Partnership does not just *happen*. It takes a person or a team of committed people acceptable to all the partners to facilitate the work of the partnership, who serve the whole partnership, enabling it to function effectively.
3. Effective partnerships have a clear purpose.
   Only a partnership that is formed to fulfil a specific vision or purpose is likely to be effective. Partnership for partnership's sake spells failure.
4. Effective partnerships identify needs before shaping structure.
   An effective partnership starts by identifying barriers to progress and from these agrees on priorities for action; it does not start by trying to establish conditions for membership or write a common Statement of Incorporation. *Function* (what the partnership can do) should always come before *form* (how the partnership is structured). Consensus is usually better than constitution.
5. Effective partnerships have clear, well-defined objectives.
   Initially, these will be limited and must be achievable. However, they must also be significant enough to provide motivation for partnering. As the partnership experiences progress, the objectives can become more challenging.
6. Effective partners keep their eyes on the ultimate vision.
   It is easy to focus on the 'means' rather than the 'end'. An effective partnership focusses on the long-term vision and what should be achieved to reach that end goal. It is important not to get distracted by maintaining the structure.
7. Effective partnerships are built on relationships of trust, openness and mutual concern.

Partnership is more than coordination and planning. The heart of partnership is strong and effective relationships demonstrated in action. Developing such relationships requires time and intentional effort. Effective partners are especially sensitive towards those from cultures and backgrounds other than their own.

8. Effective partnerships focus on what the partners have in common rather than on what makes them different.
   Unity is encouraged by sharing things of the heart, like vision, values, and common goals. Discussing differences in philosophy, history and work experience divides. However, it is important to acknowledge—even celebrate—these differences at times.
9. Effective partnerships maintain a high level of participation and ownership by the partners.
   Ownership and commitment to the process of effective partnering is encouraged by wide participation of all the partners in decision-making.
10. Effective partnerships impart the vision and skills for partnership development to all the partners continuously.
    It is important for partners to catch the vision for partnership and develop skills in partnering. This may include skills in partnership development and reinforcing the vision and goals of the partnership when the partnership meets. An effective partnership expects problems, especially at times of leadership change, and develops processes for managing them.
11. Effective partnerships do not come free of charge.
    Just participating in a partnership costs time and money, so all partners are investing in some way. Deeper commitment involves an even greater investment, but the benefits more than outweigh these costs.
12. Effective partners recognise that partnership is an on-going process, not an event.
    The early stages of developing a partnership take time. Call a meeting too soon and the process is likely to fail. The development of trust is essential before the potential partners come together. Once established, time for nurturing trust and processing issues is equally

important. It is even more challenging to maintain a partnership than to launch one.

13. Effective partners recognise that they have various constituencies whose needs must be acknowledged and whose contributions must be valued.
    There are more people and interests involved in a partnership than those sitting around the table. These include those who serve and support the partnership, the leaders and staff of the partner organisations, the people and entities the partnership is seeking to serve (users and providers of health and social services, systems for health, etc.), and the partnership itself. Effective partners understand the needs of each of these groups and seek to meet them. They also acknowledge and value the contributions each makes.
14. Effective partners celebrate.
    It is important for partners to frequently celebrate the achievements of the partnership as a whole, as well as those of individual partners.
15. Effective partners have an 'advocate' for partnership in their own organisation.
    This is a person who sees how their own organisation can benefit from practical cooperation and who will share this vision with colleagues. Without such a person, the commitment of the organisation to the partnership is likely to be half-hearted at best.
16. Effective partners have clear identities and visions.
    Partners who have a strong sense of their own identity, vocation, and calling are likely to be most effective. If the individual partners do not have a clear vision for their own organisation, they will have difficulty seeing what they can contribute to the overall partnership or how they can benefit from the joint effort.

Organisations and individuals that are serious about successful partnering with others should keep these principles in mind as they work with others to achieve the vision and objectives. Following these principles will enhance the likelihood of partnership being successful and sustained. Ignoring them is most likely to result in a failed attempt to work with others, which will make any subsequent attempts to work together much more difficult (Butler, 2006). Founding partners of both AfrIPEN and

Interprofessional.Global subscribed to this set of principles for the development of consensus-based partnerships.

The Role of the Facilitator or a Facilitation Team

The second of these partnering principles states, 'effective partnerships have a facilitator or a facilitation team'. This is such a key principle that it needs developing.

There must be a person (or a small team) with the heart, vision, and commitment to make the partnership work effectively, who connects the various members of the partnership, who is aware of the contribution to the wider whole of the partnership of each partner member, and who is able to build relationships which are the heart-beat of any partnering approach (Bentley, 1995; Grymonpre et al., 2016; Kiser, 1998). Graham Moore (2019) describes a facilitator as somebody enabling something to happen, who aids or assists in a process, especially by encouraging people to find their own solutions to problems or tasks. The partnership facilitator also brings the various elements of the partnership together and keeps communication flowing between each individual partner member. Sometimes the facilitator is an individual; sometimes two or three (but rarely more) people undertake this function. There are various functions that the partnership facilitator fulfils and an understanding of each function is important when seeking to establish any partnering approach.

One of the roles of the partnership facilitator or facilitation team is to connect people to other people—and to the partnership, in that the central task of the facilitator is to enable access to participation in the process of partnership by all those who wish to participate (Taket & White, 2000). For example, in the IPECP field, the partnership facilitator establishes who is involved in educational practice in a professional or geographical area, establishes whether they are interested in collaborating with others and helps them meet like-minded others. They form people into a partnership or, if the partnership already exists, help people become integrated and involved in what is already happening (Box 4.2).

Box 4.2 Example of how a partnership facilitation team connects people

AfrIPEN's partnership facilitation team realised that nursing students are often not included in IPE activities which typically involve medical students and those from the rehabilitation professions. Furthermore, we have found that nurses often feel that doctors look down on them and that they are not regarded as equal members in health care teams. With the increasing focus on primary healthcare and sustainable development goals, nurses are pivotal in the realisation of universal health coverage in Africa. To bring more leaders in the nursing profession into the IPE community, AfrIPEN's partnership facilitation team invited two nursing associations to co-host the Second Interprofessional Education and Collaborative Practice for Africa conference in Nairobi in 2019, namely Sigma Theta Tau International's Tau Lambda at Large Chapter—an association focussing on the development of nursing leadership globally—and the Anglophone Africa Advanced Practice in Nursing Coalition. This resulted in more than 60 nursing leaders from all over Africa attending the conference. Subsequently more than 40 nursing leaders volunteered to collaborate in AfrIPEN's working groups and are now advocates for IPECP in their respective institutions (see Partnership Principle #15 above).

The president of WONCA Africa (World Organisation of Family Doctors Africa Region) also attended the conference. This led to discussions on how the Third Interprofessional Education and Collaborative Practice for Africa conference could be co-hosted between associations for family physicians, nurses, and AfrIPEN in 2022.

Another role of the partnership facilitator or facilitation team is to identify resources needed to enhance the partnership, such as people, funding, equipment, or access to training. The partnership facilitator sees what new resources are needed and makes the connections which enable those resources to be available to the partnership (Kiser, 1998) (Box 4.3).

Box 4.3 Example where a partnership facilitator connects people to needed new resources

During a three-day partnership development meeting, AfrIPEN prioritised the development of a continuing interprofessional education (CIPE) short course in IPECP to equip faculty, staff, facilitators, preceptors, and service providers. A framework was developed by a working group for the various modules of the planned short course. The challenge was to find the people and resources to develop the modules. The facilitator learnt about the Health Professional Education Partnership Initiative (HEPI), a grant awarded to various institutions in Africa that complements and enhances the training of a workforce to meet the biomedical, behavioural, and clinical research needs in low-resource, high HIV-burden countries in Africa, including Ethiopia, Kenya, Malawi, Mozambique, Tanzania, Uganda, Zambia and Zimbabwe. The HEPI recipients identified IPECP as a critical part of their planned training. The AfrIPEN facilitation team approached the HEPI institutions, inviting them to help develop the various modules needed for the continuing interprofessional education short course with the full support of experts from AfrIPEN and Interprofessional.Global.

Connecting opportunities for IPECP is another key role for the partnership facilitator. Such connections not only bring people together to enable them to work together effectively, but also promote the *multiplication* of IPECP and its impact. In connecting people to opportunities the partnership facilitator needs both vision and initiative (Bentley, 1995). The facilitator needs to be constantly on the lookout for opportunities, see the potential in different situations and take initiatives needed to make the appropriate connections (Box 4.4).

Box 4.4 Connecting opportunities for IPECP

AfrIPEN was invited to conduct a pre-conference workshop on IPE at the 3rd Annual AFREhealth Symposium in Lagos in 2019. The African Forum for Research and Education in Health is a constitution-based partnership, well-funded by the USA. AfrIPEN's past and present facilitators did not expect much enthusiasm for the workshop, because the ethos of the organisation is very high on "form" and "funding" (constitution-based) rather than "function" (consensus-based). Much to their surprise nearly 100 people participated in the workshop, most of whom indicated interest in collaborating on a longitudinal study to determine the impact of IPECP. African governments and other decision-makers need evidence before they are willing to fund and implement radical policies to make IPECP the norm. They need evidence that IPECP improves health outcomes and patient safety, reduces cost and the burden on human resources for health and that it strengthens systems for health. AfrIPEN's "Impact Evaluation Project" was conceptualised a few days earlier in negotiations between the World Health Organization (WHO) Regional Office for Africa, the

WHO Collaboration Centre for IPE and AfrIPEN. This serves as an example how partnership facilitators can create opportunities for IPECP.

The ideal leadership style of a partnership facilitator is what Robert Greenleaf describes as the 'strong natural servant' (Greenleaf, 1970, p. 13). Such a leader assumes leadership because they see it as a way in which they can serve. They see leadership as a function and not a position; they are leading because it is their desire to serve and to promote the needs of other people and of other organisations as opposed to just their own. This should be the approach of the partnership facilitator; someone who leads through serving the partnership.

Three Stages of Consensus-Based Partnership Development

As we begin to outline the stages that a consensus-based partnership is likely to go through, it is important to note that every partnership is different. There is not what could be described as a 'typical' or even an 'ideal' partnership. Each partnership has its own personality. However, from our experience of working with emerging and operating partnerships over a period of 30 years, a consensus-based partnership will typically go through three phases or stages. These are the (1) exploration stage, (2) the formation stage, and (3) the operation stage.

Exploration Stage of Partnership Development

When establishing a partnership for any collaborative initiative, you need to begin with a very clear perspective that working together with others is really important and that working with others will help deliver the objectives you are seeking more effectively than working individually. You must be convinced that a partnering approach is the best way of providing the service you need to deliver. If you are not completely committed to a partnering approach, you are unlikely to be able to convince others to work in partnership.

The exploration stage is the period when time is spent exploring whether a partnership might be possible and what purpose it might serve. This is a critically important stage in the development of a partnership. Although it can be tempting to try to start the partnership by calling a meeting to 'form' the partnership, it is important not to rush the process. You need to give sufficient time to effective exploration. Research what others might be doing and build relationships, otherwise you can be creating problems for the future effectiveness of the partnership. It is important that time is spent building a strong, firm, and deep foundation. This is something which must be done before you can expect any real commitment on the behalf of potential partners to the development of a partnership. It takes time: most partnerships take at least a year, some up to two years, and some take much longer in the exploration stage.

For the successful exploration of a partnership, you—as the advocate for partnership who is seeking to put together a group of people who could collaborate—must demonstrate a number of characteristics and undertake a number of tasks. Perhaps the most important task is to identify and build trust relationships through holding one-on-one meetings with representatives from other organisations and institutions who are seeking to improve the standard of IPE. You need to spend time *really* listening to what 'they' are saying, not trying to gain their support for your own agenda or vision. It is also important to go to these meetings with an attitude of a learner, not as someone who has 'all the answers'.

The primary objectives of the one-on-one exploration meetings are, (1) to get to know and build relationships with everyone who is engaged in IPE, (2) learn about their organisation, (3) identify issues which need to be addressed and problems which may arise, (4) discover their opinion of others, and (5) identify and develop their perceived need for collaboration with others. During these meetings you should develop an understanding of these organisations, including:

- their vision, history, structure, objectives and relationships
- their involvement in and plans for IPECP

- their perceptions of the situation and needs regarding IPECP
- their perceptions of others who might be drawn into the partnership
- their interest in the possibility of co-operation.

Throughout the exploration process you need to demonstrate your impartiality. This is not an attempt to absorb other organisations into your own, or to take over the work of others. Then you have to encourage those you are meeting with to think seriously about a partnership approach to enhance IPE. Finally, you need to be assiduous in your follow-up. Document the discussions you have had with potential partners; thank those you meet with for their time and e-mail them with any information you have promised to send them. (See the online *Toolkit #1* for a template that can be used to record one-on-one meetings during the exploration stage.)

As the exploration stage draws to a close, you should expect to have achieved:

- good relationships with leaders of other organisations you want to draw into the partnership
- a good basis of knowledge of the overall picture of IPECP in the area
- a willingness of the key people and organisations to meet and explore the possibility of co-operation (Box 4.5).

Box 4.5 The exploration phases of AfrIPEN and Interprofessional.Global

In the case of AfrIPEN the exploration phase took four years. As often happens, the partnership developer did not have funding available to do the exploration on a full-time basis, so the process took much longer. Instead of the recommended method of exploring a partnership by visiting potential partners on their home turf, Stefanus Snyman, who undertook the exploration of the partnership, had to meet people at conferences or when they visited the university he was working at. In some cases, Skype calls were used. These methods were far from the ideal, which meant that the process took far longer than would otherwise have been the case.

With Interprofessional.Global the exploration process took only a few months. Representatives of all established and emerging networks were very eager to meet to build trust relationships and to explore opportunities for collaboration in the true spirit and ethos of interprofessionalism. It only took a few video calls and emails to explain to stakeholders how a consensus-based partnership operates and how the formation meeting would work. The short exploration stage was due to the suggestions and commitment from regional and emerging IPECP networks for the need of a consensus-based and sustainable partnership to truly model interprofessionalism.

Formation of a Partnership

Once you have completed the exploration stage you can begin the process of planning the formation meeting for your partnership. Partnership is about relationships. Experience suggests it will need a three- to four-day meeting for a successful formation meeting to happen, especially if your partnership is an international one. You may experience some resistance to such a lengthy meeting. However, taking sufficient time over the process is really important for success. Try to ensure there is equality among participants. It is best to avoid the use of titles (such as 'doctor' or 'professor', etc.). It's also helpful to discourage the wearing of formal clothing.

Meetings do not just happen, they need detailed preparation and the success of the initial partnership meeting is dependent on some key decisions as you plan the meeting. We suggest that you should invite everyone you know who is engaged with IPECP, even if, when you met them, they did not seem very enthusiastic about collaborating with others. In this way you are inclusive rather than exclusive. Leadership of the meeting is also important. Whoever leads the meeting should adopt a 'facilitative' approach rather than acting as a directive 'chair'. The leader must be perceived as being completely neutral, whose sole objective is to help the group make decisions. Sometimes it can be helpful to have a small group of up to three people take turns in facilitating different parts of the meeting (Taket & White, 2000).

Notice of meetings should be given well in advance, because people are busy. Check dates of other local and international events that might have an impact on attendance at this meeting and keep in mind annual weather conditions that might impact travel. It can be helpful to arrange the formation meeting immediately before or after another meeting that a number of interested parties will be attending. It is often easier for people to get funding to attend a conference than a meeting, and it can be easier for people to 'add-on' a meeting. Hold the meeting in a location where people can stay, eat and meet. It complicates matters if people stay in one location and the meeting is elsewhere. Both the venue and the accommodation need to be affordable. It is important to have a spacious location where the meetings can be held, and where the networking facilities are good.

There will be costs which need to be considered. These include name tags, stationery, flip charts and markers, etc. To cover these costs, you should consider charging a registration fee. When informing people about the plans for the meeting, it is important to make sure that they understand the reason for calling the meeting, which should be to encourage information sharing between people who are engaged with IPECP, and to explore possible co-operation on a task that is too big for any single organisation. Communicate clearly that no decision has been made about future co-operation, what form such co-operation will take or the purpose it might serve. This will be discussed by the group itself. The convenor of the meeting should also consider co-opting an advisory or steering group which reflects the membership of the entire potential partnership. This helps to underline that others are committed to the process and thereby widens the leadership base within the potential partnership.

Planning is important, but so is the process of the meeting itself. (See the online *Toolkit #2* for an outline agenda which you can use for a formation meeting of a partnership.)

To reach an agreement to work together and form a partnership a number of components should be incorporated in the meeting, which include:

- introductions: people sharing about themselves and their work
- a reminder of the purpose of the meeting as not everyone present may fully understand why the meeting is taking place
- organisations sharing in detail what they have done regarding IPECP so that everyone hears what each is doing
- discussion on what is working effectively
- identifying both duplication and gaps regarding IPECP provision
- discussion on challenges experienced
- an extended time in which you build consensus on two to four priorities that will be addressed together as a partnership. By consensus we mean that the group together reach an agreed decision on which priorities to focus on
- time for relationship building; it is important to allow adequate time for meals and coffee/tea breaks, because it is during those times that relationships are further developed and a lot of small-scale cooperation is agreed on (Box 4.6).

Box 4.6 The formation meeting in an African context

At the AfrIPEN formation meeting, and at all subsequent meetings, we started with ample time for partners to introduce themselves. The time allocated is likely to vary according to the number of people present, but it can take up to three hours, and sometimes even longer. We encourage participants to share about themselves as human beings, not human doings: not about what people are doing and their accolades, but to get to know them as individuals. We encourage sharing about family, upbringing, neighbourhood, where they are now in their lives, and what encouragements they need. As an example, one facilitator usually started the process by sharing about his upbringing. Another shared his story of how he never fitted in with his peers, about his burnout as a young doctor and the devastating experience of depression on his life. Sharing of stories is highly appreciated in most African contexts usually resulting in more people being eager to share their own stories. A senior leader of a very bureaucratic organisation stated at the end of one meeting that sharing his story, and listening to others, was the highlight of the event. It helped him to have compassion with others and to trust them.

The way this formation meeting is facilitated is critical if the partnership is going to be successful in the long term. Equally important is including an extended time during the meeting where you run a process to help the group decide by consensus a limited number of projects that the partnership will initially work on together. The way you approach both the facilitation of the meeting and the consensus-building approach is so important. (See the online *Toolkit #3* for a step-by-step process which you can use to achieve consensus in a partnership meeting.) Both Interprofessional.Global and AfrIPEN followed the consensus-building process outlined, one which has worked successfully many times in partnership meetings.

Having identified two to four priorities during the formation meeting, it is important to establish working groups, each focusing on a different priority. This is where most of the work of the partnership will get done. The value of working groups is that it divides the work of the partnership into manageable segments, and also provides forums for specialists to work together on projects. Time needs to be planned in the schedule for working groups to begin their work, with most continuing to meet and work on the priorities identified after the initial meeting has concluded. Working groups should come to agreement by consensus, because if anyone in the group tries to dominate, the working group will most likely fail. Each working group should report to the full membership of the partnership; in the initial formation meeting this can be through a brief report to the whole group. At subsequent meetings, always schedule time for the working groups to report to the whole partnership, and to receive feedback from others about what they have achieved. Early in a partnership, there may only be three or four working groups. As the partnership develops, and as new issues are identified, more working groups may be established. As the partnership matures, it is possible that ten or more working groups may meet. Do not maintain working groups that are no longer contributing valuable input to the partnership.

Before the formation meeting ends there are some practical issues to be addressed. These include whether the group wants to continue to meet, who the partnership facilitator might be, whether you want a partnership facilitation team (what Interprofessional.Global calls the 'Partnership Facilitation Working Group') and to celebrate what has been achieved during the time the group has been together. At the conclusion of the meeting, you may decide that it has been a good meeting, but there is nothing specific you want to work on together. If so, you have not formed a partnership. If a partnership is to be formed, at least the following three aspects should be agreed:

- when to meet again
- the appointment of someone to be the facilitator, or the appointment of a facilitation team
- plans to work together on some specific issues or projects.

If you have the above in place, you can celebrate the forming of your partnership, and move onto the next stage in the partnering process: the operation stage.

Operation Stage

The operation stage of a partnership should be the most productive stage, because this is where the members of the partnership are effective in working together. Significant results can be achieved by implementing the joint strategies and developing the partnership to its fullest potential. If the partnership is really going to work well, regular meetings need to be held. The regularity of these meetings will depend on the nature of the partnership, but whenever the partnership meets we encourage partnerships to schedule these meetings over a three- to four-day period. The key factor in all partnering meetings is the development and maintenance of relationships—and this takes time. Always allow time for relationship building in partnership meetings, whether it is a first meeting, or whether the partnership has met on a number of occasions. (See the online *Toolkit #4* for a sample agenda for a meeting during the operations stage.)

Typically, during the operation stage of a partnership, you are likely to experience a transition from independent activities to a mixture of independent efforts and joint actions. New joint projects will be identified. Working groups will meet and effectively accomplish the objectives they have been set and more organisations will join the partnership. See the online *Toolkit #6* for a sample template of a planning document which can be used by working groups.

The facilitator (or facilitation team) still has a critical role as the partnership continues to work together to meet the objectives for which it was formed. Meetings for the partnership to meet together, to review progress and to make further plans, need planning and preparation. The facilitator also continues to provide consistent and active communication among the partner members, to support the leaders of each of the working groups and, in addition, brings new partners into the partnership while ensuring everyone shares a sense of the impact of working together. The facilitator may also be managing conflict and ensuring that minor disagreements do not turn into major conflicts. Another task for the facilitator is to evaluate the impact of the partnership, so that all partner members can appreciate the value of the partnership.

Box 4.7 The operation stages for AfrIPEN and Interprofessional.Global

The biggest challenge for AfrIPEN's partnership facilitator and facilitation team was to effectively support and encourage the working group facilitators to formulate the objectives and key results they had set for themselves. During face-to-face meetings, working groups are encouraged to set themselves clear objectives for the next two year cycle and to set three to four key results they would like to attain for each objective (Doerr, 2018). However, both Interprofessional.Global and AfrIPEN were faced with the challenge that some working groups just did not get off the ground. It so happened that eager and enthusiastic members were appointed to facilitate a working group, but lacked follow-through to keep the team moving forward. To overcome this challenge both partnerships thought it wise to appoint co-facilitators for each working group.

One very helpful and positive development for the AfrIPEN partnership has been the offer of a South African university to serve as the secretariat for the partnership as a support to the partnership facilitator. This university made available administrative staff to assist the facilitator in monitoring the progress made by working groups. The university also serves as the partnership's "bank account" since the partnership is not a legal entity. To support the work of the partnership, AfrIPEN has a facilitation team, which consists of the partnership facilitator, the secretariat, and at least two other partner members. The facilitation team tries to meet quarterly with the working group facilitators to monitor progress and evaluate the impact of the partnership.

Interprofessional.Global, is structured around seven functioning working groups. This partnership was faced by a significant challenge, because as a consensus-based partnership it was not able to open a bank account or to sign contracts when receiving grants. To solve this challenge, they are—at the time of writing this chapter—in the process of registering as a non-governmental organisation (NGO) in The Netherlands. Although Interprofessional.Global needed a constitution to register as an NGO, the consensus was that it should not have to function as a constitutional-based partnership. The roles of the board members of the NGO are purely to ensure there is financial accountability, they can sign legal contracts, and they are compliant with Dutch law. In terms of the functioning of Interprofessional.Global, the Directors of the NGO form the "Legal and Finance Working Group" of the partnership. The Board Members of the NGO are elected by both the facilitators of the established regional networks affiliated to Interprofessional.Global. In this way, Interprofessional.Global is able to function with a flat consensus-based structure and at the same time be a registered NGO.

Every operating partnership is likely to look different from other partnerships. That is because the issues being addressed, and the environment in which they are operating, will be different for every partnership. However, consensus-based partnerships all have one thing in common: they have been created to solve a problem—or a series of problems—and to achieve things together that they cannot achieve on their own. They can do more together than they can do alone (Taket & White, 2000, p. 6).

Conclusion

In this chapter, we have explored practical ways to develop a consensus-based partnership between stakeholders who have the vision to establish IPECP as an integral part in training the health workforce and in the effective functioning of systems for health.

The task to transform health professions education and to reform systems for health to embrace IPECP as the norm, is too big for any one agency to tackle alone. We need numerous consensus-based partnerships across the globe—in institutions, cities, provinces, countries, and regions—to collaborate in bringing about this change in approach. A change which will significantly improve the provision of health and social care across communities, across countries and across the world. In the process, we must model the competencies and ethos of IPECP. What better way than developing consensus-based partnerships.

Additional Resource

A toolkit for the development of consensus-based partnerships for IPECP is available online at https://doi.org/10.13140/RG.2.2.33337.93285 (Rogers & Snyman, 2019). The toolkit contains forms and more techniques for developers and facilitators of consensus-based partnerships. These include:

- #1 Exploration Stage of a partnership: Report form for one-on-one meetings
- #2 Formation stage of a partnership: Agenda for a formation meeting
- #3 An approach to build consensus in a partnership meeting
- #4 Operation stage of a partnership: Draft agenda for three- to four-day partnership meeting
- #5 Operation stage of a partnership: Handling organisations' reports when large numbers are present
- #6 Operation stage of a partnership: Template for planning document for working groups.

Acknowledgements We appreciate the dedication of Helen du Preez (SS's mother, who always critically reviews his work!), Champion Nyoni (AfrIPEN's facilitator) and Johanna Dahlberg (Interprofessional.Global's facilitator). They provided valuable contributions to the content and style of this chapter.

References

Addicott, E. (2005). *Body matters*. Edmonds, WA: Interdev Partnership Associates.

AfrIPEN. (2016, June 20–21). *African interprofessional education network: Report of planning workshop held at the Nelson Mandela Metropolitan University*. Port Elizabeth. Retrieved from https://afripen.org/events-2/archive-of-previous-events/.

Ansari, W. E., & Phillips, C. J. (2001). Partnerships, community participation and intersectoral collaboration in South Africa. *Journal of Interprofessional Care, 15*(2), 119–132. https://doi.org/10.1080/13561820120039856.

Bentley, T. (1995). *Facilitation: Providing Opportunities for Learning*. New York, NY, USA: McGraw-Hill.

Bitzer, E. (2004). Cooperative learning. In S. Gravett & H. Geyser (Eds.), *Teaching and learning in higher education* (pp. 41–66). Pretoria: Van Schaik Publishers.

Bleakley, A. (2013). Working in 'teams' in an era of 'liquid' healthcare: What is the use of theory? *Journal of Interprofessional Care, 27*(1), 18–26. https://doi.org/10.3109/13561820.2012.699479.

Botma, Y., & Snyman, S. (2019). Africa Interprofessional Education Network (AfrIPEN). *Journal of Interprofessional Care, 33*(3), 274–276. https://doi.org/10.1080/13561820.2019.1605236.

Butler, P. (2006). *Well connected*. Huntington, CA, USA: Authentic & World Vision.

Doerr, J. (2018). *Measure what matters—OKRs: The simple idea that drives 10x growth*. London, UK: Portfolio Penguin.

Fehrsen, G. (2015). A framework for a clinical method fit for persons in community. In B. Brom, J. Kriel, & J. Viall (Eds.), *Conversations 2—Mind, matter and medicine* (pp. 26–33). Stellenbosch: African SUNMedia.

Greenleaf, R. K. (1970). *The servant as leader*. South Orange, NJ: Robert K. Greenleaf Center for Servant Leadership.

Grymonpre, R., Bowman, S., Rippin-Sisler, C., Klaasen, K., Bapuji, S. B., Norrie, O., & Metge, C. (2016). Every team needs a coach: Training for interprofessional clinical placements. *Journal of Interprofessional Care, 30*(5), 559–566. https://doi.org/10.1080/13561820.2016.1181611.

Interprofessional.Global. (2018, September 6–9). *Interprofessional.Global: Report of the strategic planning workshop held at the Waipuna Hotel, Auckland, New Zealand*. Auckland. Retrieved from https://interprofessional.global/interprofessional-global-strategic-planning-retreat/.

Interprofessional.Global. (2019). *The confederation.* Retrieved from https://interprofessional.global/the-confederation/.

Kiser, A. (1998). *Masterful facilitation: Becoming a catalyst for meaningful change.* New York, NY, USA: AMACOM.

McDonald, J., Davies. G. P., & Harris, M. F. (2009). Interorganisational and interprofessional partnership approaches to achieve more coordinated and integrated primary and community health services: The Australian experience. *Australian Journal of Primary Health, 15*, 262–269. https://doi.org/10.1071/PY09017.

Moore, G. (2019). *Facilitation.* Retrieved from http://mooresuccessme.com/facilitation/.

Rogers, J., & Snyman, S. (2019). *Toolkit for the development of consensus-based partnerships for interprofessional education and collaborative practice.* https://doi.org/10.13140/RG.2.2.33337.93285.

Taket, A., & White, L. (2000). *Partnership and participation: Decision-making in the multiagency setting.* Hoboken, NJ, USA: Wiley.

5

Starting, Growing and Sustaining Leadership in Interprofessional Collaboration in Thailand

Wanicha Chuenkongkaew

What Is Interprofessional Education (IPE) and Interprofessional Practice (IPP)?

Health care is dramatically changing in response to the increasing magnitude of future health and health-related complex challenges. In 2010, the World Health Organization defined IPE as learning about, from and with different professions to collaborate effectively for achieving better health care and outcomes (World Health Organization, 2010). IPE is determined as an educational approach for collaborative health care providers while IPP describes a team-based approach to strengthen health systems for better health outcomes, with strong evidences such as shorter lengths of hospitalisation, improving mental health and end-of-life care. Therefore, in enabling effective IPE and IPP there needs to be synergistic strategies for health and education systems to build future health

W. Chuenkongkaew (✉)
Siriraj Hospital, Mahidol University, Bangkok, Thailand

D. Forman et al. (eds.), *Sustainability and Interprofessional Collaboration*,
https://doi.org/10.1007/978-3-030-40281-5_5

professionals capable of tackling urgent global challenges. Global dynamics such as increasing average life spans, emerging and re-emerging infectious diseases, disruptive technology and climate change, have moved the world into a situation of Volatility, Uncertainty, Complexity and Ambiguity (VUCA).

Health Profession Education generally needs reform alongside the global changing health care context which includes having continuous dialogues to bridge the gap between health care providers and academia so as to support the change. Thus, student learners and practitioners must learn how to collaborate more effectively, as it is challenging if academic institutions stay firm and won't change. It is important that the academics and practitioners understand this. IPE emphasises interprofessional teamwork in the teaching and learning processes at undergraduate level and further continues to postgraduate level. In addition, IPP plays a key role in enhancing people-centred care, in response to populations' health needs in an equitable and efficient manner with existing resources. This is a change still in process.

Why Are IPE and IPP Important?

Health systems throughout the world have been evolving over time from controlling the spread of specific communicable diseases to having an equitably integrated health service working together in the focus on health promotion and disease prevention. Currently, both Universal Health Coverage (UHC) and Health System Strengthening are needed to respond to current health threats. The Health Workforce (HWF) is identified as one of the core building blocks of the health system.

Transformative HWF training and education is an innovative strategy for the development of a highly competent HWF to strengthen the health system. 'Competency' is more than knowledge and skills, it is the capability of bringing on or provisioning of psychosocial resources to tackle complicated needs within a specific context. Since academic tribalism or discipline-led silos in academic institutes is one of the key challenges for transformative education, changing educational cultures and paradigms is quite difficult and requires both institutional and instructional reforms as well as mutual recognition on learning and working. To optimise health professional learning, the transformation should also focus on system- and team-based learning in addition to competency-based learning. After the Lancet Commission launched a report on 'Education of health professionals for the 21st century: a global independent Commission' (Frenk et al., 2010), there was a movement in reforming health professional education and IPE with respect to the nation's socio-economic and cultural status, as well as domestic health service systems in Thailand, Vietnam, Bangladesh, China and India.

Key challenges on implementing IPE in Thailand include traditional cultural ways of learning and silos in academic institutes and professional organisations at both policy maker and faculty staff levels along with inflexible regulatory systems.

IPE and IPP have been gradually embedded in teaching and learning processes to better equip the HWF to meet population health needs of Thailand. To improve IPE, an integrated care delivery model provided by a health care team in a collaboratively interprofessional manner needs to engage the broader scale of the HWF and the non-traditional HWF in Thailand including engineers, patients, families and communities. Further collaboration with social scientists in economics, sociologists, public policy makers and social workers is also needed. The most favoured population-based model of health care needs a holistic approach, involving effective teamwork and effective leadership and interprofessional working.

Current Situation and Trend of IPE in Thailand

In 2010, the launch of a global commission on *Education of health professionals for the 21st century: a global independent Commission* chaired by Professor Lincoln Chen (President of China Medical Board) and Professor Julio Frenk (Dean of Harvard School of Public Health), triggered a solid movement of transformative health professional education in Thailand. In 2012, the Thai National Health Assembly approved the National Strategic Plan for the Development of HWF education in the twenty-first century (2014–2018). As a result a national commission was appointed by the Prime Minister to promote the strategic plan on a participatory and voluntary basis among nine health professional organisations and associations including those of the nursing, physicians, dentistry, pharmacy, physical therapy, medical technology, veterinary, public health and alternative medicine. The National Health Professional Education Foundation (NHPE) works as the secretariat for the commission. Subsequently, the Commission appointed an IPE subcommittee to implement IPE on five key activities including

- Development of national IPE framework and guidelines;
- Promotion of institutional reform and policy advocacy;
- Capacity leadership building;
- Evaluation of IPE programme; and
- Collaboration on IPE research.

The practical steps for implementation of national IPE are shown in Table 5.1.

Movement on IPE in the World Health Organization (WHO) South-East Asia Region (SEAR)

The World Health Organisation South-East Asia Region has some well-known HWF challenges and needs transformative HWF education and training. These include shortages of staff, unequal distribution of the HWF across countries, difficulty in retention of staff, adapting the HWF's education to fit rapidly changing needs and improving the performance of the HWF.

In 2012, the 65th World Health Organization Regional Committee meeting for South-East Asia met to endorse the resolution 'Strengthening HWF Education and Training in the Region' (2014–2019) (WHO, 2012). Among other initiatives, it urged SEAR countries to conduct an assessment of their HWF education using modified Asia-Pacific Network on Health Professional Education Reform (ANHER) tools

Table 5.1 Practical steps for implementation of IPE at national level in Thailand

Practical steps	Objectives	Tactics
Formulate	Constitute a commission Build leadership capacity of champions	A national IPE commission was established comprising of distinct health professions (nurse, physician, dentist, pharmacist, physical therapist, medical technologist veterinarian, public health worker and alternative medicine doctor etc.) to develop and implement the IPE strategy. Potential health professional educators, who showed a real passion for IPE, attended a series of national/international leadership or IPE training workshops. It aimed to equip educators for inter and intraprofessional knowledge and provide a skillset to achieve common desires and decisions
Integrate	Align a national conceptual framework and integrate systematically throughout the curricular	A commission developed an innovative IPE competency conceptual framework and guideline to ensure the acquisition of interprofessional knowledge and skillsets in new generations of health professions. The educators integrated the guidelines into the existing course and resources or developed new activities for implementation, assessment and further evidence-informed policy formulation on IPE

(continued)

Table 5.1 (continued)

Practical steps	Objectives	Tactics
Advocate	Raise nationwide awareness for deep understanding value and impact of IPE	An annual national health professional education reform forum was organized as a key mechanism for advocacy and momentum building, movement of the strategic plan, knowledge generation, management and sharing, in addition to capacity building including networking Pilot studies on IPE were conducted and reflected on learning experiences at different health science training institutes as a workplace-, scenario-, technology- or simulation-based course or at the community level to attain good quality patient care
Engage	Contribute to achieve a common vision	Engaged health professions featured a strong emotional connection as part of a team and understood their contribution to pursue a common vision. An institute could not afford to ignore team engagement which enabled health professions to maximize their energy, creativity and to allow the team to thrive. A storytelling of those cases would promote inspiration, relationships and networking

Practical steps	Objectives	Tactics
Evaluate	Design assessment and evaluation for evidence-informed policy	An interprofessional team collaborated to design and deliver IPE research with assessment and evaluation tools to develop an evidence-informed policy for sustainability and improvement based on the assessment result and the defined competency
Disseminate	Increase visibility and impact of IPE for sustainability	IPE activities were disseminated through various communication channels of different health professional organizations, educational institutions and communities with an expansion to a broad continuum of interprofessional activities, a support of new IPE initiatives, and grant funding for successful cases with an impact on IPE

Source Author's own creation

(Chuenkongkaew et al., 2016; Zodpey et al., 2018). The common protocol included national, institutional, and graduate surveys for assessment of medical, nursing, and public health education and training in five countries: Bangladesh, China, India, Thailand and Vietnam. The World Health Assembly subsequently endorsed a resolution (WHA 66.23) 'Transforming HWF education in support of UHC' (WHO, 2013). The resolution called for reform in all member states.

In 2014, Thailand organised a national meeting on transformative education and training among health professions, with the other member States participating. The most commonly adopted is IPE, which has now been initiated in Bangladesh and Sri Lanka, but is still in a process of development. The national IPE commission, which comprised various health professional experts who were appointed to implement a strategic action plan for IPE, developed an innovative IPE competency conceptual framework (see Fig. 5.1 and Table 5.2) and guidelines (Chuenkongkaew, 2018). The framework stemmed from the WHO Conceptual Framework on IPE (WHO, 2010), the Framework for action on IPE and Collaborative Practice, Canadian Interprofessional Health Collaborative (Canadian Interprofessional Health Collaborative, 2012) and Core Competencies for Interprofessional Collaborative Practice (Interprofessional Education Collaborative Expert Panel, 2011). The guidelines indicated IPE principles and approaches including examples of modules, course specification and assessment to ensure the successful acquisition of interprofessional knowledge and skillsets in new generations of health professionals in Thailand. The educators integrated the guidelines into the existing course and resources or developed new activities for implementation, assessment and further evidence-informed policy formulation on IPE.

IPE Experiences in Thailand: Past and Present

The past experience of collaborative practices across multiple academic institutes in Thailand was demonstrated at two outstanding institutions which were the Faculty of Public Health, Mahidol University and the Faculty of Medicine, Khon Kaen University. The term IPE has been quite

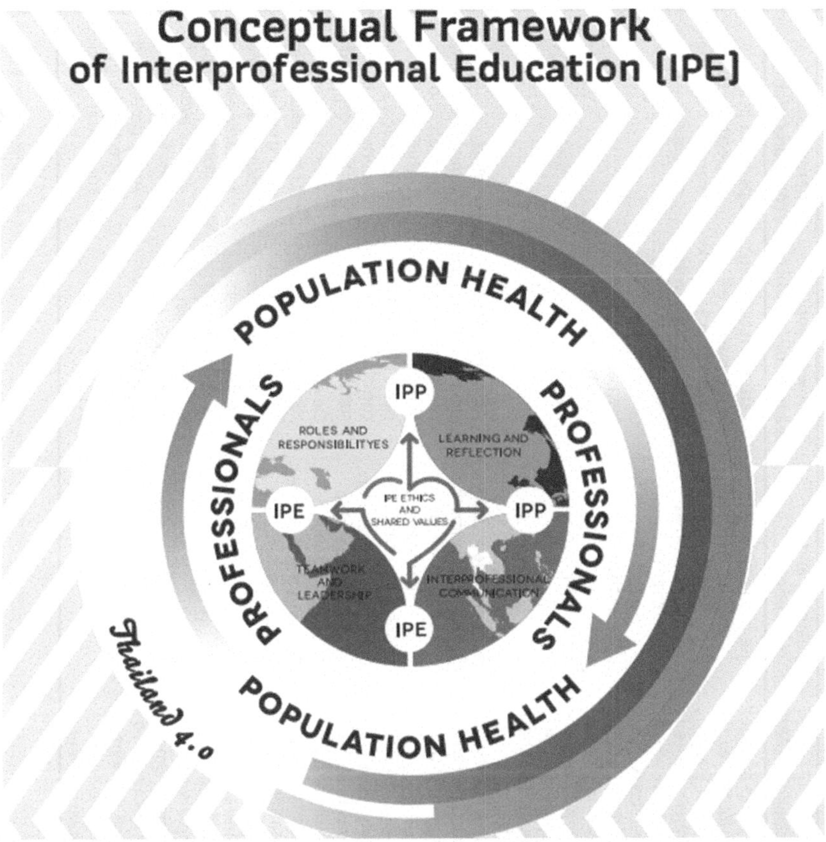

Fig. 5.1 Conceptual framework of Interprofessional education (IPE) (*Source* Chuenkongkaew, 2018)

new to Thai educators. Those two activities were continuously implemented though they were previously not named as IPE.

Faculty of Public Health, Mahidol University in Bangkok

Public health education programmes represent the population-based health sciences and deliver high-quality public health training through

Table 5.2 Competency domain, general competency statement and subcompetency of IPE

Competency domain	Ethics and shared values	Roles and responsibilities (R&R)	Learning and reflection	Team work and leadership	Interprofessional communication
General competency statement	Determine and do what professions judge to be right Create an environment of mutual respect and trust	Understand member's contribution to the team and learn member's desire for the success Use member's knowledge and experience to efficiently determine and describe the patients' healthcare needs	Be aware of and describe member's own thinking in a way that allows member to close the gap between what they know and what they need to learn	Create team building and dynamics of relationship to work collaboratively with others in achieving common goal to plan and deliver health care	Open and listen respectfully to member's divergent opinions
Subcompetency	• Set common interest at the center of health care team • Value member's dignity, privacy and keep confidentiality • Embrace the cultural diversity in team engagement • Appreciate individual difference on culture, values, R&R and expertise • Collaborate with those who contribute to health care delivery	• Clarify member's expectation to complete tasks • Communicate member's R&R clearly to other members and patients and be aware of the limitations • Engage diverse healthcare professions who complement member's expertise, and resources, to evolve efficient strategies for population needs	• Explore learning and developmental needs of a team or common interests through reflection • Reflect critically on their relationship within a team • Learn through peer support • Transfer team learning to clinical setting • Self-questioning of individual belief and stereotyped views	• Activate effective team building, sense of ownership and the roles and participation that contribute to the success • Develop clear direction and priority on the ethical principles of health care and team work • Enhance other members in shared patient-centered care	• Select comprehensive set of tools and techniques for discussion and interaction in patient-centered care • Communicate team in a trustful and respectful manner, for complementary effort to each other and by avoiding specific terminology • Apply gentle and respectful language for critical situation

Competency domain	Ethics and shared values	Roles and responsibilities (R&R)	Learning and reflection	Team work and leadership	Interprofessional communication
		• Explain R&R of other members and how the team works together for sustainable provision of health care • Use member's competencies to appropriately provide safe, efficient and effective patient care in an equitable manner • Communicate with team members to concretely accountable in executing components of disease prevention and treatment • Cultivate trustful relationship with others for better health care • Engage in sustaining high-performance team building • Apply member's skill, knowledge and attitude to optimize health care		• Interact with members to manage conflicts about values, roles, goals, and practices with patients and family • Enhance member's knowledge and experience to inform decisions and apply leadership practices • Share accountability with other members, constructively reflect on individual and team performance in a climate of trust by respectful behavior • Use evidence and process of improving strategies to ensure success • Encourage and support group participation in different team roles and in different settings	• Deeply understand member's experience, expertise, effort, culture and hierarchical relationship in team

Source Adapted from: Chuenkongkaew (2018)

competency-based education and research. Since 1958, a field training course has been running for the graduate students of public health programme at Mahidol University. All students who register in this field-training course participate in a classroom field training preparation session for three hours a week over 15 weeks and undergo field training in a district community for five weeks. The 4th year medical students from the Faculty of Medicine, Srinakharinwirot University, within their five-week field course of community medicine, jointly attend the public health programme at the district community. Comprehensive public health skills have been developed as an interprofessional approach for field training. It is system-based education for providing learners with experience on population-centred health systems, practising teamwork, leadership and networking across disciplines. The learning process includes:

- Community diagnosis, health problems identification, prioritisation, and selection;
- Community survey and analysis of selected health problem risk and protective factors;
- Drawing a web of causation of a selected health problem;
- Planning and implementing public health development programmes in the community;
- Programme evaluation and reporting; and
- Submission of a written report to the local administrative community office and health office by the students under university administrator and faculty members' supervision for continuing community programme activities.

Moreover, integration of academic knowledge, ethics, local wisdom and culture for promotion of a sustainable humanised public health development is taken into account within the programme design. The programme has been sustained under strong, collective and committed leadership at academic institutes with policy makers' and local governors' support.

Faculty of Medicine, Khon Kaen University

Since 1983, 10-day fieldwork for community medicine has been set up at the Faculty of Medicine, Khon Kaen University in north-eastern Thailand. Subsequently, the students from the Faculty of Veterinary Science, Dentistry and Physical Therapy, from Khon Kaen University and the Faculty of Nursing from the College of Asian Scholars, have been participating in this interprofessional fieldwork. It aims to inspire health science students to gain a positive attitude towards the community, as healthy people are based on community health care, and community sociocultural exposure. By mutual learning with people in the community to meet population health needs, and through health promotion and disease prevention, students gain a community-oriented skillset and sense of achievement via their effective contribution for a future health care system. The students establish their own recognition of appropriate skills, understanding of existing sociocultural activities, lifestyle, beliefs on healthcare, social determinants of health, working relationships through interactive action-based learning, and therefore eventually serve a community as highly competent health care providers. Moreover, a rural community background is assessed and analysed in terms of a sustainable health care service. The programme has impacted on the educational long-term bond and consistently improved quality of care in the district community under strong, collective and committed leadership from the faculty members and local communities.

More Recent IPE Experiences

Since 2014, different IPE activities and networks under the Strategic Movement Plan on Health Professional Education for the 21st Century (2014–2018) have been implemented. One of the key mechanisms is to organise the Annual National Health Professional Education Reform Forum (ANHPERF) with nine Thai health professional leaders and an international delegation. The forum focuses on policy-related health professional education issues. A number of academic institution policies were identified during these conferences encompassing both instructional and institutional educational reform. The need for transformative learning on institutional educational reform included collaboration among health professions from health service, professional education institutes and councils. Alongside the collaboration, faculty development, institutional management, legal instruments and measurement included processes such as instructional reform needed to encompass learner competency, learning process, assessment and environment. Empowering HWFs through transforming learning and practice in the community is a critical component to strengthen community health systems in the country. In 2016, the conference theme was *IPE toward Thai health team* and Professor Emeritus John H.V. Gilbert, the founder of IPE at the University of British Columbia, addressed the basic knowledge of IPE for Thai and SEAR's educators (Health Professional Foundation of Thailand, 2016). This included the definition, benefits and challenges of IPE and why as well as how to implement IPE.

One Health University Network

An example of IPE was from the H5N1 highly pathogenic Avian influenza (HPAI) outbreak in Thailand between 2004 and 2008. To solve this serious disease outbreak, health workers in Thailand including public health, veterinarians, environmental workers, nurses and physicians, invested a lot of effort to control the spreading of Avian influenza virus via several strategies, predominantly focused on active and passive surveillance, culling infected flocks, prohibition of poultry movement, and people education for disease control. Since the H5N1 had a multidimensional impact on human, animal, and environmental health, and the socio-economy and food security, multiple professions from both private and government sectors collaboratively controlled the disease nationally. Many new food products, new diagnostic tools and vaccines, were also created and developed for commercial export and utilised within the country during that period. Learning from this valuable H5N1 experience, multi-disciplinary collaboration is a key to successfully managing disease outbreaks and could be helpful in the anticipation of new emerging infectious diseases. Therefore, an IPE programme, with the aim of promoting learners' soft skill competency, is crucial for the formulation of the One Health University network. The development of this network was based on collaboration between multiple professions in order to eliminate H5NI. Through learning to work together, the professionals from different disciplines were inspired to develop IPE for their students. Thus, in 2011, Indonesia, Malaysia, Vietnam, and Thailand jointly established a network, namely Southeast Asia One Health University Network (SEAOHUN), to strengthen the One Health network and build the capacity of health professions in the region. Subsequently, in 2012, Thailand One Health University Network (THOHUN) conducted training platforms for One Health students' future roles in terms of disease detection, surveillance, response, control and prevention of emerging or re-emerging diseases by embedding core competency into curricula based on research or case studies in the classroom or community.

Community Setting, Project-Based IPE Network

In 2014, a joint effort from 15 health and health-related faculties at Mahidol University in Bangkok initially designed a project-based IPE programme in a community setting. It aimed to enhance interprofessional competencies and skills among different health professional students through an integrative and collaborative approach on education. The programme is now embedded into the educational curriculum to improve quality of care in the district community at a university campus in western Thailand. It has contributed to strengthening the country's health system performance with an adequate, efficient and effective health care delivery system. Subsequently, both extracurricular and intracurricular IPE courses were implemented across the university to promote quality health care systems through IPP (Mahidol University, 2018).

Humanised Home Care with INHOMESSS (Immobility, Nutrition, Housing, Others, Medication, Examination, Safety, Spirituality, Services)

In 2015, a humanised, homecare based IPE programme was jointly created from the Faculties of Medicine, Pharmacy and Architecture with an additional extension to the Faculties of Nursing and Informatics at Mahasarakham University (MSU) in north-eastern Thailand. MSU is a public higher education institution focusing on social and community-based engagement incorporating the philosophical statements of: 'Public devotion is a virtue of the learned' and 'Students with contribution to society and community'. The programme aimed to equip students to collaboratively motivate health behaviour change and promote health prevention and medical care, with support from the existing multiprofessional team in community settings in achieving humanised home care with INHOMESSS skills and encompassing five domains of students' outcomes, including teamwork with trust and respect, leadership, communication and problem solving skills, and patient care plan and goal setting skills (Unwin & Jerant, 1999).

Steps of IPE priority activities for humanised patient home care were:

1. Interprofessional Educational preparation to build the capacity of committed faculty members and recruitment of targeted learners.
2. Learner preparation, featured through having an icebreaker game for team building activities among different health professional students who underwent an IPE learning process stemming from their existing intra-curricular professional courses.
3. A Community plan established through requesting approval from the local municipality office for coordinating necessary health information data gathering at the primary care unit.
4. Learner Assessment, analysed in three domains including learners' competencies, course and community satisfaction, by using questionnaire, direct observation, reflection and peer review. Its results, assessed by faculty staffs, home health care nurses and patients, showed improvement in health outcomes and learning experiences, with a statistically significant increase in attitude scores. The students'

attitudes showed satisfaction on IPE behaviours such as friendship, new viewpoints on other professionals, learning in real life, love and understanding from friends and patients, inspiration from working in the community with an interprofessional team attitude.

Home Visits with Service in Mind Model

In 2016, workplace-based IPE learning through patient home visits with service in mind was established in five faculties at Huachiew Chalermprakiet University in Bangkok including the Faculties of Nursing, Pharmacy, Medical Technology, Physical Therapy, and Social Work/Social Welfare, and the Faculties of Communication, Art, and Science and Technology later joined in. Collaborative and multidisciplinary teams proactively provided preventative care through the development of an application to continuously monitor patients' health status. This IPE activity is still being undertaken and has been continuously evaluated from the outset.

Interprofessional Training and Practice Model

In 2009, workplace-based in-service training, through a context-based learning approach, was carried out to strengthen health care delivery for frontline health workers at Rasisalai Hospital in north-eastern Thailand (Pongsupap et al., 2016). It shed light on interprofessional training and practice for better health outcomes at primary care level by use of guidelines, supervision, communication and information systems. All health professions at the training centre contributed to enhance trainees' capacities through creating a trusting relationship, and the development of a sustainable network through the strong leadership of the hospital director and improvement of health outcomes in the community.

Implementation and Challenges of IPE

IPE in Thailand is now practical and effective but needs more systematic analysis and development, the generation of evidence to evaluate the outcome, and a scale-up and creation of policy dialogues for sustainability. The assessment on attitudes towards interprofessional health care teams in undergraduate students before, during, after training, and after graduation also needs to be implemented. In addition, faculty development, in particular for collective leadership, is an ongoing process of building on trust, involving horizontal or equitable and collegial-based relationships among professions, with an appreciation of hard work and collective effort, while avoiding high expectations from merely token efforts. This needs to happen simultaneously while IPE is gradually and continuously integrated into each University's curricula. To tackle challenges with IPE sustainability, in Thailand the 4Cs are applied. These include: to strongly **C**larify common goals; **C**ollect champions and potential people to support and help; **C**reate possible actions; and, **C**ollaborate with no conflict. The common goal is to improve learner outcomes through a health system- based approach to practice collaboratively to achieve better quality of care.

Conclusion

Thailand is moving to something new, with IPE and IPP developing throughout the health care system. Since the terms of IPE and IPP were quite new to us, we have not yet fully assessed the long term outcome of IPE for learners, such as changes in learners' views and attitudes. However, the marked improvements in health care delivery have convinced us to continue with the programme. The lessons learned and shared so far will continue to motivate health professionals through the opportunities for doing things differently and better.

Acknowledgements I would like to extend my grateful thanks to the Thai Health Professional Education Reform commission (Professor Vicharn Panich as Chair and Dr. Suwit Wibulpolprasert as Vice-chair) and IPE subcommittee, Professor Emeritus John H.V. Gilbert University of British Columbia, Canada,

Professor Hideomi Watanabe and team, Gunma University, Japan, Professor Dr. Prasit Watanapa, Dean of Faculty of Medicine, Siriraj Hospital, Professor Lincoln C. Chen, President of the China Medical Board, Dr. Poonam Khetrapal Singh, Regional Director of the WHO South-East Asia Region who have been very supportive and continually provided extremely useful advice, and thanks to Miss Dusita Krawanchid and Miss Manuschon Kunapornsujarit, researchers for data collection, Health Professional Education Foundation, Thailand and Thai Health Promotion Foundation, China Medical Board, and the World Health Organization (South-East Asia Regional Office) for grant support of IPE initiatives in Thailand.

References

Canadian Interprofessional Health Collaborative. (2012). *An inventory of quantitative tools measuring interprofessional education and collaborative practice outcomes.* The Canadian Nurses Association.

Chuenkongkaew, W. (2018). *Interprofessional education guideline.* Bangkok, Thailand: P.A. Living Co., Ltd. http://www.healthprofessionals21thailand.org/download/?cat_ID=174&y=2018.

Chuenkongkaew, W., Negandhi, H., Lumbiganon, P., Wang, W., Mahmud, K., & Cuong, P. V. (2016). Attitude towards working in rural area and self assessment of competencies in last year medical students: A study of five countries in Asia. *BMC Medical Education, 16,* 238. https://doi.org/10.1186/s12909-016-0719-9.

Frenk, J., Chen, L., Bhutta, Z. A., Cohen, J., Crisp, N., Evans, T., ... Zurayk, H. (2010). Health professionals for a new century: Transforming education to strengthen health systems in an interdependent world. *The Lancet, 376,* 1923–1958.

Health Professional Foundation of Thailand. (2016). http://www.healthprofessionals21thailand.org/media/?type=video.

Interprofessional Education Collaborative Expert Panel. (2011). *Core competencies for interprofessional collaborative practice: Report of an expert panel.* Washington, DC.

Mahidol University. (2018). *Faculty of nursing together with the faculty of medicine Siriraj Hospital Mahidol University NSID 332 offers enhanced patient safety through inter-professional collaborative practice.* http://www.ns.mahidol.ac.th/nurse_th/annual_activities/2561/07/IPE_th.html.

Pongsupap, Y., Archananuparp, S., Boonyapaisarncharoen, T., Srimuang, P., Ngamkham, S., Tiptiengtae, C., … Martiny, P. (2016). District health system management learning: A big leap forward to people-centred District Health System in Thailand. *Journal of Public Health Development, 14*(3), 3–12. http://www.bcnu.ac.th/research/attachments/documents/2559/2559/08in2559.pdf.

Unwin, B. K., & Jerant, A. F. (1999, October 1). The home visit. *American Family Physician, 60*(5), 1481–1488. https://www.aafp.org/afp/1999/1001/p1481.html.

World Health Organization (WHO). (2010). *Framework for action on interprofessional education and collaborative practice.* http://www.who.int/hrh/resources/framework_action/en/.

World Health Organization (WHO). (2012, September 7). *Resolution of the WHO Regional Committee for South-East Asia: SEA/R65/R7 'Strengthening health workforce education and training in the region'.* https://apps.who.int/iris/handle/10665/128331.

World Health Organization (WHO). (2013, May 27). *Resolution of the World Health Assembly (WHA 66.23) resolutions on Transforming health workforce education in support of universal health coverage.* https://apps.who.int/iris/handle/10665/150174.

Zodpey, S., Lumbiganon, P., Evans, T., Yang, K., Thi Thu Ha, B., Negandhi, H., … Al-Kabir, A. (2018). Assessment of health professional education across five Asian countries-a protocol. *Human Resources for Health, 16,* 52. https://doi.org/10.1186/s12960-018-0316-6.

6

The Resurgence of the Global Research Interprofessional Network

Hossein Khalili

This chapter describes the development of the global interprofessional research network (IPR.Global) from its roots in the Global Research Interprofessional Network (GRIN) and the In-2-Theory network (see Fig. 6.1).

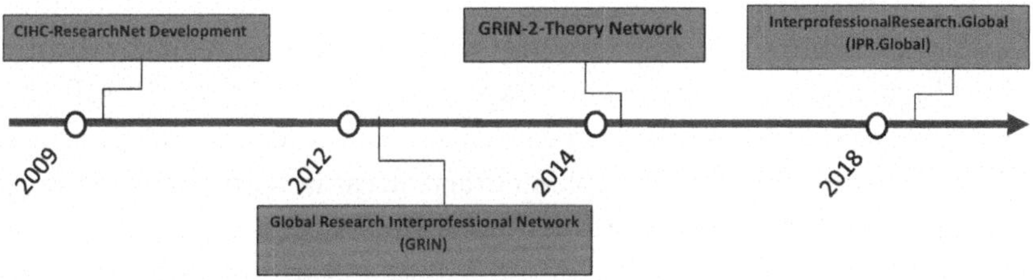

Fig. 6.1 IPR.Global development timeline

H. Khalili (✉)
University of Wisconsin-Madison, Madison, WI, USA
e-mail: hkhalili@wisc.edu

D. Forman et al. (eds.), *Sustainability and Interprofessional Collaboration*,
https://doi.org/10.1007/978-3-030-40281-5_6

The Journey to GRIN and In-2-Theory

In late 2009, Dr. John Gilbert,[1] Dr. Ruby Grymonpre[2] and other members of the Canadian Interprofessional Health Collaborative (CIHC) Research and Evaluation Committee invited me to lead the development of a national network of (post)graduate students who were involved in interprofessional education for collaborative practice (IPECP) research. The initiative was later expanded beyond students and was named the CIHC-ResearchNet. In 2005 Health Canada (the Canadian Ministry of Health) had invested over Can$20 million through its Health Human Resource Strategy to support 21 projects focusing on the development of Interprofessional Education for Collaborative Patient-Centred Practice (IECPCP) in the Canadian context. In 2009 I was a graduate-student representative on three of these projects:

1. **The Institute of Interprofessional Health Sciences Education (the institute)** was a virtual institute (2006–2009) made up of four universities in Ontario (McMaster University, University of Ottawa, Laurentian University, and University of Western Ontario) and the Council of Ontario Universities. The institute aimed to encourage interprofessional learning among students and providers, through building a virtual network of expertise and skills in IPECP, and promoting cultural change in health science students and providers. The institute had two complementary streams with different target groups: (a) Pre-licensure Student Stream, with a focus on learners from selected health sciences professions learning and practising skills associated with well-functioning teams, and (b) Post-licensure Practice Stream with a focus on health care providers learning how to become better role models for effective teamwork (Luke et al., 2009).

   The institute developed and offered more than ten web-based self-directed learning modules on key topics that facilitated interprofessional knowledge and skill development for health professional

[1] Professor Emeritus at the University of British Columbia.

[2] Professor at the University of Manitoba.

students and practising health professionals. My role within this multisite and multiphase institute research project resulted in:

- The development of two modules, including, 'How to Assess Team Effectiveness Module' as part of a series of self-directed interprofessional team modules for the practice stream, and the 'Communication with Diverse Population Module' for the student stream;
- The establishment and evaluation of the pre- and post-licensure streams at Western University; and
- The facilitation and evaluation of an interprofessional student placement within one of our practice team sites, and an online IPE student module at Western University.

2. **Creating Interprofessional Collaborative Teams for Comprehensive Mental Health Services (CIPHER-MH)** was developed to explore interprofessional client-centred education, within a mental health context (2006–2008). The overall project goal was to facilitate interprofessional collaborative mental health care in both education and practice settings, while augmenting the work toward provincial priorities such as mental health care reform, care of the homeless, and the development of local health integration networks within the London and Western community (Forchuk & Vingilis, 2008). This project, in which I was a member of the steering and evaluation committees, assisted with the development, facilitation, and evaluation of a series of 12 IPE workshops and the publication and dissemination of the project outcomes (Vingilis et al., 2011).
3. **The Canadian Interprofessional Health Collaborative (CIHC)** was established in 2006 by Professor Emeritus John Gilbert as a complementary IPECP project. Following the initial 20 funded IECPCP projects, CIHC was also funded by Health Canada (i.e. 21 projects in total) to facilitate and foster cross-IECPCP project communication, collaboration, and knowledge/findings exchange. In doing so, CIHC, with a number of committees and working groups, quickly became the central 'hub' for IPECP in Canada and globally. CIHC has since evolved in 2012 into a not-for-profit corporation with a board of directors, of which I am a member, and continues to play a major role

in supporting interprofessional education and collaborative practice development in Canadian health care and social services.

In the autumn of 2008, I was invited to participate in the CIHC Research and Evaluation Committee (R&E) retreat to discuss the possibility of creating a national network of graduate students with interest in conducting their research on IPECP. The CIHC R&E committee included researchers, faculty/educators, providers, administrators, organisational leaders and students who worked together as a 'community of practice' (CoP) (Wenger, McDermott, & Snyder, 2002). The members had a shared passion for research capacity building (RCB) in the field of IPECP (Suter et al., 2011).

The Conception of the Canadian Interprofessional Research Network

During 2008 and 2009, the R&E committee conducted a mapping exercise, using the Cooke RCB Framework (2005), to strategize and prioritise best approaches towards building research capacity in IPECP. In this mapping process, the R&E committee identified three of the six Cooke principles (Principle 2—support research and evaluation close to practice; Principle 3—build linkages, partnerships and collaboration; and Principle 4—dissemination) as the priorities to pursue. The idea of establishing a national research network in IPECP was developed in response to two of these three priorities (Principles 3 and 4) (Suter et al., 2011).

The main argument was that, in the context of a rapidly evolving Canadian health care system, there was an increasing need to foster on-going dialogue and collaboration between different actors in the health care system with regards to several aspects of interprofessional care partnerships. Researchers, faculty, providers, and students were often struggling to interact and collaborate with each other because of the lack of a structured interprofessional network. Collaboration between interprofessional communities was mostly happening on an ad hoc basis, through contacts between experts, researchers and academics in regular conference settings (Suter et al., 2011). The coordination of the diverse interprofessional research activities across Canada into a unified, publicly accessible research database was therefore considered to be a vital function of CIHC, and it was identified as one of the three priorities of the CIHC R&E committee. The committee proposed the formation of a national research network to fill this gap through sharing information and facilitating collaboration.

In December 2009, at the R&E committee's request, I had the privilege of leading the development of this national research network. The initial steps toward its development included: (a) identifying the underpinning frameworks for the network, (b) (re)building the working group—later called CIHC-ResearchNet Working Group, (c) expanding the scope of the network beyond graduate students to be inclusive of all IPECP community Canadian Interprofessional Research Network members, and (d) developing the CIHC-ResearchNet synopsis (Khalili, 2010).

This network development project was underpinned by two conceptual frameworks:

1. The IECPCP framework by D'Amour and Oandasan (2005). The IECPCP framework reinforced the interconnectivity of different sectors (i.e., education, practice, administration, and policymaking) in health care and interprofessional research.

   To reach the goal of creating the CIHC-ResearchNet, a collaborative group of researchers, educators, providers, and students from across Canada and different professions and programmes formed the CIHC-ResearchNet Working Group subcommittee of the CIHC R&E committee. CIHC-ResearchNet was envisioned as an interprofessional health research network among and between Canadian health programme students, faculty/educators, researchers, providers/practitioners, administrators, and organisational leaders who are engaged in collaborative research and knowledge translation (KT) to advance interprofessional education and practice. This network created an environment for different health care actors to interact and collaborate on a regular basis. One tool utilised to facilitate this communication and share information between members was the interactive Google map that localised each member's institutional information and which has now been updated and integrated into the global interprofessional network (Fig. 6.2). In addition, in this role CIHC-ResearchNet performed as supporter, facilitator, knowledge disseminator, a discussion forum, and a resource for information and guidance in suggesting best practices for IPECP (Suter et al., 2011; Thistlethwaite et al., 2013).

2. The Network Life Cycle framework developed by Browne, Campion, and Stenger (2001). This framework was used to guide the development of CIHC-ResearchNet. According to this framework, the life cycle of the CIHC-ResearchNet was considered as a three-phase process including formative (12 months), evolving (6–12 months), and maturing (6–12 months) phases.

   The one-year formative project was envisioned in three interrelated steps: Step A: Preliminary Network Structure (2–3 months); Step B: Survey Development and Implementation (4–5 months); and Step C: Database Development and Management (4–6 months).

   In its formative phase, the CIHC-ResearchNet working group was formed, and the working group developed and submitted a project application entitled 'Formation of the Canadian Interprofessional Health Research Network' to the Ontario Health Human Resources Research Network (OHHRRN) for funding in Feb 2010. Despite the

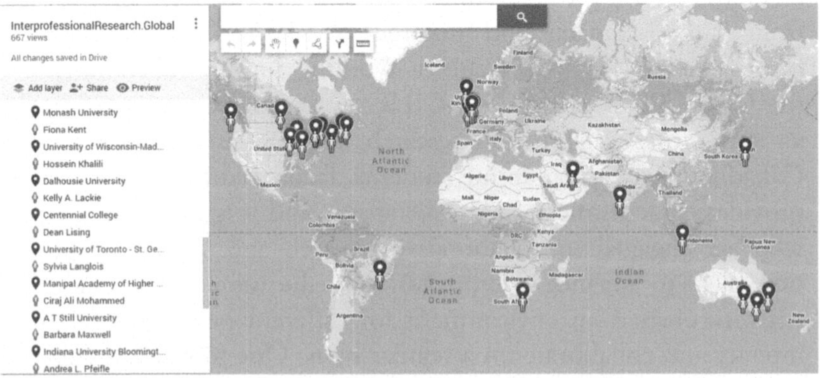

Fig. 6.2 IPR.Global interactive map, 2019

application being unsuccessful, the members of the working group were highly motivated and committed to continue with the network development. The group met regularly via telephone and Skype for over two years to formulate plans for developing and expanding the CIHC-ResearchNet. During the evolution phase, members of the working group assisted with a journal publication developed by the CIHC R&E committee (Suter et al., 2011), presented two workshops in national and international meetings and conferences, conducted a national interprofessional research survey, and wrote a grant application to secure funding for the third phase of the network (maturation) (Thistlethwaite et al., 2013).

On February 14, 2011 we received an email from Dr. Christopher Green, at that time a PhD student co-coordinator of the United Kingdom (UK) 'Interprofessional Research Student Network (IRSN)'. He indicated his network's interest to collaborate with CIHC-ResearchNet in developing a 'thriving potentially global network'. This email was perfectly timed as CIHC-ResearchNet, as part of its third phase, was working to expand the scope of the network beyond Canada to become a global network through the development of a grant proposal.

Drivers of Success

As a collaborative of researchers, the efforts of CIHC-ResearchNet were largely targeted to stakeholders at the national level. Evidence indicated that rich, intense communication with individuals and groups across the globe can stimulate creativity and research productivity (Adams, Black, Clemmons, & Stephan, 2005; Heinze, Shapira, Rogers, & Senker, 2009; Lee & Bozeman, 2005; Ordóñez-Matamoros & Cozzens, 2010) and help consolidate research agendas. Research collaboration is largely viewed as an important enabler; it supports the exchange of ideas, experience and information. Global collaboration by increasing research unit size and involving multiple sites can strengthen the generalisability of research results and support international visibility (Horta & Lacy, 2011).

In 2011, the CIHC-ResearchNet working group developed and submitted a meeting and planning grant proposal, entitled 'International Research Network in IPE/IPP' to the Canadian Institutes of Health Research (CIHR) Open Competition. The main goal of the proposal was to bring together international IPECP research experts in order to create a comprehensive strategic plan to guide the expansion of the CIHC-ResearchNet into a global IPECP research network (Khalili et al., 2013).

This grant development was an exemplar of virtual teamwork in action. During this process, several of the working group collaborated virtually over eight months, by using email, Google docs, Dropbox, and other online open source/asynchronised communication and videoconferencing media, to put forward a quality proposal for the highly competitive open funding opportunities provided by the CIHR.

In February 2012, we received the exciting news that CIHC-ResearchNet had been successful in receiving funding through the CIHR Meeting and Planning Grant Award. This was a milestone for the CIHC-ResearchNet working group. This grant was the first and only funding that CIHC-ResearchNet had received since its conception in 2009. The work and activities of CIHC-ResearchNet thus far had been mainly based on the goodwill of its members. The CIHC-ResearchNet grant funding was crucial because CIHC was transitioning from a Health Canada funded organisation into a not-for-profit organisation.

Network Sustainability

With the success of the meeting and planning (M&P) project, our goals were to:

- Build international capacity for and facilitate research in IPECP
- Foster new, and enhance existing, international interprofessional collaborations among and between students, faculty/educators, practitioners, organisations and other knowledge users interested in conducting, funding or the uptake of research in IPECP

- Provide a virtual forum/platform for international knowledge generation and translation (synthesis, dissemination, exchange and application) relevant to IPECP
- Advance innovation in IPECP by providing an international vehicle for translating the research-based evidence for best practice into interprofessional education and practice
- Apply for peer reviewed funding.

To ground our work, we conducted a scoping review with: (1) a database search (CINAHL and Academic Search) for 2005–2012 literature on best practices to support international research collaboration and (2) an internet search to identify website models of international collaboration. A two-day international summit was subsequently held in May 2012 in Toronto, Ontario, involving 15 participants from Canada, United States, United Kingdom and Australia. Participants were invited to ensure both knowledge producer and knowledge user representation including educators, providers, graduate students, researchers and international collaborators (Thistlethwaite et al., 2013). The overarching goal of the summit was to discuss how the research agenda for IPECP might be advanced and translated globally with an emphasis on the nurturing and development of new researchers in the field, using insights from the scoping review.

The objectives of the workshop included:

- To motivate participants regarding the need for and benefits of an international e-research network in IPECP
- To understand the evidence around international and e-platform networking/collaboration
- To obtain consensus on the purpose, structure and function of an international e-research network in IPECP
- To develop a strategy on how to create a virtual international research collaborative in IPECP
- To commit to a formal plan of 'next steps' in developing the international e-ResearchNet.

The main outcome of the 2-day summit was the emergence of the *Global Research Interprofessional Network (GRIN)*:

GRIN Vision: Research and values informed/based interprofessional collaboration for global health.
GRIN Mission: To advance global collaborative interprofessional research and practice in IPECP.
GRIN Values:

- Cultural sensitivity and inclusivity
- Respect for diversity
- Knowledge sharing
- Interprofessional collaboration
- Quality inquiry
- Supportive mentorship
- Theory-based research (Thistlethwaite et al., 2013).

Sustainability was a challenge identified by all summit participants, who recommended that GRIN needed to be innovative and offer something unique and of value. Lessons from the scoping review indicated that key factors for a sustainable interprofessional collaboration would need to include the maintenance of dialogue, ensuring clarity, respecting diversity, and engagement in process/contextual factors. Relevance, buy-in and social capital for members were key principles explored in the summit, and were seen as imperative for ensuring a sustainable network. Several other recommendations and action items were generated from the meeting including developing a stakeholder map, conducting a needs assessment, developing a website, participating in a diverse KT and dissemination strategy, and seeking collaborative funding from international peer reviewed granting agencies. Later, we continued our conversations via telephone, Skype, and email to further formulate plans, follow through with deliverables and to host a final face-to-face meeting (Thistlethwaite et al., 2013).

An important first step for GRIN was the creation of a stakeholder map (Fig. 6.3) inclusive of a broad range of target groups (service users/consumers/patients/clients, students, policy makers, and health

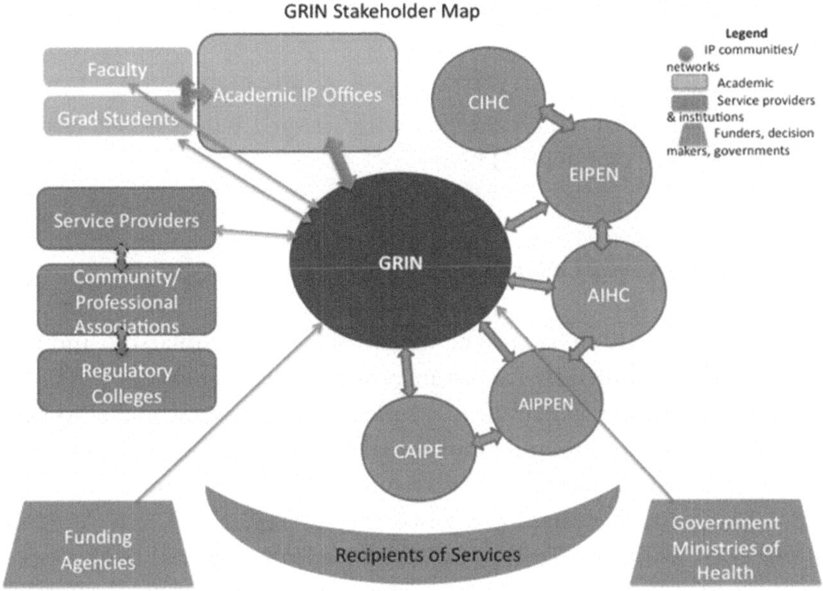

Fig. 6.3 GRIN stakeholder map

and education administrators). GRIN strived to promote an interdisciplinary approach inclusive of all disciplines beyond the traditional health professions such as linguistics, sociology, anthropology, economics, political sciences and others. GRIN recognised that its work would be strengthened by numbers, diversity and quality. Since IPECP networks already existed, the emerging GRIN needed to ensure that it was complementary rather than competitive or duplicative. However, core members agreed that GRIN was unique in having as its primary foci research in IPECP and integrated KT with global participants. While several other organisations were advocates for research in this area, GRIN uniquely promoted idea sharing, mentorship and knowledge generation and translation (Thistlethwaite et al., 2013).

We published an editorial in the *Journal of Interprofessional Care* introducing GRIN to the world (Thistlethwaite et al., 2013). The working group presented two pre/conference workshop presentations at the Collaborating Across Borders IV (CAB IV) conference in Vancouver, Canada and at the All Together Better Health VII Conference in Pittsburgh USA.

From GRIN to GRIN2Theory

In 2014, the scope of the GRIN was expanded to include theory in IPECP as a result of which the Network merged with GRIN, resulting in the emergence of GRIN2Theory.

In-2-Theory Network

In-2-Theory was an international, interprofessional scholarship and practice network developed by Dr. Sarah Hean and her colleagues in the UK. In-2-Theory formed as a result of a series of interprofessional workshops funded by the UK Economics and Social Research Council (2007–2009) with the goal to build theoretical rigour in IPECP (Hean et al., 2013). In-2-Theory members have published several papers and have presented a number of workshops and presentations at international conferences.

On April 23, 2014, Dr. Ruby Grymonpre and I, as the co-leads of GRIN, received an encouraging email from In2Theory Network indicating their willingness to merge with GRIN. Later that year, during the GRIN workshop at ATBH conference in Pittsburgh, the GRIN2Theory network was announced, which was positively received by the participants.

At the end of the Pittsburgh ATBH conference, we hosted the first GRIN2Theory meeting with members of the GRIN and In-2-Theory groups who were attending the conference. More than 30 members participated and developed an action plan for creating a shared strategy for the GRIN2Theory network. A number of taskforce groups were tasked with the next steps to help ensure the success of the new merged network. A main accomplishment of GRIN2Theory was hosting a pre-conference workshop at CAB V in Virginia, USA, in which over 60 interprofessional researchers and leaders participated.

Despite the movement towards joint strategic planning and next steps, there were challenges resulting in long delays to the work of the taskforces. These challenges included: time zone differences between members in the taskforce; new members working together without enough time to build trusting relationships; and lack of funding to support long-distance synchronised communication between members. These issues, together with the retirement and migration of some of the key members of GRIN2Theory, caused the new network to become silent for a period of time.

On reflection, an area that GRIN (and later GRIN2Theory) seemed to struggle with was the recommendation to seek collaborative funding from international peer reviewed granting agencies. Despite a great effort from the GRIN working group to submit a CIHR project grant to develop an interprofessional research summer Institute, we were unsuccessful in securing any new funding, leading to uncertainty and insecurity among the members about the future of GRIN and later of GRIN2Theory. One thing that we could have done differently to maintain and build upon the momentum would have been to reach out to other national and international IPECP organisations and institutions for their support. Some members of the GRIN working group were tasked to seek collaborative funding from other international peer reviewed granting agencies but this was done to support IPECP at national and international levels, rather than to ensure the sustainability of GRIN and GRIN2Theory.

Resurgence of GRIN2Theory

In 2018, two factors helped to revive GRIN2Theory. First, the financial support received through my new employment and, secondly, collaboration with Interprofessional.Global. As part of my employment agreement and through my professional development fund, I was provided with the opportunity to support the GRIN2Theory.

This financial support arrived at the time that the World Coordinating Committee on Interprofessional Education and Practice (WCC) was working to expand its scope beyond facilitating the ATBH conference to providing support to regional, national and international IPECP-related networks. The WCC held a 3-day retreat following the ATBH IX conference in Auckland, New Zealand in 2018, where the GRIN2Theory network was seeking partnerships. During ATBH IX GRIN2Theory's vision, mission and goals were displayed at the WCC booth. The ATBH IX conference was the best opportunity for me to bring back the team to 'resuscitate' the GRIN2Theory network.

It worked. After a few years of silence, we were beginning to see the light at the end of the tunnel. The GRIN2Theory poster-display was well received by the conference attendees. We invited members and non-members who indicated their interest to join the network to meet during the conference, using the conference app. While some members sent regrets due to scheduling conflicts, the GRIN2Theory meeting was held on 4 September 2018 with ten participants. The meeting provided an opportunity for returning and new members to share their thoughts, reflections and concerns on how to move forward with the network. Four common themes emerged from the discussion: (1) How GRIN2Theory and WCC could collaborate with each other. (2) How GRIN2Theory could move forward. (3) GRIN2Theory visibility; and (4) GRIN2Theory sustainability. A brief action plan was created to address the themes.

From GRIN2Theory to InterprofessionalResearch.Global (IPR.Global)

The ATBH momentum for GRIN2Theory helped to rebuild and restructure the network. Following the conference we accomplished the following: renaming the GRIN2Theory network InterprofessionalResearch.Global (IPR.Global); developing a two-year strategic plan; and building partnership with the WCC, which was renamed Interprofessional.Global—the Global Confederation for Interprofessional Education and Collaborative Practice—following the retreat.

The establishment of Interprofessional.Global catalysed the transfiguration of GRIN2Theory to InterprofessionalResearch.Global (IPR.Global): The Global Network for Interprofessional Education and Collaborative Practice Research. Around that time, November

2018, IPR.Global became a new member of Interprofessional.Global as a special interest group.

IPR.Global mission: We provide global leadership in interprofessional education and collaborative practice (IPECP) research. We engage world-renowned and emerging scholars, leaders, service providers, decision-makers, administrators, service-users, and students in research collaborations. We promote and advocate for evidence-informed policies and practices and we foster and facilitate theory-driven, methodologically rigorous IPECP research.

IPR.Global vision: We strive to enhance evidence-informed interprofessional collaboration for global and population health; to improve care access and quality; to achieve positive patient and community outcomes; to enhance cost-effectiveness, ensuring the provision of high-value care; and to improve the experience of service providers.

Sustainability and Resilience—Lessons Learned

IPR.Global Actionable Strategies

IPR.Global is committed to building and supporting a culture of global IPECP research, which is essential to generating evidence-based, theoretically informed, and methodological sound strategies for IPECP research. In leading the advancement of global IPECP research, IPR.Global is committed to achieving the following over the next two years:

1. Establishing strategic partnerships with diverse regional and global stakeholders to ensure the inclusivity of interprofessional research.
2. Conducting a comprehensive literature review.
3. Disseminating and exchanging knowledge and expertise.
4. Recognising and celebrating excellence in IPECP research.
5. Developing a globally agreed set of definitions and descriptions that capture interprofessional education, learning, practice, and care.

To meet the IPR.Global mandate and strategic plan, the continuous development of IPR.Global as a CoP is a crucial step. IPR.Global's development and planned activities are underpinned by the seven principles of communities of practice (Wenger et al., 2002), which include recognising that CoP development is an evolutionary process. Public and private community spaces need to be created, and a focus on the value IPR.Global offers members is essential. Finally, IPR.Global activities need to be established on a regular basis with events combining familiarity and stimulation within a safe environment.

Key to the development of a CoP such as IPR.Global is the 'practice' element. RCB is our practice. IPR.Global's focus is the enhancement of the evidence base and the research capacity of practitioners, educationalists, students and researchers in the IPECP field and its translation. This practice develops from our domain of shared interest and competence in IPECP research and our wish to build research capacity in the wider IPR.Global membership. We continue adopting two of the six principles of RCB developed in the 'Research Capacity Building in Health Care Framework' (Cooke, 2005) to direct our network: principle 3 (build linkages, partnerships and collaboration) and principle 4 (dissemination). Through interacting regularly (virtually and at times face to face through conferences and presentations), IPR.Global as a CoP will be building relationships and learning better ways of working together (Wenger et al., 2002). We anticipate that community members will engage in these and other joint activities, help and learn from each other, share information and build relationships.

IPR.Global incorporates a unique core team of world-renowned and emerging scholars, leaders, service providers, decision-makers, administrators, service-users, and students in research collaborations from diverse geographical areas/countries, disciplines, and institutions with diverse, but strong, expertise in RCB, KT, CoP, IPECP, international collaboration and information technology. Our global representation in the core team has significantly improved in the past year and we now have members from more than ten different countries represented and we are actively seeking broader global membership.

The unique structure of the membership makes IPR.Global and its strategic plan more sustainable and viable in our agreed timeline. The IPR.Global membership structure includes:

1. Members—currently IPR.Global has over 750 members from more than 50 countries, of which 30 members are part of the core team.
2. IPECP networks—There are more than ten networks represented in IPR.Global, including:
   a. AfrIPEN (African Interprofessional Education Network),
   b. AIHC (American Interprofessional Health Collaborative),
   c. APIPECnet (Asia Pacific Interprofessional Education and Collaboration Network),
   d. AIPPEN (Australasian Interprofessional Practice and Education network),
   e. Arab-speaking countries
   f. CAIPE (Centre for the Advancement of Interprofessional Education),
   g. CIHC (Canadian Interprofessional Health Collaborative),
   h. IndIPEN (Indian Interprofessional Education Network),
   i. IPE in World Health Organization global Initiatives
   j. Interprofessional.Global (Global Confederation for Interprofessional Education and Collaborative Practice),
   k. REIP (Regional Network for Interprofessional Education in the Americas),
   l. Student IPECP Research Network
3. Working Groups—IPR.Global has six active working groups of which two are joint working groups with Interprofessional.Global:
   a. Partnership development
   b. Research awards and fellowships
   c. Knowledge exchange
   d. Research institute
   e. IP terminology (Joint)
   f. Global situational analysis (Joint)

4. Sponsors—to sustain and advance IPR.Global core activities as outlined in the strategic plan, IPR.Global is looking for institutions and networks to sponsor us. While IPR.Global accepts different types of sponsorship, it has created a five-level sponsorship package that is available on our website and is open to all organisations, institutions and networks to consider. At this time, IPR.Global has received sponsorship from three organisations as listed on our website.

In providing global leadership in interprofessional education and collaborative practice (IPECP) research, and to promote and advocate for evidence-informed policies and practices, IPR.Global has released a joint publication with Interprofessional.Global: 'Guidance on Global Interprofessional Education and Collaborative Practice Research: Discussion Paper' (Khalili, Thistlethwaite, et al., 2019). The discussion paper offers perspectives to inform the global research agenda for IPECP by identifying research priorities and providing guidance to theoretical frameworks, research methodologies, and composition of research teams. A proposed lexicon for the interprofessional field is also available (Khalili, Gilbert, et al., 2019). The lexicon serves as a working document towards developing consensus on terminology related to interprofessional education, learning, practice, and care.

IPR.Global, with CIHC and AIHC, facilitated a pre-conference workshop entitled '*Global Leadership in IPECP Research; an Intro to Co-Creation of Best Practice Guidelines*' at CAB VII). IPR.Global presented its Distinguished Global IPECP Research Awards to three interprofessional leaders at the CAB VII Conference in Indiana in 2019: Hugh Barr, Barbara Brandt and John Gilbert. At the same conference it launched its Global Best Research Awards named after the above global leaders as follows:

- The InterprofessionalResearch.Global Barbara Fifield Brandt Award
- The InterprofessionalResearch.Global John H.V. Gilbert Award
- The InterprofessionalResearch.Global Hugh Barr Award.

The application calls for nomination for the awards opened in early 2020 through the IPR.Global website at www.research.interprofessional.global.

IPR.Global, in collaboration with Interprofessional.Global, is co-leading the situational analysis working group that is developing and conducting a global survey to identify the status and the needs of our IPECP stakeholders. The survey explores the global status of interprofessional education, collaborative practice, and IPECP research at macro, miso, and micro levels, with the intent to share the survey outcomes during the next ATBH conference in Doha, Qatar in October 2021.

Conclusion

In striving to achieve its mission and vision, IPR.Global is currently collaborating with more than ten global and regional IPECP networks, three sponsors, and over 750 members from more than 50 countries. To accomplish its strategic actions, IPR.Global continues to seek collaborative partners and sponsorship from individuals, educational institutions, health care organisations, interprofessional networks and centres from around the globe to ensure sustainability.

Similar to other IPECP networks, sustainability remains a high priority for IPR.Global. It is therefore imperative that IPR.Global be innovative and offer something unique and of value. Lessons learned from our experience and from our scoping review on collaborative networks indicate that key factors for a sustainable interprofessional collaboration need to include a committed membership, the maintenance of dialogue, ensuring clarity, respecting diversity, and engagement in process/contextual factors. Relevance, buy-in and social capital for members are key principles for ensuring a sustainable network. IPR.Global will remain focused on global leadership in IPECP Research, as our practice, and will continue to promote and advocate for evidence-informed policies and practices. We foster and facilitate theory-driven, methodologically rigorous IPECP research to achieve better health, better care, better value and better work experience for all.

Acknowledgements The ongoing process of creating, maintaining and advancing the global research interprofessional network has been possible through an incredible team effort in which many people and groups have significantly contributed. I would like to thank all the contributors and members of the current IPR.Global and its original network/s discussed in this chapter. My special thanks also goes to John Gilbert, Ruby Grymonpre, Barbara Maxwell, Sarah Hean, Christopher Green, and Jill Thistlethwaite along with others who have been instrumental in the expansion of the network.

References

Adams, J. D., Black, G. C., Clemmons, J. R., & Stephan, P. (2005). Scientific teams and institutional collaborations: Evidence from US universities, 1981–1999. *Research Policy, 34*(3), 259–285.

Browne, K., Campion, D., & Stenger, R. (2001). *Strategic planning for rural health networks, academy for health services research and health policy*. Retrieved from http://www.academyhealth.org/ruralhealth/strategicplanning.pdf.

Cooke, J. (2005). A framework to evaluate research capacity building in health care. *BMC Family Practice, 6*(1), 44.

D'Amour, D., & Oandasan, I. (2005). Interprofessionality as the field of interprofessional practice and interprofessional education: An emerging concept. *Journal of Interprofessional Care, 19*(sup1), 8–20.

Forchuk, C., & Vingilis, E. (2008). *Creating Interprofessional Collaborative Teams for Comprehensive Mental Health Services (CIPHER-MH)*. Health Canada: Final Report.

Hean, S., Anderson, E., Bainbridge, L., Clark, P. G., Craddock, D., Doucet, S., … Oandasan, I. (2013). IN-2-THEORY—Interprofessional theory, scholarship and collaboration: A community of practice. *Journal of Interprofessional care, 27*(1), 88–90.

Heinze, T., Shapira, P., Rogers, J. D., & Senker, J. M. (2009). Organizational and institutional influences on creativity in scientific research. *Research Policy, 38*, 610–623.

Horta, H., & Lacy, T. A. (2011). How does size matter for science? Exploring the effects of research unit size on academics' scientific productivity and information exchange behaviors. *Science and Public Policy, 38*(6), 449–460.

Khalili, H. (2010). Canadian Interprofessional Health Collaborative Research Network (CIHC-ResearchNet) Synopsis. In *A report for Research and Evaluation Committee, Canadian Interprofessional Health Collaborative.*

Khalili, H., Gilbert, J., Lising, D., MacMillan, K., Maxwell, B., & Xyrichis, A. (2019). *Proposed lexicon for the interprofessional field.* A joint publication by InterprofessionalResearch.Global, & Interprofessional.Global. Retrieved from www.research.interprofessional.global.

Khalili, H., Gilbert, J., Soubhi, H., Grymonpre, R., Tam, S., Atack, L., ... and Moravac, C. (2013). March. Canadian Interprofessional Health Collaborative Research Network (CIHC-ResearchNet): Make it a Global Initiative. *Journal of Interprofessional Care, 27*(supl), 154–155.

Khalili, H., Thistlethwaite, J., El-Awaisi, A., Pfeifle, A., Gilbert, J., Lising, D., ... Xyrichis, A. (2019). *Guidance on global interprofessional education and collaborative practice research: Discussion paper.* A joint publication by InterprofessionalResearch.Global, & Interprofessional.Global. Retrieved from www.research.interprofessional.global.

Lee, S., & Bozeman, B. (2005). The impact of research collaboration on scientific productivity. *Social Studies of Science, 35*(5), 673–702.

Luke, R., Solomon, P., Baptiste, S., Hall, P., Orchard, C., Rukholm, E., & Carter, L. (2009). Online interprofessional health sciences education: From theory to practice. *Journal of Continuing Education in the Health Professions, 29*(3), 161–167.

Ordóñez-Matamoros, H. G., & Cozzens, S. E. (2010). International co-authorship and research team performance in Colombia. *Review of Policy Research, 27*(4), 415–431.

Suter, E., Lait, J., MacDonald, L., Wener, P., Law, R., Khalili, H., & McCarthy, P. (2011). Strategic approach to building research capacity in interprofessional education and collaboration. *Healthcare Quarterly, 14*(2), 54–60.

Thistlethwaite, J. E., Khalili, H., Grymonpre, R., Gilbert, J., Atack, L., Espin, S., ... Namavarian, A. (2013). Introducing the global research interprofessional network (GRIN). *Journal of Interprofessional Care, 27*(2), 107–109. https://doi.org/10.3109/13561820.2012.718814.

Vingilis, E., Forchuk, C., Orchard, C., Shaw, L., King, G., McWilliam, C., ... Edwards, B. (2011). Development, implementation and formative evaluation of pre-licensure workshops using participatory action research to facilitate interprofessional, client-centred mental health care. *Journal of Research in Interprofessional Education (JRIPE), 2*(1), 25–48.

Wenger, E., McDermott, R. A., & Snyder, W. (2002). *Cultivating communities of practice: A guide to managing knowledge.* Boston: Harvard Business Press.

7

Qatar—Sustaining Interprofessional Collaboration in Collaborative Partnership with Other Universities

Alla El-Awaisi

Health Care in Qatar

The State of Qatar, an oil and gas rich nation, is a sovereign Arab state situated in the Arabian Gulf Region of the Middle East. The country's population has grown significantly in the last twenty years, due to the large expatriate influx to the country, with a current estimated population of around 2.8 million, predominantly Arab, Indian, Nepali and Filipino (Forstenlechner & Rutledge, 2011; World Population Review, 2019). Qatar's economy is claimed to be one of the highest in the world with a gross domestic product per capita of $124,500 (Central Intelligence Agency, 2017). There has been significant investment in the health care system and health care education in Qatar in the last 15 years. Most health care facilities are public, mainly run by expatriate health care professionals who completed their education and training outside Qatar. As an example, Hamad Medical Cooperation (HMC), which is the main

A. El-Awaisi (✉)
College of Pharmacy, QU Health, Qatar University, Doha, Qatar
e-mail: elawaisi@qu.edu.qa

D. Forman et al. (eds.), *Sustainability and Interprofessional Collaboration*,
https://doi.org/10.1007/978-3-030-40281-5_7

provider for secondary and tertiary care in the country and consists of 12 hospitals, has about people of 90 different nationalities working within it (Hamad Medical Cooperation, 2019).

Qatar has published its National Health Strategy for the period between 2018 and 2022 focused on 'Our Health, Our Future', which includes initiatives and projects to achieve the Qatar National Vision 2030 and its four pillars focused on human, social, economic and environmental development. The strategy advocates that health is a shared responsibility and lays down seven principles to achieve this including one on teamwork and collaboration. This principle is defined as:

> A call to come together and work together with mutual respect and trust to improve the health of the people of Qatar. A call for improved teamwork across the health system and increased collaboration across all sectors including the community. (Ministry of Public Health, 2018, p. 11)

Another principle is focused on patient-centred care and, to achieve this, the strategy advocates for having experienced and expert health care professionals who are working in teams to deliver high quality care for their patients (Ministry of Public Health, 2018). The strategy is based on an integrated system and model of care centred around better health, better care and better value delivered by interprofessional teams working together across different health care settings (Ministry of Public Health, 2018). Developing interprofessional education (IPE) and promoting collaborative practice will help Qatar meet the goals of Pillar 1: promoting human development which focuses on a population that is healthy and an educated workforce that is capable and motivated in a comprehensive world class health care system (General Secretariat for Development Planning, 2008). One proposed initiative for building a skilled national health care workforce, in the Qatar National Development Strategy, is to optimise the skill mix by encouraging the establishment of interprofessional health care teams working towards patient-centred care, recruiting health care professionals with expanded roles, and fostering a collaborative practice environment (Qatar General Secretariat for Development Planning, 2011).

Furthermore, in an effort to establish the educational and research infrastructure and build a high quality health workforce with Qatari nationals who are domestically trained, Qatar currently accommodates branch campuses of some of the leading universities in North America. These include Weill Cornell Medicine—Qatar (based in the United States), the University of Calgary School of Nursing (based in Canada), and the College of the North Atlantic (based in Canada). In 2007, the College of Pharmacy was established in the only national institution in the country: Qatar University. Qatar University College of Pharmacy is the first and only pharmacy degree programme in the State of Qatar. It is accredited by the Canadian Council on Accreditation of Pharmacy Programs (CCAPP) and was the first institution outside Canada to achieve this accreditation. In line with the country's growing health care sector and increasing need for health care professionals, Qatar University has been playing a key role through the establishment of Colleges of Medicine, Health Sciences and Dental Medicine (Table 7.1). Another notable positive move is that in 2017 Qatar University established a health cluster, referred to as QU Health, that brought the health related colleges of Qatar University under one administrative organisational umbrella to work together and maximise efficiencies with a mission to 'prepare competent graduates capable of shaping the future of health care in Qatar' (QU Health, 2019). QU Health focuses on four key areas including research & graduate studies, clinical affairs, interprofessional education and continuous professional development. In addition, QU works closely with the colleges on business operations, engagement and communication.

In June 2009, the Qatar Interprofessional Health Council (QIHC) was formed to help address health care needs in Qatar. The council was keen to drive IPE forward in Qatar and foster collaborative initiatives locally, regionally and internationally (Johnson et al., 2011). Members of the QIHC included deans of the above four health care educational institutions in Qatar as well as members from HMC and Sidra Medicine (Johnson et al., 2011). One of the council's main outcomes was securing a three-year National Priorities Research Program (NPRP) project from the Qatar National Research Fund entitled 'Implementing Interprofessional Undergraduate Health Professional Programs Health Care

Table 7.1 Healthcare academic institutions and program offered in Qatar

Institution	College	Date established	Programs offered
Weill Cornell Medicine—Qatar (WCM-Q)		2001	• Medicine
College of North Atlantic	School of Health Sciences	2002	• Advanced care paramedicine • Occupational health • Safety and environment • Environmental health • Medical radiography • Pharmacy technician • Respiratory therapy • Health education: diabetes • Dental hygiene
Qatar University	College of Pharmacy	2006	• Pharmacy
	College of Medicine	2014	• Medicine
	College of Health Sciences	2016	• Biomedical sciences • Public health • Human nutrition • Physical therapy and rehabilitation
	College of Dental Medicine	2019	• Dental Medicine
University of Calgary—Qatar		2007	• Nursing

Education in Qatar'. The project investigated the development of shared competencies to be used by faculty while integrating IPE into the undergraduate curriculum. Unfortunately, the council has been dormant since 2013 due to many of the key personnel in the council relocating to outside Qatar, affecting the sustainability of this IPE initiative. However, the College of Pharmacy took the lead with the establishment of the interprofessional education committee (IPEC), in 2014 as discussed below.

Development and Implementation of IPE in Academic Institutions

Accreditation as a Driver

The main initial drive to integrate IPE was achieving the Canadian accreditation of the pharmacy programme. IPE is an important element in the accreditation standard for pharmacy for CCAPP. Many western accreditation bodies call for incorporation of IPE into the curricula of health care programmes. However, there is lack of collective global IPE standards for the different health care professions and a need for different accrediting bodies to collaborate to have common IPE standards (Zorek & Raehl, 2013). Recognising the importance of incorporating IPE, CCAPP standards, effective from January 2013, have addressed the necessity to provide IPE experiences within the pharmacy curricula (Canadian Council for Accreditation of Pharmacy Programs, 2014). In their latest standards, 3, 4, 6, 11 and 19 explicitly focus on the necessity of incorporating IPE within pharmacy curricula as highlighted in the following (Canadian Council for Accreditation of Pharmacy Programs, 2018, pp. 4–5):

- Standard 3 (curriculum): The professional degree programme in pharmacy has a minimum of four academic years, or the equivalent number of hours or credits, including a series of core courses, practice experiences and interprofessional experiences that support educational outcomes.

- Standard 4 (curriculum): The curriculum includes foundational content in: biomedical, pharmaceutical, behavioural, social, and administrative pharmacy sciences; clinical sciences including clinical practice skills; practice experiences; and intra- and interprofessional collaborative practice skills.
- Standard 6 (curriculum): The curriculum includes required intra- and interprofessional learning experiences, offered throughout the professional programme, to enable a graduate to provide patient care as a collaborative member of a care team.
- Standard 11 (university structure and commitment): The curriculum includes required intra- and interprofessional learning experiences, offered throughout the professional programme, to enable a graduate to provide patient care as a collaborative member of a care team.
- Standard 19 (planning and evaluation): Interprofessional education and collaborative practice is embedded in Faculty policy and/or strategic plans.

Establishment of the Interprofessional Education Committee

The College of Pharmacy at Qatar University took the lead to incorporate IPE initiatives formally into the pharmacy curriculum, with other health care students in Qatar aligned to CCAPP accreditation standards, and to fulfil the recommendations set in the World Health Organization (WHO) framework (Canadian Council for Accreditation of Pharmacy Programs, 2018; World Health Organization, 2010). Taking into account recommendations and perspectives from research findings, and support from the college administration, the college led the integration and implementation of IPE through the establishment of IPEC. The aim was to provide guidance and support in implementing IPE within the pharmacy curriculum, as well as in our partner health care training programmes in the country. The committee was dedicated to facilitating awareness and understanding of IPE for interprofessional collaboration (IPC) for students and faculty members. In addition to creating enthusiasm and motivation for planned IPE activities (Acquavita, Lewis,

Aparico, & Pecukonis, 2014), it was imperative to engage stakeholders in IPE planning steering committees. The committee includes representatives from all the health care schools in Qatar as nominated by the respective deans based on their academic portfolio and familiarity with their respective curriculum (Table 7.1).

Another opportunity to improve and ensure that planned IPE initiatives work best in the context of their institutions was to measure stakeholder readiness for IPE (El-Awaisi, El Hajj, Joseph, & Diack, 2018a, 2018b; El-Awaisi, Joseph, El Hajj, & Diack, 2019). Overall, the process provided opportunities for key stakeholders to plan IPE activities that are effective and relevant to our students. The process was used as a catalyst to incorporate more IPE into their curriculum and to better prepare our students to engage with others in a collaborative practice environment. This is evident in that the college has been successful in integrating IPE into their curriculum and these IPE activities have gained positive attention from all the stakeholders with all activities incorporated in the different professional years of pharmacy and sustained for the last five years (El-Awaisi, Wilby, et al., 2017).

Interprofessional Education Committee Moving Beyond College Level

Academic institutions need to facilitate and support the integration of IPE into health care programmes and direct resources to IPE for it to thrive. As such, IPEC moved to QU Health level in 2017 to strengthen IPE with a vision 'to be recognised regionally for excellence in interprofessional health education and interdisciplinary health research; a first choice for students and scholars, and a national catalyst for innovation in the field' (QU Health, 2019). IPEC deliverables were based on four key pillars including IPE curriculum, faculty development, student led initiatives and research. Therefore, it is planned that QU health will serve as a catalyst for IPE, facilitating and strengthening IPE initiatives suitable for the Qatari and Middle Eastern context and meeting the highest standard of excellence in the field. The IPEC website can be viewed at the following link: http://www.qu.edu.qa/health/ipe.

IPE Curriculum

The model adopted as the base for the IPE activities was that of the University of British Columbia (UBC) with its three main levels: exposure, immersion and mastery (Charles, Bainbridge, & Gilbert, 2010; El-Awaisi, Wilby, et al., 2017). All learning outcomes for the IPE activities are based on the interprofessional shared competencies developed for the Qatar context which include: role clarification, interprofessional communication, shared decision making and patient centred care (Johnson et al., 2015). IPE is currently integrated across the professional years of the different curricula. Activities are shown in Table 7.2. Professions participating in the different activities vary across the years but usually include between two and six health care professions. Activities are usually held in different campuses depending on availability (El-Awaisi, Wilby, et al., 2017).

Table 7.2 Examples of IPE activities across the professional years

Professional Year	Fall semester	Spring semester
Professional Year 1	Introducing the concept of IPE I	Introducing the concept of IPE II
Professional Year 2	Case based interprofessional discussion on chronic obstructive pulmonary disease (COPD) and smoking cessation	Case based interprofessional discussion on being an effective team player
Professional Year 3	Cased based interprofessional discussion on diabetes	Cased based interprofessional discussion on infection and antibiotic stewardship
Professional Year 4	Practice based IPE activities	Interprofessional simulation focused on mental health

Faculty Development

Faculty IPE development and facilitator training with effective preparation and orientation are critical for effective implementation of IPE, especially as many faculty have little or no previous experience of IPE (Ratka, 2013; Reeves, Goldman, & Oandasan, 2007). Faculty development (FD) initiatives are key drivers to overcoming barriers, facilitating a positive culture change in academic institutions, and encouraging short and long term commitment by faculty (Lawlis, Anson, & Greenfield, 2014). FD sessions need to focus on familiarising faculty with the different health care professions' roles and responsibilities, current challenges to collaboration in the practice setting, the interprofessional learning programme, and the skills needed for effective collaboration (Holland, 2002). FD needs to be ongoing and offered on a regular basis with opportunities for participants to reflect and learn from any IPE experiences they have undertaken. These are also opportunities to promote IPE, recruit faculty members, and network with each other.

The College of Pharmacy at Qatar University led the first IPE symposium for academic health care faculty in Qatar in February 2015 to equip over 50 faculty members with the knowledge to develop IPE content and with the skills to impart curricular change for IPE implementation (El-Awaisi, El Hajj, Joseph, & Diack, 2016; El-Awaisi, Wilby, et al., 2017). This was followed by the First Middle Eastern Conference on IPE, in December 2015, which attracted more than 300 participants, faculty, and practitioners from 13 countries: Australia, Bahrain, Canada, Egypt, Iraq, Kuwait, Lebanon, Oman, Saudi Arabia, the United Arab Emirates, Turkey, the United Kingdom and the United States. Attendance exceeded the organisers' expectations and was a strong indicator of the need for such conferences in the region. Some of the attendees were novices in relation to the concept of IPE and hence had the opportunity to learn and explore strategies for how IPE can be integrated into their institutions. For others, it was an opportunity to reflect on how they may improve the delivery of IPE in their institutions. During the 3-day conference, there were six workshops, 37 oral presentations, and 40 posters displayed (El-Awaisi et al., 2016; El-Awaisi, Wilby, et al., 2017). Further information about the conference can be found at http://www.qu.edu.qa/IPE2015/.

As a result of the conference, the conference advisory committee proposed a set of actions to strengthen and support IPE in the region, emphasising that Qatar can lead the way in creating opportunities for IPE initiatives in the region. These include promoting an interprofessional culture at both educational and health care institutions with the intent of developing new frontiers in health care education, and collaborating and working closely with the World Confederation for Interprofessional Practice and Education (Interprofessional.Global). Additionally, Qatar plans to lead the way in establishing a Middle Eastern network in collaboration with other countries in the Middle East, as there is currently no Middle Eastern representation at Interprofessional.Global (El-Awaisi & Barr, 2017; El-Awaisi et al., 2016). Regional interprofessional networks affiliated with Interprofessional.Global are from the Americas, USA, Canada, UK, Europe, Africa, India, Southeast Asia and the Pacific Rim, Japan and Australasia. Discussion has started about creating an IPE network in this region that works collaboratively to foster partnerships and enable opportunities to share experiences and contribute to the global perspectives on IPE and collaborative practice. The second Middle East Conference is planned to take place in Lebanon. Another important milestone is that Qatar University was successful in its bid to host the tenth event of the All Together Better Health (ATBH) conference in October 2020, taking this biennial event to the Middle East for the first time. However, due to the current COVID-19 pandemic, the conference has been rescheduled to October 25–27, 2021. The theme of the conference will be: ‘Cultivating a collaborative culture: sharing pearls of wisdom’, advocating for people-centered care, health and wellbeing; embracing diversity of stakeholders; informing regional and global interprofessional education and collaborative practice conference (IPECP) policies and standards; promoting safety in and beyond health and social care settings and sharing models of best practice in IPECP. All Together Better Health is the leading global interprofessional education and collaborative practice conference under the direction of Interprofessional.Global.

In addition to faculty development, health care professional training is of paramount importance. Continuing professional development (CPD), participating in interprofessional committees, interprofessional ward rounds, interprofessional meetings, participating in research, and journal clubs are effective strategies for promoting IPC between health care team members (Curran, Sargeant, & Hollett, 2007; Luetsch & Rowett, 2015; Price, Doucet, & Hill, 2014). The College of Pharmacy led the way in establishing an interprofessional CPD programme in 2011, which was expanded to incorporate QU Health in 2017. CPD for health care professionals is regulated by the Qatar Council for Healthcare Practitioners. The programme attracts health care professionals from different fields and it is a requirement when designing these activities to demonstrate the principles of IPE (McMahon et al., 2016). However, many negotiated efforts are still needed to drive the integration and implementation of IPE forward including collaboration with patient and service users who are key stakeholders and central to the development of IPE.

Student Leadership

It is important to engage students in IPE initiatives and, consequently, members selected a student representative from a group of interested students to serve on the IPEC. The students were tasked to form an IPE student society and assume, with a student executive committee, leadership roles in promoting IPE amongst students from the different health care disciplines. The society executive committee includes student representatives from all health care programmes in Qatar. Two of their major events include the annual IPE student forum and organising interprofesssional outreach events focused on chronic conditions such as hypertension and smoking cessation. In addition, they host an annual research day for health care students. Further information about the society can be accessed at: http://ipestudent-qatar.weebly.com.

Research

Since the establishment of IPE, research in this area has started to emerge. This varies from projects focused on the perspective of various key stakeholders to IPE (El-Awaisi, Diack, Joseph, & El Hajj, 2016; El-Awaisi et al., 2016; El-Awaisi, El Hajj, et al., 2018a, 2018b; Wilbur & Kelly, 2015; Zolezzi et al., 2017) to others focused on the actual experiences of IPE (El-Awaisi, Awaisu, et al., 2017; Wilby, Al-Abdi, El-Awaisi, & Diab, 2016; Wilby et al., 2015). There are also reviews (El-Awaisi, Joseph, El Hajj, & Diack, 2017; El-Awaisi, Wilby, et al., 2017; Johnson & Carragher, 2018) and a description of the steps to follow in introducing IPE into health care curricula (El-Awaisi et al., 2016).

With the integration of IPE into the health care curricula in Qatar, it is important to evaluate the longitudinal impact of IPE on collaboration and quality of care delivered to patients. The hierarchical culture prominent in this region reinforces the idea that the physician is always at the top of the organisational structure, and this is usually instilled in the mind-set of health care students. It would be useful to investigate how this mind-set is instilled, how it affects interprofessional working, and how to manage the behavioural change needed to change the culture. In this region, patient perception towards health care professionals in general, and interprofessional teams in particular, also needs to be explored further, in the context of continuously working toward patient-centred care.

Promotion and Implementation of IPC in Practice Settings

Although the focus in Qatar has been on integrating IPE within the curriculum, there are many challenges and barriers in the practice settings that need to be explored and addressed. Aligning the efforts of academic institutions with practice is of crucial importance and has the potential to enhance the value and quality of experience for patients, their families, communities, and learners (Earnest & Brandt, 2014; Institute of

Medicine, 2015). The transformation to an environment where interprofessional working and collaborative practice are fostered and promoted will be challenging and disrupt the longstanding hierarchical structure within the team by levelling status among the members (Ginsburg & Tregunno, 2005; Solimeo, Ono, Lampman, Paez, & Stewart, 2015). The process will be facilitated if organisational leaders dedicate resources, advocate for this change, and raise awareness and understanding about the contributions of every member of the health care team and the importance of interprofessional working (Solimeo et al., 2015). These measures, combined with evaluation and feedback, are important to convey the importance of IPC, assist health care professionals toward achieving IPC in their settings, motivate changes toward successful implementation, and increase sustainability (Ginsburg & Tregunno, 2005).

There is a need to build on the established success to date. Students have to be provided with learning opportunities to implement what they are taught. Practice settings should be collaborative environments with positive role models where students are educated and trained (Thibault, 2013). Institutional support, working culture, and environment are all important factors contributing to the effectiveness of collaborative practice in health care settings (World Health Organization, 2010). Careful 'needs assessment' to improve IPC in the practice setting is required to identify the facilitators and challenges from multiple perspectives to create an action plan for implementation. It is important to note that changing the existing culture will be a complex and lengthy process and many unidentified barriers might appear in the process. However, instead of emphasising hidden curriculum messages, the focus should be on reinforcing skills needed to overcome and deal with challenges (Hafferty & O'Donnell, 2015).

Hospitals, primary care centres and even the Ministry of Public Health need to raise awareness and send positive messages that convey respect and trust to health care providers about the importance of collaboration, its link to better patient outcomes and the unique contribution each brings to the health care team. Creating a positive collaborative environment will help negate stereotypes and barriers that may arise from the lack of understanding of the contribution each health care professional makes to the interprofessional team (Price et al., 2014).

Policies and Governmental Vision

Reforming health care curricula to lead to better health care outcomes and improve quality of care for the patient will require a cultural change at all stages with an emphasis on linking IPE experiences with practice (Thibault, 2013). In addition to this, institutional and public policies need to promote and support reform in both health care curricula and the health care delivery system (Thibault, 2013). Governments and health care institutions play a critical role in initiating and sustaining IPE and IPC initiatives (Lawlis et al., 2014). Regulatory bodies have been identified as having an important impact on facilitating collaboration between health care professionals (Bourgeault & Grignon, 2013). The Qatari Ministry of Public Health can play a key role but needs to accelerate the promotion and implementation of IPE and collaborative practice. As an example, the Qatar Council for Healthcare Practitioners, the regulatory body for all health care practitioners working in both governmental and private health care sectors in Qatar (McMahon et al., 2016), could play a key role by mandating and promoting IPE and collaborative practice as part of its accreditation standards to create a culture that promotes interprofessional collaboration. Additionally, national and internal funding agencies such as NPRP need to fund development and provide opportunities for IPE and collaborative practice to be researched and included within their priorities. This would be an excellent strategy to recruit and engage faculty and practitioners into such initiatives to provide a sustainable programme from IPE to IPC (Brashers, Owen, & Haizlip, 2015).

Identified Challenges

Though the implementation and integration of IPE has been a success in the last five years, there have been many challenges and obstacles to overcome. Some of the key challenges encountered during the implementation process of the IPE programme in Qatar include (El-Awaisi, Wilby, et al., 2017):

- Curriculum alignment with partnering institutions
- Current status of collaboration in practice
- Workload and faculty recognition
- Logistical difficulties in terms of coordinating scheduling and finding a suitable space to conduct the activity
- Geographical location of the partnering institutions
- Lack of a structured IPE assessment plan
- Lack of adequate IPE training and sufficient IPE experiences.

However, the existence of highly motivated facilitators eager to integrate IPE into health care curricula has leveraged many of the difficulties faced (El-Awaisi et al., 2019; El-Awaisi, Wilby, et al., 2017). During the integration of IPE, political considerations may surface in different ways and need to be dealt with cautiously and diplomatically (Interprofessional Education Consortium, 2002). Tension and competition for prestige, resources and influence are present when IPE is implemented across institutions and has been observed in Qatar. As an example, IPE activities are usually advertised through a press release to promote an interprofessional culture. Initially these press releases were sent through Qatar University, as IPEC is part of this institution. However, to acknowledge all efforts and avoid any unnecessary tension, it was decided that press releases should be sent from the institution that hosts the event with full recognition of all participating institutions.

Recommendations for Sustainability

Though IPE implementation has been achieved and IPE is now part of the QU health strategy, the lack of a dedicated unit for IPE and the lack of dedicated IPE personnel are key challenges we face to ensure the sustainability of IPE. Sustainability planning needs to be considered right from the beginning (Interprofessional Education Consortium, 2002). Sustainability should be a long-term strategy to work toward though it is not always easy to achieve. To ensure the sustainability of IPE programmes, a proposal is currently under discussion to establish a dedicated academic office to be called the Office of IPE at a QU health level that will replace the currently operating QU Health IPEC. The IPE office at QU health level will build on the success of the IPEC, which was able to develop a leadership role in IPE in Qatar within a short period since its establishment. The creation of QU Health provides a unique opportunity for Qatar University to further develop and become a leader of IPE in the region. The formation of a dedicated office will help towards expanding IPEC initiatives, and planning activities according to evidence, best practice and contemporary models of health care is consistent with the QU Health vision.

Another proposal to ensure sustainability is to have a dedicated IPE credit-bearing course formally embedded into the different health care curricula at Qatar University. The course will be compulsory for all QU health students in their third or fourth year of study. This will ensure all health care students receive the same IPE exposure and experiences and will perceive it as a key part of their programme.

Conclusion

Readiness assessment conducted prior to the implementation of IPE was important to formulate and inform strategies for implementation and enhancement of IPE and IPC. The findings have had significant implications already on the development of IPE in Qatar and the region with the establishment of the interprofessional education committee with its focus on IPE curriculum integration into the health care programmes in Qatar. Faculty development, hosting the first Middle East conference on interprofessional education in the region, research and student led initiatives through the IPE student society have also contributed to the development of IPE. However, aligning efforts of academic institutions with practice is of crucial importance. While a tremendous amount of work has occurred already with many positive changes, it is important to capitalize on these opportunities and establish sustainable mechanisms to pave the way for meaningful integration of interprofessional learning and practice both in educational and practice settings with a commitment for continuous improvement through innovation and creativity.

References

Acquavita, S. P., Lewis, M. A., Aparicio, E., & Pecukonis, E. (2014). Student perspectives on interprofessional education and experiences. *Journal of Allied Health, 43*(2), e31–36.

Bourgeault, I. L., & Grignon, M. (2013). A comparison of the regulation of health professional boundaries across OECD countries. *The European Journal of Comparative Economics, 10*(2), 199.

Brashers, V., Owen, J., & Haizlip, J. (2015). Interprofessional education and practice guide no. 2: Developing and implementing a center for interprofessional education. *Journal of Interprofessional Care, 29*(2), 95–99. https://doi.org/10.3109/13561820.2014.962130.

Canadian Council for Accreditation of Pharmacy Programs. (2014). *Accreditation standards for the first professional degree in pharmacy programs.* Retrieved from http://www.ccappaccredit.ca/site/pdfs/university/CCAPP_accred_standards_degree_2014.pdf.

Canadian Council for Accreditation of Pharmacy Programs. (2018). *Accreditation standards for Canadian first professional degree in pharmacy programs.* Retrieved from http://ccapp-accredit.ca/wp-content/uploads/2016/01/Accreditation-Standards-for-Canadian-First-Professional-Degree-in-Pharmacy-Programs.pdf.

Central Intelligence Agency. (2017). *The world factbook.* Country comparison: GDP—PER CAPITA (PPP). Retrieved from https://www.cia.gov/library/publications/the-world-factbook/rankorder/2004rank.html.

Charles, G., Bainbridge, L., & Gilbert, J. (2010). The University of British Columbia model of interprofessional education. *Journal of Interprofessional Care, 24*(1), 9–18. https://doi.org/10.3109/13561820903294549.

Curran, V., Sargeant, J., & Hollett, A. (2007). Evaluation of an interprofessional continuing professional development initiative in primary health care. *Journal of Continuing Education in the Health Professions, 27*(4), 241–252. https://doi.org/10.1002/chp.144.

Earnest, M., & Brandt, B. (2014). Aligning practice redesign and interprofessional education to advance triple aim outcomes. *Journal of Interprofessional Care, 28*(6), 497–500. https://doi.org/10.3109/13561820.2014.933650.

El-Awaisi, A., Anderson, E., Barr, H., Wilby, K. J., Wilbur, K., & Bainbridge, L. (2016). Important steps for introducing interprofessional education into health professional education. *Journal of Taibah University Medical Sciences, 11*(6), 546–551. https://doi.org/10.1016/j.jtumed.2016.09.004.

El-Awaisi, A., Awaisu, A., El Hajj, M. S., Alemrayat, B., Al-Jayyousi, G., Wong, N., & Verjee, M. A. (2017). Delivering tobacco cessation content in the Middle East through interprofessional learning. *American Journal of Pharmaceutical Education, 81*(5), 91. https://doi.org/10.5688/ajpe81591.
El-Awaisi, A., & Barr, H. (2017). Editorial: East meets West: Working together in interprofessional education and practice. *Journal of Interprofessional Education & Practice, 7*, 72–74.
El-Awaisi, A., Diack, L., Joseph, S., & El Hajj, M. (2016). Perspectives of pharmacy students, pharmacy academics and practicing pharmacists on interprofessional education and collaborative practice: A comprehensive systematic review protocol. *JBI Database of Systematic Reviews and Implementation Reports, 13*(12), 70–92. https://doi.org/10.11124/jbisrir-2015-2115.
El-Awaisi, A., El Hajj, M.S., Joseph, S., & Diack, L. (2016). Interprofessional education in the Arabic-speaking Middle East: Perspectives of pharmacy academics. *Journal of Interprofessional Care*, 1–8. https://doi.org/10.1080/13561820.2016.1218830.
El-Awaisi, A., El Hajj, M. S., Joseph, S., & Diack, L. (2018a). Perspectives of practising pharmacists towards interprofessional education and collaborative practice in Qatar. *International Journal of Clinical Pharmacy, 40*(5), 1388–1401. https://doi.org/10.1007/s11096-018-0686-9.
El-Awaisi, A., El Hajj, M.S., Joseph, S., & Diack, L. (2018b). Perspectives of pharmacy students in Qatar toward interprofessional education and collaborative practice: A mixed methods study. *Journal of Interprofessional Care*, 1–15. https://doi.org/10.1080/13561820.2018.1498466.
El-Awaisi, A., Joseph, S., El Hajj, M. S., & Diack, L. (2017). A comprehensive systematic review of pharmacy perspectives on interprofessional education and collaborative practice. *Research in Social and Administrative Pharmacy, 14*(10), 863–882. https://doi.org/10.1016/j.sapharm.2017.11.001.
El-Awaisi, A., Joseph, S., El Hajj, M. S., & Diack, L. (2019). Pharmacy academics' perspectives toward interprofessional Education prior to its implementation in Qatar: A qualitative study. *BMC Medical Education, 19*(1), 278. https://doi.org/10.1186/s12909-019-1689-5.
El-Awaisi, A., Wilby, K. J., Wilbur, K., El Hajj, M. S., Awaisu, A., & Paravattil, B. (2017). A Middle Eastern journey of integrating interprofessional education into the healthcare curriculum: A SWOC analysis. *BMC Medical Education, 17*(1), 15. https://doi.org/10.1186/s12909-016-0852-5.
Forstenlechner, I., & Rutledge, E. J. (2011). The GCC's 'demographic imbalance': Perceptions, realities and policy options. *Middle East Policy, 18*(4), 25–43.

General Secretariat for Development Planning. (2008). *Qatar National Vision 2030*. Retrieved from http://www.mdps.gov.qa/portal/page/portal/gsdp_en/qatar_national_vision/qnv_2030_document.

Ginsburg, L., & Tregunno, D. (2005). New approaches to interprofessional education and collaborative practice: Lessons from the organizational change literature. *Journal of Interprofessional Care, 19*(Suppl 1), 177–187. https://doi.org/10.1080/13561820500083105.

Hafferty, F. W., & O'Donnell, J. F. (2015). *The hidden curriculum in health professional education*. Lebanon: Dartmouth College Press.

Hamad Medical Cooperation. (2019). *Our people*. Retrieved from https://www.hamad.qa/EN/About-Us/Our%20People/Pages/default.aspx.

Holland, K. (2002). Interprofessional education and practice: The role of the teacher/facilitator. *Nurse Education in Practice, 2*, 221–222.

Institute of Medicine. (2015). *Measuring the impact of interprofessional education on collaborative practice and patient outcomes*. Washington, DC: The National Academies Press.

Interprofessional Education Consortium. (2002). *Creating, implementing and sustaining interprofessional education*. San Francisco: Interprofessional Education Consortium.

Johnson, B., Abi-Hayla, M., Jewesson, P., Byrne, C., El Tawil, M., & Verjee, M. (2015). Core Interprofessional Education (IPE) health competencies: The process of adaptation and implementation for a local environment. *Journal of Local Global Health Science, 1*(3). https://doi.org/10.5339/jlghs.2015.3.

Johnson, B., Pyburn, R., Bolan, C., Byrne, C., Jewesson, P., Robertson-Malt, S., ... Verjee, V. (2011). Qatar Interprofessional Health Council: IPE for Qatar. *Avicenna, 2*. https://doi.org/10.5339/avi.2011.2.

Johnson, J. M., & Carragher, R. (2018). Interprofessional collaboration and the care and management of type 2 diabetic patients in the Middle East: A systematic review. *Journal of Interprofessional Care, 32*(5), 621–628. https://doi.org/10.1080/13561820.2018.1471052.

Lawlis, T. R., Anson, J., & Greenfield, D. (2014). Barriers and enablers that influence sustainable interprofessional education: A literature review. *Journal of Interprofessional Care, 28*(4), 305–310. https://doi.org/10.3109/13561820.2014.895977.

Luetsch, K., & Rowett, D. (2015). Interprofessional communication training: Benefits to practicing pharmacists. *International Journal of Clinical Pharmacy, 37*(5), 857–864. https://doi.org/10.1007/s11096-015-0130-3.

McMahon, G. T., Aboulsoud, S., Gordon, J., McKenna, M., Meuser, J., Staz, M., & Campbell, C. M. (2016). Evolving alignment in international continuing professional. *Health Professions, 36*(Suppl 1), S22–26. https://doi.org/10.1097/ceh.0000000000000075.

Ministry of Public Health. (2018). *National Health Strategy 2018–2022: Our health, our future.* Retrieved from https://www.moph.gov.qa/HSF/Documents/short%20report%20eng%2020.03.2018.pdf.

Price, S., Doucet, S., & Hall, L. M. (2014). The historical social positioning of nursing and medicine: Implications for career choice, early socialization and interprofessional collaboration. *Journal of Interprofessional Care, 28*(2), 103–109. https://doi.org/10.3109/13561820.2013.867839.

Qatar General Secretariat for Development Planning. (2011). *Qatar national development strategy (2011–2016).* Retrieved from http://www.nhsq.info/app/media/139.

QU Health. (2019). *Mission and vision.* Retrieved from http://www.qu.edu.qa/health/about-us/vision-mission.

Ratka, A. (2013). Transition of pharmacy educators to faculty champions of interprofessional education. *American Journal of Pharmaceutical Education, 77*(7), 136. https://doi.org/10.5688/ajpe777136.

Reeves, S., Goldman, J., & Oandasan, I. (2007). Key factors in planning and implementing interprofessional education in health care settings. *Journal of Allied Health, 36*(4), 231–235.

Solimeo, S. L., Ono, S. S., Lampman, M. A., Paez, M. B., & Stewart, G. L. (2015). The empowerment paradox as a central challenge to patient-centred medical home implementation in the veteran's health administration. *Journal of Interprofessional Care, 29*(1), 26–33. https://doi.org/10.3109/13561820.2014.937480.

Thibault, G. E. (2013). Reforming health professions education will require culture change and closer ties between classroom and practice. *Health Affairs (Millwood), 32*(11), 1928–1932. https://doi.org/10.1377/hlthaff.2013.0827.

World Health Organization. (2010). *Framework for action on interprofessional education and collaborative practice.* Retrieved from: https://www.who.int/hrh/resources/framework_action/en/.

Wilbur, K., & Kelly, I. (2015). Interprofessional impressions among nursing and pharmacy students: A qualitative study to inform interprofessional education initiatives. *BMC Medical Education, 15*(1), 1–8. https://doi.org/10.1186/s12909-015-0337-y.

Wilby, K. J., Al-Abdi, T., El-Awaisi, A., & Diab, M. I. (2016). Changes in student perceptions after a semester-long interprofessional education activity in Qatar. *Journal of Taibah University Medical Sciences, 11*(6), 541–545. https://doi.org/10.1016/j.jtumed.2016.08.009.

Wilby, K. J., Al-Abdi, T., Hassan, A., Brown, M. A., Paravattil, B., & Khalifa, S. I. (2015). Attitudes of pharmacy and nutrition students towards team-based care after first exposure to interprofessional education in Qatar. *Journal of Interprofessional Care, 29*(1), 82–84. https://doi.org/10.3109/13561820.2014.933949.

World Population Review. (2019). *Qatar population 2019.* Retrieved from http://worldpopulationreview.com/countries/qatar-population/.

Zolezzi, M., Abdallah, O., Aden, S., Major, S., White, D., & El-Awaisi, A. (2017). Perceived preparedness of health care students for providing cardiovascular disease risk assessment and management. *Pharmacy, 5*(1), 9.

Zorek, J., & Raehl, C. (2013). Interprofessional education accreditation standards in the USA: A comparative analysis. *Journal of Interprofessional Care, 27*(2), 123–130. https://doi.org/10.3109/13561820.2012.718295.

Part III

Key Drivers

8

Developing an Australia Wide Approach to IPE Leadership and Sustainability

Monica Moran, Dawn Forman, Maree O'Keefe, Carole Steketee, Gary D. Rogers, and Roger Dunston

Introduction

Australia is a country and a continent. Whilst health standards are ranked amongst the best in the world, its immense size and distributed population creates unique challenges for the delivery of integrated health and

M. Moran (✉)
WA Center for Rural Health, University of Western Australia, Geraldton, WA, Australia
e-mail: monica.moran@uwa.edu.au

D. Forman
University of Derby, Derby, UK

M. O'Keefe
University of Adelaide, Adelaide, SA, Australia

C. Steketee
University of Notre Dame, Fremantle, WA, Australia

G. D. Rogers
Griffith University, Brisbane, QLD, Australia

D. Forman et al. (eds.), *Sustainability and Interprofessional Collaboration*,
https://doi.org/10.1007/978-3-030-40281-5_8

social care services. The fragmentation of current health service delivery across tertiary and primary care, poor integration with health professional education functions, and the lack of over-arching governance models to facilitate coordinated team based care pose major challenges to the sustainability of Australian health services (Swerissen, Duckett, & Moran, 2018).

This chapter reports on the outcomes of a nationally funded project to develop a leadership and governance structure to span the Australian higher education and health sectors and support the roll out of interprofessional education (IPE) for sustainable interprofessional collaborative practice (IPCP).

Proposing a national action plan, and then moving towards activating it, is no small undertaking. This project was supported by multiple universities, professional representative organisations and individual experts. Their involvement in spanning the sectors has strengthened the development and provides optimism for the sustainability of project outcomes.

Background

Commencing in 2015, the Securing an Interprofessional Future (SIF) project drew together a substantial body of work undertaken as related projects and funded by the Australian Government:

1. Interprofessional health education in Australia: The way forward (Dunston et al., 2009).
2. Interprofessional health education: A literature review (Nesbit, Lee, Kumar, Thistlethwaite, & Dunston, 2011).
3. Interprofessional education for health professionals in Western Australia: Perspectives and activity (Nicol, 2011).

R. Dunston
Faculty of Arts and Social Sciences, University of Technology Sydney (UTS), Ultimo, NSW, Australia

4. Curriculum renewal for interprofessional education in health (Interprofessional Curriculum Renewal Consortium, Australia, 2014).
5. Work based assessment on teamwork (The iTOFT Consortium, Australia, 2015).
6. Collaborating across boundaries: A framework for an integrated interprofessional curriculum (O'Keefe, 2015).
7. Developing sustainable and embedded interprofessional education: Threshold learning outcomes as a potential pathway (O'Keefe, Henderson, & Chick, 2015).
8. Curriculum renewal in interprofessional education in health: Establishing leadership and capacity (Dunston et al., 2016).
9. Defining a set of common interprofessional learning competencies for health profession students (O'Keefe, Henderson, & Chick, 2017).
10. Securing an interprofessional future (SIF). Establishing an Australian interprofessional education governance and development framework.
    (Dunston et al., 2018). [NB: This is an interim report; the final report will be available in late 2019.]

Many examples of impactful IPE were identified across these projects. However a number of serious barriers to sustainability were also identified. These included:

- an over-dependence on local champions,
- time limited local funding opportunities,
- a lack of recognised national standards,
- no accepted national governance framework,
- no leadership structures, and
- significant gaps in planning for an interprofessional health workforce between the key sectors of higher education, health and community services.

Combined, these barriers created an environment of constraint and instability which prevented IPE from growing and sustaining itself. The SIF Project, therefore, focussed on creating a sustainable model for interprofessional education and practice across Australia.

Aims of the SIF Project

The SIF Project was designed to springboard from the previous projects' contributions, and to address the lack of a national system for ensuring the quality of interprofessional provision. It aimed to do this via the development of governance structures and mechanisms to ensure integration and sustainability.

The specific aims of the SIF project were to:

1. Make a significant contribution to optimising the employability skills of health professional students in Australia.
2. Position Australia as a global leader in its approach to the incorporation and development of IPE as a core element of health professional curricula so that all graduates are prepared to take their place in a more collaborative workforce.
3. Implement an innovative, consensus-based and sustainable approach to the governance and further development of IPE across Australian health professional education. We refer to this approach in its entirety as the National Interprofessional Education for Collaborative Practice Governance and Development Framework (see Fig. 8.1). Such an approach does not currently exist in Australia.
4. Make a significant contribution to ensuring that health professional education is aligned with the changing needs and requirements of contemporary and future health practice.

(Dunston et al., 2018)

Over the course of the project, the need for a uniting national 'whole-of-system' governance and development plan was recognised. This resulted in the establishment of a framework that represents all conditions required for the governance of a national approach.

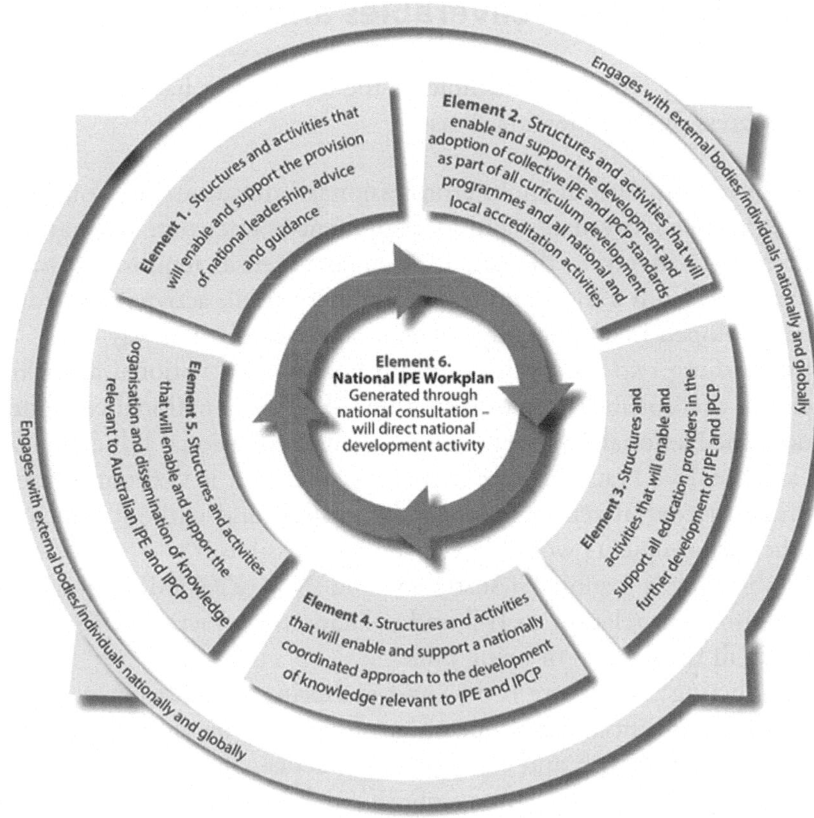

Fig. 8.1 National Interprofessional Education for Collaborative Practice Governance and Development Framework

Project Approach

The project utilised a range of socio-cultural and socio-material theorisations of practice, learning and change. These theories addressed the complex nature of the various bodies involved and their respective cultural, social and historical values. Key to achieving the project aims was to build trust and strong working relationships to support collaborative outcomes.

Project Outputs, Deliverables and Resources

Working closely with key stakeholders the SIF project has made significant progress in the following areas:

1. Finalising an Australian Interprofessional Education for Collaborative Practice Governance and Development Framework. The national framework identifies the activity elements seen as required to transform IPE from a local and isolated activity to an activity that could be developed in a nationally coherent and coordinated way.
2. Establishing two national leadership bodies: (i) a national auspicing group, the 'collaborating organisations', and (ii) a national collaboration, the National Advisory Group on Interprofessional Education for Collaborative Practice. Achievement in this area is without a doubt the most central achievement of the project, and without which all other achievements would have been less possible.
3. Establishing a regional (Australian and New Zealand) 'knowledge repository' in relation to IPE and collaborative practice. This is currently in the process of being built.
4. Conducting a literature review and authoring a discussion paper on how the concept and practice of 'governance' is being utilised in the development of IPE and collaborative practice.
5. Developing a National Interprofessional Education Workplan. This will be presented to the national advisory group and collaborating organisations at their first formal meeting in late 2019.
6. Other project materials and resources, such as journal publications, the project blog, ResearchGate page, conference presentations and workshops.

(Dunston et al., 2018)

National IPE for Collaborative Practice Governance and Development Framework

The national framework (see Fig. 8.1) is a conceptual model that gives us a road map for future focused, systems-wide approaches for the development of Australian IPE and IPCP. It has been constructed as an evidence-based and consensus-informed platform drawing on the findings of multiple previous studies and the results of consultative processes with numerous organisations and key informants across the duration of the SIF project. It is designed to illustrate and articulate the national developmental processes that are required to support the progress of Australia-wide IPE. It is constructed around a set of core principles as follows:

- The development of IPE and IPCP must be seen as a national, system-wide and coordinated undertaking.
- Work underpinning the development of IPE and IPCP must be co-located and concurrently progress a number of national agendas including leadership, faculty development, knowledge development and knowledge dissemination.
- IPE and IPCP will only succeed with system-wide ownership—all stakeholders including the health professions and key national leadership bodies must work together on the shared development and operationalisation of Australian IPE and IPCP.

The Road to Developing a Sustainable National IPE and Collaborative Practice Leadership Structure

A significant risk related to project funded IPE development activities is the loss of momentum between funding cycles. The SIF project team endeavoured to create a set of circumstances to manage this risk by generating organisational structures to facilitate national and sustainable IPE for collaborative practice leadership.

The project team facilitated numerous face-to-face and virtual consultative meetings and extensive correspondence with national peak bodies that could be positioned to take on a leadership role. These consultations included co-generation and working through a range of different arrangements to support a national leadership model.

Early in the project, the team recognised that the promotion of effective IPE for collaborative practice would articulate with a number of other national priority areas. A series of engagement activities with the peak organisations concerned with these areas evolved. The priority areas included:

- regulation of the health professions
- provision and accreditation of health professional education programmes
- promotion of quality and safety in health care
- provision of hospital and other health services
- partnership with the patients, clients and communities that the health system serves
- professional development of health professional educators
- partnership with health professional students
- promotion of the interests of the health professions themselves.

(Dunston et al., 2018)

Following this widespread engagement process the project team coordinated a national round table meeting with representatives of thirteen national organisations concerned with these priority areas. The leadership organisations that attended the day long round table meeting workshopped a series of questions and ideas that helped identify how their missions and priorities could be advanced though the development of a national structure to drive the roll out of Australian IPE for collaborative practice. The outcomes of these discussions were collated and disseminated to the attending groups for reflection and consideration.

The next phase of the project involved the project team progressing discussions with the thirteen national organisations that had participated in the national round table meeting and additional national organisations who identified as having an interest in the project. Multiple individual face-to-face and virtual consultations were held to advance the round table outcomes into a robust structural model that would bring interested organisations together to drive national IPE development.

The structure for the formation of a new national leadership organisation was a major discussion point and various models were posited as options for the development of such an organisation. This stage of the project highlighted the complexities that a national undertaking of this scale can generate. Interestingly, several organisations who wanted to participate in the national IPE leadership strategy were hampered by their own governance structures that disallowed participation in an external organisation operating outside their internal terms of reference. Nevertheless, following detailed negotiations, four national organisations representing hospital and health services, licensing and accreditation processes, health professions education and consumer engagement, agreed to the formal formation of a new group which was named the *Collaborating Organisations* (CO) group. An exchange of letters outlining their commitment to the group was the primary strategy that facilitated this process.

Whilst the four leadership organisations are the first to exchange letters of intent and engage in the formal leadership processes, the CO group is in a developmental phase and is open to other national organisations joining. The next steps for the CO group will be the formation of a larger advisory group representing a much wider group of stakeholders across the health, health education, policy, safety, disability and community sectors. Further work remains to be done on the processes for establishing an advisory group and this will continue to be honed over time. There is significant interest in the group and the CO group will engage with individual leaders and organisational champions in this formation process.

National IPE Workplan

The National Interprofessional Education Workplan has been developed by the SIF team as a resource for the CO group and the Advisory Group. It provides them with a foundational operational plan for a coordinated approach to the development of critical work. The broad foci of the national workplan are identified in Table 8.1. It is designed to facilitate a series of national activities that can be instigated by the CO group and the Advisory Group to tackle the existing barriers to an integrated national roll out of IPE for collaborative practice. Some of these activities have been commenced by the SIF team including the development of the national IPE knowledge repository and the completion of a literature review on IPE governance models. These resources will inform and equip the CO and Advisory groups as they move forward with the national work plan.

The Australian and New Zealand IPE for Collaborative Practice Knowledge Repository

Based on feedback from national organisations regarding the need for local support, evidence and resources to support the development of IPE for collaborative practice, a subgroup of the SIF team undertook to develop a sustainable Australasian interprofessional education (IPE) knowledge repository and dissemination hub. The project commenced with a comprehensive scoping review of international interprofessional websites, resource repositories and databases to understand the challenges of developing such a tool and explore the conditions to ensure success and best practice (Fig. 8.2).

As a result of the scoping exercise and collaborative arrangements, an alliance with the National Centre for Interprofessional Practice and Education (NEXUS) was established to create an Australasian special collection knowledge repository that would not only address the needs identified but would also allow users to access international resources from a well-established website. The working group also developed the specification for a website and resourced the Australian and New Zealand Association for Health Professional Educators to enhance their existing website in relation to IPE and IPCP content and sustain this facility for a five year period.

Table 8.1 National Interprofessional Education Work Plan—areas of focus (Dunston et al., 2018)

Benefit areas	Broad focus	Activities to	Deliverables	Approach
Safety	Governance	Establish enduring national and local IPE governance	Specified in National IPE Workplan	
	Standards	Develop and implement practice and education standards	Specified National IPE Workplan	All developed through collective consensus activities of the advisory group and collaborating organisations and established working groups/projects
Effectiveness	Accreditation	Develop and implement accreditation standards and processes	Specified National IPE Workplan	
Patient responsiveness	Faculty capability and capacity	Increase IPE capability and capacity at the institutional and faculty levels	Specified National IPE Workplan	

(continued)

Table 8.1 (continued)

Benefit areas	Broad focus	Activities to	Deliverables	Approach
Efficiency	Knowledge management and dissemination	Establish and promote the content and utilisation of the Australasian IPE knowledge repository	Specified National IPE Workplan	
	Knowledge development	Invite, encourage and enable regionally relevant knowledge development	Specified National IPE Workplan	
	Domains of practice and models of care	Develop exemplar models and related education activities	To be considered	

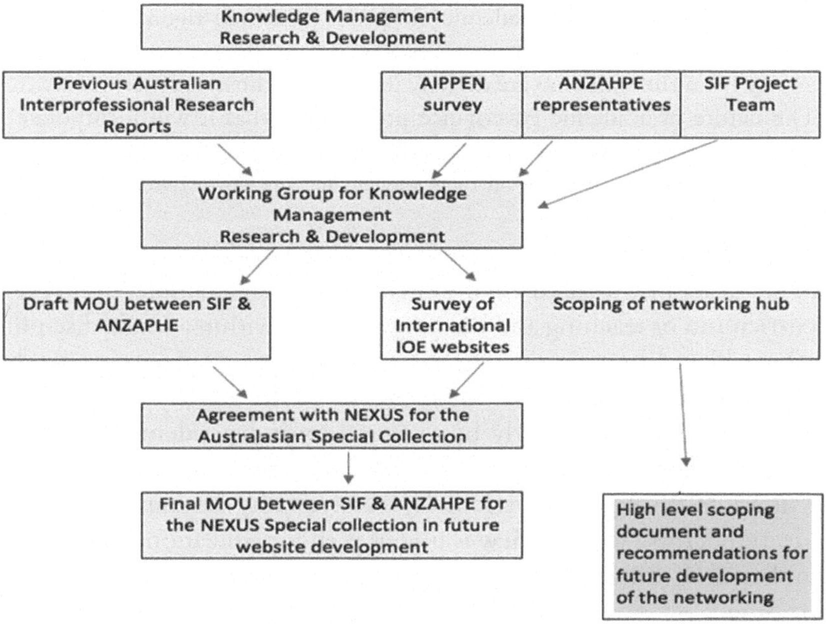

Fig. 8.2 Flow diagram of five stages of work done for the knowledge repository and collections

Models of IPE Academic Governance

The SIF team also aimed to provide a resource for faculty development. Whilst numerous curriculum resources exist, what was less accessible was a framework for monitoring the quality of IPE standards across courses, faculties and institutions. A key element of successful educational initiatives is a robust academic governance framework. Put plainly, academic governance describes the processes by which decisions are made and enacted. More specifically, it refers to the

> policies, structures, relationships, systems and processes that collectively provide leadership to and oversight of a higher education provider's academic activities … at an institutional level. (TEQSA, 2017, p. 1)

Further observation is made that

> traditional functions of academic governance include rigorous scrutiny and peer review of academic activities, carried out independently and separately from the staff who are directly involved in those activities. .... The nature of academic governance presupposes that it will incorporate academic expertise and experience sufficient to provide leadership, judgement and scrutiny at the level of academic activity concerned.

Existing models of academic governance have largely grown up within a strongly discipline focused environment where, for example, peer review of curriculum or teaching and learning activities within a single discipline can be achieved by accessing the expertise and experience of a member of the same discipline who is independent of the activity. Proposals for new curriculum can similarly be reviewed by independent expert peers who understand and appreciate any particular discipline nuances. Moving upwards through the various layers of quality assurance within an institution, cross faculty review is undertaken for educational quality and compliance with institutional policies and procedures. Although relying increasingly on peer review by academics with a broad perspective of different disciplines, it can be argued that these quality assurance and review processes still rely on a disciplinary lens. Once the focus shifts to more interdisciplinary offerings, the standard higher education academic governance models start to fall short. Crossing disciplinary boundaries still poses a significant challenge to traditional models of academic governance (Hannon, Hocking, Legge, & Lugg, 2018).

Echoing the increasing challenges that higher education institutions are facing as they grapple with the complexities of interdisciplinary academic governance, the project team found much the same situation in relation to effective academic governance models for IPE. Although there is a plethora of literature around curriculum models and pedagogical approaches for IPE, there is very little available by way of descriptions of effective models of academic governance to support high quality IPE. Whether this be in relation to increasing academic teaching staff capacity and capability to the delivery of high quality IPE curriculum, or to ensure achievement of specific IPE competencies, it was very difficult to locate a substantial body of work to guide institutions. As with many previous reports, the Curriculum Renewal Studies Programme noted that the lack of apparent guidance in this area constrains development of IPE at any level other than the micro level (Dunston et al., 2016).

Given the importance of effective governance to further the cause of realising successful and sustainable implementation of IPE, we undertook a systematic review of the literature published over a 10 year period ending in 2018. This yielded 13 articles that addressed academic governance at least in part. Rather than a consideration of formal academic governance models or structures, the most common approach to addressing academic governance was to describe organisational structures for implementation and administration. Any real contemplation of academic standards was notably absent.

Within the small subset of 13 articles, the most common model for IPE administration was one that was centralised within the senior academic administration of the higher education institution. Responsibility for design, implementation and evaluation sat within a central entity that was distinct to and separate from any of the participating disciplines. Although most reports were descriptive, success was most often linked to the extent to which stakeholder disciplines were represented on key decision-making bodies. Two other models that received more limited attention were the decentralised models (usually faculty based and led by champions), and the stand-alone centres which are essentially similar to the centralised models but that are physically discrete. As noted above, these reports are limited and considerable further work is required to identify optimal academic governance models to support effective and sustainable IPE.

As a final comment, there has been a strong focus on the structural elements associated with implementing and administering IPE in the literature that appears to continue given the substantial logistical challenges associated with implementing IPE (Pecukonis, Doyle, & Buss, 2008; McKimm et al., 2010). However, to move forward we encourage future work that considers the wider aspects and requirements of effective governance such as the maintenance of academic standards, documenting achievement of requisite learning outcomes and competencies for all students who successfully complete an interprofessional course, considerations of appropriate academic professional development, capacity and capability to deliver quality learning experiences, and developing robust, reliable and valid assessment methods.

Impact of the Project—Alignment with Project Aims

The deliverables produced by the SIF Project are significant. While each one in and of itself is valuable, the overarching outcome is that for the first time in Australia a national infrastructure will act as a single point of reference and advice for Australian IPE. The establishment of the national advisory group is a major step in addressing the existing fragmented and patchy approach to IPE and will provide much needed leadership and central oversight of IPE standards across Australia. Furthermore, the model created by the SIF team is unique and, as far as is known, is unprecedented in any other global jurisdiction. The two-tiered governance model is structured such that an overarching collaboration which is comprised of national peak health professional bodies will be guided by a National Advisory Group that will bring together a wide variety of relevant organisations and individuals to formulate and advise government on IPE development priorities and policies. This model is intended to provide stability to IPE development and implementation, something that it has not enjoyed to date.

While medium to longer term sustainability of the two-tiered model is dependent on on-going support from the peak bodies, the SIF team are confident that the robust nature of national governance model will secure its future. For the first time the national body provides a central platform for organisations who have a shared interest in IPE priorities to come together and to combine efforts (and resources) to lobby government and other relevant stakeholders about the importance of IPE. The capacity to provide a coordinated approach to influence change is the model's strongest feature and will likely be its key to an enduring future.

In addition to the establishment of the two-tiered model, another significant outcome of the SIF Project has been a notable shift in IPE discourse at the level of national peak bodies. IPE has become a common term and focus point for these bodies as a result of the activities of the

SIF team. Whilst these bodies have largely operated in isolation from one another, IPE has brought them together to discuss a shared interest that has been an elusive and difficult construct to manage singlehandedly. For example, the national round table fora that was part of the SIF process was an exercise in interprofessional collaboration in itself. Of the 13 national peak bodies invited to participate in the fora, all organisations energetically participated and contributed as all were eager to unite around a common concern about the state of IPE policy. International colleagues have also taken a keen interest in the system-wide and cross-sectoral approach of the SIF project.

Factors Critical to the Success and Impeding the Success of the Project Approach

Enabling and Supporting Factors

In attempting to unpack why the SIF Project has been so successful, one obvious reason relates to 'timing' and the collective desire across the health and education sectors to identify solutions for the sustainable implementation of IPE. This collective need was undoubtedly at the heart of the positive response the SIF team received by all organisations and stakeholders who were contacted about the Project. The clear message here is that most, if not all, stakeholders recognise the importance of establishing a central and coordinated approach to IPE. This was a strong outcome of the earlier Curriculum Renewal Studies (CRS) project where stakeholders called for a resounding 'stop' to the inefficient and ineffective localised approach to IPE development and implementation, and instead advocated for a centralised national approach.

A paradigm change was evident at the time of the CRS project and continues to grow in momentum with the work of the SIF Project. Given that many of the researchers who were involved in the CRS project were also involved in SIF, there was a strong recognition that the SIF Project remit had been founded on solid ground as was the next level in turning IPE from an important but peripheral and local activity to an activity that would and should be central to the development of effective health professional education and health professional practice.

Global developments by peak groups have also contributed to this paradigm shift. For example, work carried out by The Centre for the Advancement of Interprofessional Education and the World Health Organization have been instrumental in advocating for IPE and IPCP. These collective global efforts to raise the profile of IPE and IPCP are fundamental to its sustainability. They do not however, suggest that operationalising IPE as a central part of day-to-day education and practice has suddenly become easy. That is not the case. What it does mean, however, is that the significant effort expended on arguing the case on behalf of IPE can now be redirected to more productive tasks.

A third factor that has enabled the success of the SIF Project is its methodology. Given the complex social and cultural context within which IPE plays out, adopting a sociocultural methodology was key. This methodology facilitated the researchers' need to work across multiple interprofessional disciplines and sectors and to negotiate a common language that could traverse traditionally rigid boundaries. As mentioned before, the development of a national infrastructure is a good example of interprofessional collaboration in itself. The sociocultural methodology was sensitive to all parties' nuances, all the while uniting them under a shared goal.

Constraining Factors

It is well recognised that the design and implementation of IPE for IPCP is constrained by a wide variety of factors across multiple organisational levels. Similarly, complete achievement of the goals of the SIF Project faced a range of constraints including its scope and complexity, as well as elements of its sociopolitical context, the relatively short time frame in which it was to be completed, and the challenges of managing the engagement and decision-making processes of multiple diverse stakeholder organisations.

It was clear from the beginning that the project was highly ambitious, seeking as it did to implement a new and enduring national system of governance and leadership in a complex environment involving multiple stakeholders and interests.

Scope

Defining the precise scope of the project was perhaps the greatest challenge. The earlier 'Curriculum Renewal for Interprofessional Education in Health' project had suggested a broad design for an enduring governance and leadership system (2014) but it was particularly difficult to determine how much of this plan would be feasible to implement in the available time, and which elements should be prioritised. These decisions were also highly contingent on the responsiveness of, and positions taken by, the diverse stakeholder organisations, and this further impeded the a priori definition of scope. Often, particular areas of activity were pursued for a period, with the investment of significant time and resources, only to encounter an unanticipated and insurmountable roadblock before the work could be completed.

Ultimately, the scope of the project was defined, retrospectively, by what proved to be *possible* to achieve after concerted 'diplomatic' efforts in multiple directions. This led, though not especially by design, to a focus on the national leadership elements of the framework and closest engagement with a relatively small number of receptive national peak bodies.

Complexity/Context

The prior completion of the Curriculum Renewal for Interprofessional Education in Health project over nearly 10 years had prepared the team to anticipate the complexity that inheres in the systems of health professional education, practice and regulation. The socio-cultural and relational approach adopted was also fit for purpose and allowed the team to gain perspective and build on the positive orientation brought to the project by many stakeholders.

One result of this complexity was, however, that each area of activity focus required protracted discussion with stakeholders, brokering of possible resolutions to conflicting priorities and enormous amounts of time while organisations completed their own decision making processes. Further, the closer the project moved toward finalising stakeholder commitments, the more time these processes took.

Management

In addition to the external constraints imposed by the scope and complexity of the project's context, overall management by the project team was also intricate and challenging. The decisions with which we were faced about which possible pathways of action to prioritise and pursue were highly contingent and difficult to adjudicate. At multiple points along the implementation trajectory for the project, the project team itself felt a sense of impasse, where the 'right' choices to make in terms of commitment of its resources were extremely difficult to discern. Accordingly, the management of the project involved a great deal of extended debate and in the end we tried to make the best decisions we could without any certainty about how each would contribute to fulfilment of our goals.

International Transferability

Although it had a clear focus on Australia, the project endeavoured to draw from international experience and facilitate the transferability of its outcomes to other jurisdictions. It set up an esteemed reference group of international experts who monitored its progress carefully and provided invaluable advice about how the project's achievements might inform future work in their own settings. Some members of this group are closely connected with the World Health Organization, which has espoused the implementation of IPE for IPCP for more than a decade. In their judgement, the project was seen as unique and ground-breaking at a global level. Accordingly, the SIF Project's outcomes are likely to have transferability, with appropriate modifications, around the world. Of particular note is the project's interaction with IPE leaders in New Zealand. Whilst the project was funded with an Australian focus, close collaboration has occurred with our near neighbours throughout its implementation.

Another endeavour in the global sphere that had deep links with the project was the process to formulate an International Consensus Statement on the Assessment of Interprofessional Learning Outcomes (Rogers et al., 2017). In this activity, 75 scholars from 15 countries were consulted and its leadership included two members of the project management team. The resultant consensus statement (which has 36 citations so far on Google Scholar) has already impacted significantly on the assessment of interprofessional learning outcomes in multiple countries and will provide a starting point for the ongoing scholarly practice in this area that will be undertaken as a result of the enduring governance and leadership systems that the project has brought into existence.

Closing Remarks

This project has been ambitious in its scope and aims. The development of such a strategic governance framework has not been achieved elsewhere in the world and there are many lessons which have been learnt from this work which will be useful to other countries. The methodology we have used has ensured an open, dynamic and inclusive implementation process. We believe that through the collaborating organisation group, the advisory group and the work plan we have firm foundations for the sustainability of IPE and IPCP in Australia. In addition the work we have done in identifying the challenges and gaps around available governance structures for IPE and IPCP provides a reference point for organisations and jurisdictions beyond Australia in building their own governance structures.

We are optimistic that sustainability is enhanced by robust outcomes of the project including resources such as the knowledge repository for our Australian developments in collaboration with NEXUS. Our major concern is the absence of explicit ongoing commitment of public resources and we continue to advocate in our various roles for this commitment to be realised.

Acknowledgements Australian Office of Learning and Teaching, Department of Education and Training, International Review Panel.

References

Dunston, R., Canny, B., Fisher, A., Steketee, C., Forman, D., Rogers, G. D., … Yassine, T. (2018). *Securing an interprofessional future: Establishing an Australian interprofessional education governance and development framework—A compelling case.* Information brochure. Canberra: Australian Government Department of Education and Training.

Dunston, R., Forman, D., Moran, M., Rogers, G. D., Thistlethwaite, J., & Steketee, C. (2016). *Curriculum renewal in interprofessional education in health: Establishing leadership and capacity.* Canberra: Commonwealth of Australia, Office for Learning and Teaching.

Dunston, R., Lee, A., Matthews, L., Nisbet, G., Pockett, R., Thistlethwaite, J., & White, J. (2009). *Interprofessional health education in Australia: The way forward.* Sydney: University of Technology Sydney.

Hannon, J., Hocking, C., Legge, K., & Lugg, A. (2018). Sustaining interdisciplinary education: Developing boundary crossing governance. *Higher Education Research & Development, 37*(7), 1424–1438.

Interprofessional Curriculum Renewal Consortium, Australia. (2014). *Curriculum renewal for interprofessional education in health.* Canberra: Commonwealth of Australia, Office for Learning and Teaching.

McKimm, J., Sheehan, D., Poole, P., Barrow, M., Dockerty, J., Wilkinson, T. J., & Wearn, A. (2010). Interprofessional learning in medical education in New Zealand. *The New Zealand Medical Journal, 123,* 1320 (Online).

Nesbit, G., Lee, A., Kumar, K., Thistlethwaite, J., & Dunston, R. (2011). *Interprofessional health education: A literature review.* Canberra: Australia Learning and Teaching Council.

Nicol, P. (2011). *Interprofessional education for health professionals in Western Australia: perspectives and activity.* Sydney: University of Technology Sydney.

O'Keefe, M. (2015). *Collaborating across boundaries: A framework for an integrated interprofessional curriculum.* Australian Government Office for Learning and Teaching. https://www.researchgate.net/profile/Maree_OKeefe/research.

O'Keefe, M., Henderson, A., & Chick, R. (2015). *Developing sustainable and embedded interprofessional education: Threshold learning outcomes as a potential pathway.* Australian Government Office for Learning and Teaching. https://www.researchgate.net/profile/Maree_OKeefe/research.

O'Keefe, M., Henderson, A., & Chick, R. (2017). Defining a set of common interprofessional learning competencies for health profession students. *Medical Teacher, 39*(5), 1–6. https://doi.org/10.1080/0142159x.2017.1300246.

Pecukonis, E., Doyle, O., & Buss, D. L. (2008). Reducing barriers to interprofessional training: Promoting interprofessional cultural competence. *Journal of Interprofessional Care, 22,* 417–428.

Rogers, G. D., Thistlethwaite, J. E., Anderson, E. S., Abrandt Dahlgren, M., Grymonpre, R., Moran, M., & Samarasekera, D. D. (2017). International consensus statement on the assessment of interprofessional learning outcomes. *Medical Teacher, 39,* 347–359. https://doi.org/10.1080/0142159X.2017.1270441.

Swerissen, H., Duckett, S., & Moran, G. (2018). *Mapping primary care in Australia.* Melbourne: Grattan Institute.

TEQSA. (2017, October). *TEQSA guidance note: Academic Governance Version 2.3* (p. 1). https://www.teqsa.gov.au/latest-news/publications/guidance-note-academic-governance.

The iTOFT Consortium, Australia. (2015). *Work based assessment of teamwork: An interprofessional approach.* Canberra: Australian Government, Office for Learning and Teaching.

9

Indigenous Health

Denise Wilson

Me ka moemoea au, ko au anake
Me ka moemoea e tatau, ka taia e tatau
If I dream, only I achieve
If we dream together, we all achieve. (Te Puea Herangi)

The whakatauakī or proverb above speaks to the need for collaboration in order to achieve our goals and highlights the futility of functioning as individuals—it speaks to an Indigenous approach to functioning driven by not only collective aspirations but achieving these by working together. For Indigenous peoples globally, there is a need for health professionals to work collaboratively to achieve Indigenous aspirations for health and wellbeing. The colonisation of Indigenous peoples has resulted in persistent and marked health and social inequities compared to other groups living in their respective countries (Mbuzi, Fulbrook, &

D. Wilson (✉)
Auckland University of Technology, Auckland, New Zealand
e-mail: dlwilson@aut.ac.nz

D. Forman et al. (eds.), *Sustainability and Interprofessional Collaboration*,
https://doi.org/10.1007/978-3-030-40281-5_9

Jessup, 2017; Wilson, Heaslip, & Jackson, 2018). Recognition of Indigenous historical and contemporary realities, coupled with the effects of ongoing colonisation, historical trauma, and socioeconomic marginalisation helps understand the complexities that impact their health and social wellbeing. A myriad of long-term effects has arisen from colonisation, which includes economic disenfranchisement, historical trauma, inadequate access to social determinants of health, and experiences of social marginalisation, systemic discrimination, and encounters of racism—all negatively affecting health (Cormack, Stanley, & Harris, 2018; Paradies, 2016; Walters et al., 2011; Whitbeck, Adams, Hoyt, & Chen, 2004). As a consequence, Indigenous peoples face persistent access, quality and safety issues when engaging with health services.

This chapter will explore the necessity for culturally responsive collaborative practice for working with Indigenous peoples and their families. For such an approach to be sustainable, this requires enabling the leadership from within Indigenous patients and their families or whānau (extended family network beyond nuclear family constructions)—essential for their active involvement in the patient's health care and subsequent decision-making. Sustainable Indigenous patient and family involvement requires health professionals to recognise them as legitimate team members, to form relationships and build trust through authenticity and consistency, all of which are essential for active collaboration between professionals, patients, and their families and quality health care (van Dijk-de Vries, van Dongen, & van Bokhoven, 2017). Interprofessional collaborative practice with Indigenous peoples holds patients and their families or whānau central to all activities, recognising the need for them as key participants in their health care experiences and decision-making.

Drawing on Māori (the Indigenous peoples of Aotearoa New Zealand) mātauranga (knowledge), the waka (canoe) will be used as an analogy to illustrate collaborative practice within this context and how patients and their families or whānau have a leadership role in their health care. Moreover, given the historical and contemporary contexts of Indigenous peoples' realities, the notion of resilience for sustainable interprofessional collaboration to establish relationships when working with Indigenous peoples will be discussed briefly.

Indigenous Peoples

The United Nations (2013) explains that Indigenous peoples:

> populated areas before the arrival of others and often retain distinct cultural and political characteristics, including autonomous political and legal structures, as well as a common experience of domination by others, especially non-indigenous groups, and a strong historical and ongoing connection to their lands, territories and resources, including when they practise nomadic lifestyles. (p. 3)

Indigenous peoples subjected to colonisation have diverse but similar experiences in that their experiences differed not only between but also within countries. They share contemporary experiences of being displaced from their land (a rightful place to stand in the world), loss of language and cultural ways of knowing and being that negatively impacted their health and social wellbeing (Atkinson, 2002; Battiste, 2000; Smith, 2012). Displacement from land and loss of language and culture left many Indigenous peoples culturally, socially, economically, and educationally marginalised, and more likely to have differential access to the essential determinants of health and health services and experience differences in the quality of care than other groups of people living in their respective countries. Differential access and quality of care is evident in the increased risk and burden of long-term non-communicable diseases and premature mortality for many Indigenous peoples (Axelsson, Kukutai, & Kippen, 2016; Jones, 2000; Mbuzi et al., 2017).

There is a tendency to explain Indigenous disparities in health status and health outcomes as some form of deficit an individual possesses, yet the majority of Indigenous peoples struggle with systemic barriers to accessing timely safe and quality health care (Browne et al., 2016; Jones, 2000; Wilson et al., 2018). Access to timely and quality health care is made difficult by having to navigate complex health services and a myriad of health professionals who act independently with often conflicting messages. These barriers are endemic, systemic and structural, and are referred to as institutional or systemic racism (Browne et al., 2016;

Came, 2014) because Indigenous peoples have different health care experiences, levels of disease burden and health outcomes compared to other people. When people and their family or whānau are seeking health care, they need respectful engagement, and people willing to listen and work with them (D. Wilson, 2008; Wilson & Barton, 2012). Instead, Indigenous peoples commonly encounter health professionals with judgmental attitudes and who engage in racist or discriminatory practices when providing health care services (Cormack et al., 2018; Goodman et al., 2017; Harris et al., 2012). Consequently, it is not uncommon for Indigenous peoples to lack trust in health care services and health professionals. Persistent adverse health care experiences and health outcomes are unfair and avoidable, indicating equity issues (Braveman, 2010; Whitehead, 1992).

Invariably, health professionals aim to improve the health and wellbeing of the people they work with and do not set out to treat people differently. However, Indigenous peoples (and other minority or marginalised groups) frequently report being treated differently (Goodman et al., 2017; Huria, Cuddy, Lacey, & Pitama, 2014; Ziersch, Gallaher, Baum, & Bentley, 2011). Compounding inequitable treatment and interactions is the divergence in worldviews between Indigenous peoples, and health professionals who work predominantly within Western and biomedically driven health care services that lead to differences in beliefs and values around health and health care. Indigenous peoples' worldviews are holistic, relational, and spiritual, with their connection to the environment an essential factor for their wellbeing (Smith, 2012; S. Wilson, 2008). Importantly, Indigenous peoples function collectively rather than as individuals, with inherent responsibilities and obligations to others and their family or whānau as a whole. Practically, this means for many Indigenous patients that the inclusion of their family or whānau is essential in their health care experiences. Therefore, forming relationships is fundamental for any interactions with health professionals before getting down to the business of health care. Recognising and responding to Indigenous worldviews contributes to patients and their family or whānau understanding the relevance and meaningfulness of health information and health regimens, but also for culturally responsive collaborative practice to occur.

Culturally Responsive Collaborative Practice

Establishing culturally responsive collaborative practice involves creating different pathways that are person- and whānau-centred, drawing on the leadership that exists (particularly from whānau Māori). Creating different pathways involves developing environments as safe places with safe spaces that establish reliable and sustainable avenues for communication and relationships to enable change and ultimately improve health care. It requires shifting conversations from being deficit-based to ones focusing on Indigenous patients' and their families or whānau strengths and potential. Health professionals need to enable alternative approaches to health care delivery and innovation as part of culturally responsive collaborative practice.

Culturally responsive collaborative practice is essential for establishing trust and relevant and meaningful health care experiences to achieve outcomes for patients and their whānau. Fundamental to culturally responsive collaborative practice is culturally competent and capable health professionals who can demonstrate culturally appropriate and acceptable practice that Indigenous patients and their family or whānau deem as safe (Bearskin, 2011; Pitama et al., 2007; D. Wilson, 2008; Wilson & Hickey, 2015).

Importantly, health professionals should be able to work collaboratively in such a manner for the benefit of the patient and their family or whānau (Wepa, 2016). For Indigenous peoples and their families or whānau, this means feeling culturally safe—that is, respectfully recognising their cultural identity and including their needs in their health care experiences (Bearskin, 2011; Wilson & Hickey, 2015). Working *with* Indigenous peoples and their whānau in culturally responsive and collaborative ways requires an equity approach. An equity approach is grounded in social justice and rights and involves acknowledging alternative ways for engagement and the implementation of interventions needed to achieve the same outcomes as for other people (Braveman, 2010; Marmot, 2013). Such an approach requires understanding Indigenous peoples' unique historical and contemporary realities, which will be different for each person and their family or whānau.

Culturally responsive collaborative practice can be achieved using the acronym KAI (knowledge-action-integration), which is the Māori word for food. Within the context of collaborative practice, KAI is used to refer to the components of cultural responsiveness (Heke, Wilson, & Came, 2019; Wilson & Hickey, 2015). KNOWLEDGE relates to health professionals having insight and understanding into the following factors:

- Being aware of personal and professional cultural values, beliefs, practices, assumptions;
- Identifying biases and stereotypes held about Indigenous peoples;
- Critically reflecting on the influence biases and stereotypes have on professional practice;
- Critically analysing the diverse realities (historical, socio-economic and political influences on health and wellbeing) of Indigenous peoples; and
- Recognising key cultural values and practices of Indigenous peoples;
- Understanding individual leadership roles in developing a collaborative mindset necessary to practise collaboratively.

ACTION relates to the activities and behaviours related to working with Indigenous peoples and their families in ways that are respectful, genuine, non-judgmental, and avoid dominant cultural imposition. It is also about recognising and responding to the diverse cultural needs of each indigenous person and their family in respectful and authentic ways, while at the same time rectifying any potential conflicts in values, beliefs, and practices. Importantly, within the context of collaborative practice, actions relate to interacting and working with both Indigenous patients and their families or whānau and other health professionals to ensure identification and meeting of their needs. It is advantageous to include community health workers to assist Indigenous patients and their families to identify their needs and requirements and work with health professionals. Community health workers know their community, the people in the community who could support the patient and family or whānau and speak the language used in their community, rather than health professionals' language and jargon.

INTEGRATION is about incorporating into their plans of care Indigenous patients and their families' or whānau cultural needs. Integrating cultural needs involves working with them to identify first who needs to be involved in their health care experience, and then negotiating the various and potentially competing needs of the various health professionals and those of Indigenous peoples and their families or whānau for inclusion in plans of care. Consideration should be given to:

- observing critical cultural practices, identified by respectfully enquiring about what is essential for the patient and their family or whānau;
- recognising and including these cultural needs and what is essential for the patient and family or whānau into intervention or care plans; and
- influencing cultural forms of shame and embarrassment related to the reluctance of patients and their families or whānau to discuss some matters or undertake health care related activities.

Leadership for Culturally Responsive Collaborative Practice

The functioning of a waka (canoe) illustrates the essential components of collaboration and leadership, and when applied to the context of health care, patient and family or whānau positions them as leaders of their care standing mid-ship to direct proceedings. The waka is a perfect example of collaboration in action, as without everyone in the waka working together, it would not propel forward to achieve its mission. It exemplifies the imperative of every person needing to collaborate, determining early the goals and directions. Effective collaborative practice requires having the right people on board with their unique capabilities, knowledge, and skills ready to work together to achieve shared goals. In this way, everyone has leadership responsibilities to make things happen.

The waka (YouTube, 2014, May 5) is a useful analogy to illustrate how culturally responsive interprofessional collaboration could work. Great collaboration between everyone in the waka is needed for it to float and move through the water. Without this collaboration, the waka does not proceed forward, and in the worst situation can capsize. It metaphorically demonstrates the pivotal need for collaboration—without interprofessional collaboration Indigenous patients' health care metaphorically capsizes with poor outcomes. Getting into the waka requires precision, cooperation, and collaboration; without these three things, it will tip over, making it difficult for everyone to get in. Each person in the waka has a role in propelling and manoeuvring the waka to its destination. The leader stands in the middle of the waka coordinating the activity within the waka, continually communicating through various chants. To propel the waka forward and manoeuvre around any obstacles, most of those on the waka paddle together to gain and maintain its momentum—they must dip their hoe (paddles) in and out of the water in perfect time with each other. Someone has the role of baling out the unwanted water to prevent the waka from sinking. The helm (rear of the waka) is the place from where the steering of the waka occurs—the role of someone with an interprofessional collaborative mind-set, either a health professional or community health worker (Brewer, Flavell, Trede, & Smith, 2016; McHugh, Margolis, Rosenberg, & Humphreys, 2016).

Culturally responsive collaborative practice requires people who can work together to achieve a shared vision for each patient and their family or whānau. The configuration of people will depend upon the patient's and family's or whānau needs. The World Health Organization (2010) reinforces this notion of working collaboratively with patients and their whānau or family: 'Collaborative practice happens when multiple health workers from different professional backgrounds work together with patients, families, carers, and communities to deliver the highest quality of care' (p. 7). Mickan, Hoffman, and Nasmith (2010) contend that collaborative practice is essential for safe, timely, and quality services. They cite several benefits for patients such as higher levels of satisfaction, greater acceptance of care, fewer visits to clinics, and improved health outcomes—all factors that health professionals, whoever they are, aim to achieve. In addition to these patient-whānau-centred benefits, culturally responsive collaborative practice reduces the incidence of adverse events and costs, improves continuity and coordination of care, and importantly improves collaborative decision-making with patients. It does so because health care services become relevant and meaningful for Indigenous peoples and their families or whanau (Boulton, Tamehana, & Brannelly, 2013; Wilson & Barton, 2012).

The functioning of the waka illustrates the nature and components of collaboration with patients and their families or whānau positioned in the mid-ship. It is an example of collaboration in action because, without the leadership and direction of patients and their families or whānau, the waka would not achieve its goal. It also illustrates how every person on the waka contributes and collaborates. If we consider that health professionals are at the "helm" of the waka steering health, it is important for Indigenous patients and their families and whānau that we have all the necessary people to achieve the desired outcomes in health and quality of care. High levels of collaboration and teamwork are more productive and are associated with sustainable quality care (McHugh et al., 2016).

Resilience

Indigenous peoples and their families or whānau have long experienced barriers to access culturally responsive health care related to accessibility, affordability, availability, and appropriateness. Furthermore, they frequently face barriers to effective interprofessional collaboration, instead experiencing fragmentation of their health care, not helped by the nature of the discipline-specific pedagogies that channel health professionals into silos. Many Indigenous peoples and their families and whānau lack trust in health care services and health professionals (Bearskin, 2011; Mbuzi et al., 2017; Wilson & Barton, 2012). The sustainability of culturally responsive collaborative practice, therefore, requires health professionals to possess the resilience necessary to secure the trust of Indigenous patients and their families or whānau so that health professionals will work with them productively—something that will take time and perseverance.

Health professionals are tested often when undertaking their roles by stress associated with inadequate staffing, unpredictable work environments, changing team membership, perceived lack of time and resource deficits, and patient contact (Nissim, Malfitano, Coleman, Rodin, &

Elliott, 2019). Expectations related to collaborative practice, being culturally responsive, and involving patients and whānau can also add to such stressors. Avrech Bar, Katz Leurer, Warshawski, and Itzhaki (2018) found a positive correlation between cooperation with other health professionals and resilience, which enables better adaptation to changing environments and overcoming obstacles. Interactions with patients require health professionals to be present, compassionate and resilient, all necessary attributes to establish trust and respect in relationships with Indigenous peoples and their family or whānau and for the provision of complex holistic care (Nissim et al., 2019). Nissim et al. (2019) found that engaging in a range of activities and practices such as self-compassion and taking time to reflect improves interactions with colleagues and improves quality of care delivered. These are all factors in building empathy and compassion, necessary for resilience in interprofessional collaboration.

Given that health professionals have undergone some form of traditional education that channelled them into professional silos, collaborative practice requires them to be re-educated and re-think *how* to engage with the patient and their family or whānau and other health professionals (McHugh et al., 2016). It involves health professionals using their leadership skills to remove the silos to enable unfettered collaboration that involves sharing, communicating, listening and working together—characteristics essential for real-world functioning (Schuetz, Mann, & Everett, 2010). Gilbert (2006) defined interprofessional collaborative practice as 'A process through which parties who see different aspects of a problem can constructively explore their differences and search for solutions that go well beyond their professional vision of what is possible' (p. 4). Indigenous patients and their families and whānau bring to their health care experiences expertise about their realities and their understanding of health and wellbeing. This expertise is essential to inform effective planning, decision-making, and interventions to evoke positive outcomes—they know what they can afford, what will work given their life contexts, and what is doable in their seemingly complex lives (Mbuzi et al., 2017; Wilson et al., 2018). Collaborative practice also includes learning to work, sometimes innovatively, with people in their worlds and realities.

Returning to the waka (canoe) analogy—if we take the helm to steer health guided by the leadership of Indigenous peoples and their families or whānau, culturally responsive collaborative practice should be informed by the following principles:

- Being committed—You are in or out of the waka
- Working together in a unified relationship with others in the group
- Sharing similar understandings
- Working toward a common goal
- Recognising it is a journey and that quitting is not an option because it gets too hard.

Just like steering a waka (canoe), sustainable collaborative practice requires sound communications skills, teamwork, respect, and importantly listening to Indigenous patients and their family or whānau and other health professionals (Nisbet et al., 2018). Sustainability also requires resilient health professionals who can work with Indigenous peoples and their family or whānau, and this requires commitment, practice, and learning how to work with other health professionals (Avrech Bar et al., 2018; Nissim et al., 2019). Effective collaboration and teamwork improves health outcomes and quality of care (Nisbet et al., 2018; van Dijk-de Vries et al., 2017). van Dijk-de et al. (2017) indicate that leaders within the interprofessional team need to be able to negotiate and navigate the array of socioeconomic and political issues necessary for collaborative relationships. Being able to function in this way may require systemic changes to support working in a culturally responsive and collaborative way with Indigenous patients and their family or whānau at the centre.

Conclusion

Nā tō rourou, nā taku rourou ka ora ai te iwi.
With your food basket and my food basket, the people will thrive.

This whakataukī or proverb above highlights the importance of working together for people to be well and thrive. Culturally responsive collaborative practice is about dreaming together with Indigenous patients and their family or whānau. It is about holding Indigenous patients and their family or whānau central at all times during their health care experience, and being guided by their leadership. Nevertheless, sustainable culturally responsive collaborative practice requires resilient health professionals who are willing to be present and compassionate and learn from others within the patient's 'team'. It is also about critically understanding the historical and contemporary contexts within which Indigenous peoples live, and involving them as key players in their health care experience.

References

Atkinson, J. (2002). *Trauma trails recreating song lines: The transgenerational effects of trauma in indigenous Australia.* North Melbourne, VIC: Spinifex Press.

Avrech Bar, M., Katz Leurer, M., Warshawski, S., & Itzhaki, M. (2018). The role of personal resilience and personality traits of healthcare students on their attitudes towards interprofessional collaboration. *Nurse Education Today, 61,* 36–42. https://doi.org/10.1016/j.nedt.2017.11.005.

Axelsson, P., Kukutai, T., & Kippen, R. (2016). The field of Indigenous health and the role of colonisation and history. *Journal of Population Research, 33*(1), 1–7. https://doi.org/10.1007/s12546-016-9163-2.

Battiste, M. (Ed.). (2000). *Reclaiming Indigenous voice and vision.* Vancouver: UBC Press.

Bearskin, R. L. B. (2011). A critical lens on culture in nursing practice. *Nursing Ethics, 18*(4), 548–559. https://doi.org/10.1177/0969733011408048.

Boulton, A., Tamehana, J., & Brannelly, P. M. (2013). Whānau-centred health and social service delivery in NZ: The challenges to, and opportunities for, innovation. *MAI Journal, 2*(1), 18–32.

Braveman, P. (2010). Social conditions, health equity, and human rights. *Health & Human Rights, 12*(2), 31–48.

Brewer, M. L., Flavell, H. L., Trede, F., & Smith, M. (2016). A scoping review to understand 'leadership' in interprofessional education and practice. *Journal of Interprofessional Care, 30*(4), 408–415. https://doi.org/10.3109/13561820.2016.1150260.

Browne, A. J., Varcoe, C., Lavoie, J., Smye, V., Wong, S. T., Krause, M., ... Fridkin, A. (2016). Enhancing health care equity with Indigenous populations: Evidence-based strategies from an ethnographic study. *BMC Health Services Research, 16,* 544. https://doi.org/10.1186/s12913-016-1707-9.

Came, H. (2014). Sites of institutional racism in public health policy making in New Zealand. *Social Science and Medicine, 106,* 214–220. https://doi.org/10.1016/j.socscimed.2014.01.055.

Cormack, D., Stanley, J., & Harris, R. (2018). Multiple forms of discrimination and relationships with health and wellbeing: findings from national cross-sectional surveys in Aotearoa/New Zealand. *International Journal for Equity in Health, 17,* 26. https://doi.org/10.1186/s12939-018-0735-y.

Gilbert, J. (2006). *The theory-practice relationship in IPE.* Retrieved from https://nexusipe-resource-exchange.s3-us-west-2.amazonaws.com/Gilbert_TheoryPracticeRelationship_HigherEdAcad2005.pdf.

Goodman, A., Fleming, K., Markwick, N., Morrison, T., Lagimodiere, L., & Kerr, T. (2017). They treated me like crap and I know it was because I was Native: The healthcare experiences of Aboriginal peoples living in Vancouver's inner city. *Social Science & Medicine, 178,* 87–94. https://doi.org/10.1016/j.socscimed.2017.01.053.

Harris, R., Cormack, D., Tobias, M., Yeh, L.-C., Talamaivao, N., Minster, J., & Timutimu, R. (2012). The pervasive effects of racism: Experiences of racial discrimination in New Zealand over time and associations with multiple health domains. *Social Science & Medicine, 74*(3), 408–415. https://doi.org/10.1016/j.socscimed.2011.11.004.

Heke, D., Wilson, D., & Came, H. (2019). Shades of competence? A critical analysis of the cultural competencies of the regulated-health workforce in Aotearoa New Zealand. *International Journal for Quality in Health Care, 31*(8), 606–612. https://doi.org/10.1093/intqhc/mzy227.

Huria, T., Cuddy, J., Lacey, C., & Pitama, S. (2014). Working with racism: A qualitative study of the perspectives of Māori (Indigenous peoples of Aotearoa New Zealand) registered nurses on a global phenomenon. *Journal of Transcultural Nursing, 25*(4), 364–372. https://doi.org/10.1177/1043659614523991.

Jones, C. P. (2000). Levels of racism: A theoretic framework and a gardener's tale. *American Journal of Public Health, 90,* 1212–1215. https://doi.org/10.2105/AJPH.90.8.1212.

Marmot, M. (2013). *Health gap: The challenge of an unequal world.* London, UK: Bloomsbury.

Mbuzi, V., Fulbrook, P., & Jessup, M. (2017). Indigenous peoples' experiences and perceptions of hospitalisation for acute care: A metasynthesis of qualitative studies. *International Journal of Nursing Studies, 71,* 39–49. https://doi.org/10.1016/j.ijnurstu.2017.03.003.

McHugh, M., Margolis, L., Rosenberg, A., & Humphreys, E. (2016). Advancing MCH interdisciplinary/interprofessional leadership training and practice through a learning collaborative. *Maternal and Child Health Journal, 20*(11), 2247–2253. https://doi.org/10.1007/s10995-016-2129-3.

Mickan, S., Hoffman, S. J., & Nasmith, L. (2010). Collaborative practice in a global health context: Common themes from developed and developing countries. *Journal of Interprofessional Care, 24*(5), 492–502. https://doi.org/10.3109/13561821003676325.

Nisbet, G., Raymond, J., Batstone, A., Barclay, T., Barraclough, F., Haq, I., … Stuart-Smith, W. (2018). Building interprofessional learning sustainability: Development and evaluation of an interprofessional learning placement resource. *Health Education in Practice: Journal of Research for Professional Learning, 1*(2), 15–38.

Nissim, R., Malfitano, C., Coleman, M., Rodin, G., & Elliott, M. (2019). A qualitative study of a compassion, presence, and resilience training for oncology interprofessional teams. *Journal of Holistic Nursing, 37*(1), 30–44. https://doi.org/10.1177/0898010118765016.

Paradies, Y. (2016). Colonisation, racism and indigenous health. *Journal of Population Research, 33*(1), 83–96. https://doi.org/10.1007/s12546-016-9159-y.

Pitama, S., Robertson, P., Cram, F., Gillies, M., Huria, T., & Dallas-Katoa, W. (2007). Meihana model: A clinical assessment framework. *New Zealand Journal of Psychology, 36*(3), 118–125.

Schuetz, B., Mann, E., & Everett, W. (2010). Educating health professionals collaboratively for team-based primary care. *Health Affairs, 29*(8), 1476–1480. https://doi.org/10.1377/hlthaff.2010.0052.

Smith, L. T. (2012). *Decolonizing methodologies: Research and indigenous peoples* (2nd ed.). London: Zed Books.

United Nations. (2013). *Indigenous peoples and the United Nations human rights system: Fact sheet No. 9/Rev.2.* New York and Geneva: Author. Retrieved from http://www.ohchr.org/Documents/Publications/fs9Rev.2.pdf.

van Dijk-de Vries, A., van Dongen, J. J. J., & van Bokhoven, M. A. (2017). Sustainable interprofessional teamwork needs a team-friendly healthcare system: Experiences from a collaborative Dutch programme. *Journal of Interprofessional Care, 31*(2), 167–169. https://doi.org/10.1080/13561820.2016.1237481.

Walters, K. L., Mohammed, S. A., Evans-Campbell, T., Beltrán, R. E., Chae, D. H., & Duran, B. (2011). Bodies don't just tell stories, they tell histories: Embodiment of historical trauma among American Indians and Alaska Natives. *Du Bois Review: Social Science Research on Race, 8*(1), 179–189. https://doi.org/10.1017/S1742058X1100018X.

Wepa, D. (2016). *Struggling to be involved: A grounded theory of Māori whānau engagement with healthcare* (Unpublished doctoral thesis). Auckland University of Technology, Auckland, New Zealand.

Whitbeck, L. B., Adams, G. W., Hoyt, D. R., & Chen, X. (2004). Conceptualizing and measuring historical trauma among American Indian people. *American Journal of Community Psychology, 33*(3–4), 119–130. https://doi.org/10.1023/B:AJCP.0000027000.77357.31.

Whitehead, M. (1992). The concepts and principles of equity and health. *International Journal of Health Services, 22*(3), 429–445.

Wilson, D. (2008). The significance of a culturally appropriate health service for Indigenous Maori women. *Contemp Nurse, 28*(1–2), 173–188. https://doi.org/10.5172/conu.673.28.1-2.173.

Wilson, D., & Barton, P. (2012). Indigenous hospital experiences: A New Zealand case study. *Journal of Clinical Nursing, 21*(15–16), 2316–2326. https://doi.org/10.1111/j.1365-2702.2011.04042.x.

Wilson, D., Heaslip, V., & Jackson, D. (2018). Improving equity and cultural responsiveness with marginalised communities: Understanding competing worldviews. *Journal of Clinical Nursing, 27*(19–20), 3810–3819. https://doi.org/10.1111/jocn.14546.

Wilson, D., & Hickey, H. (2015). Māori health: Māori- and whānau-centred practice. In D. Wepa (Ed.), *Cultural safety in Aotearoa New Zealand* (pp. 235–251). Melbourne, Australia: Cambridge University Press.

Wilson, S. (2008). *Research is ceremony: Indigenous research methods.* Nova Scotia, Canada: Fernwood.

World Health Organization. (2010). *Framework for action on interprofessional education and collaborative practice.* Geneva: WHO.

YouTube. (2014, May 5, July 28, 2019). *Waka (canoe) used by Māori for ceremonial events* [Video File]. Retrieved from https://www.youtube.com/watch?v=fk3wibr30es.

Ziersch, A. M., Gallaher, G., Baum, F., & Bentley, M. (2011). Responding to racism: Insights on how racism can damage health from an urban study of Australian Aboriginal people. *Social Science and Medicine, 73,* 1045–1053. https://doi.org/10.1016/j.socscimed.2011.06.058.

Part IV

Specific Examples

10

Embedding Interprofessional Learning into Undergraduate Health Science Programmes: Developing an Interprofessional Learning Zone (IPLZ)

Brenda Flood and C. Jane Morgan

Introduction

Interprofessional education improves students' collaboration and understanding of each other's distinct professional roles, and results in better health outcomes for clients (Institute of Medicine, 2015; Reeves et al., 2016). What is known from new graduate practitioners is that interprofessional education offers a deeper understanding of team work, an appreciation of reflective practice and a greater sense of being prepared for interprofessional practice (Pollard, Miers, & Rickaby, 2012; Thompson, Bratzler, Fisher, Torres, & Sparks, 2016). Interprofessional

B. Flood (✉)
School of Clinical Sciences, Auckland University of Technology, Auckland, New Zealand
e-mail: brenda.flood@aut.ac.nz

C. J. Morgan
School of Public Health and Interdisciplinary Studies, Auckland University of Technology, Auckland, New Zealand
e-mail: jane.morgan@aut.ac.nz

D. Forman et al. (eds.), *Sustainability and Interprofessional Collaboration*,
https://doi.org/10.1007/978-3-030-40281-5_10

practice transforms and broadens personal and professional perspectives, opens minds to difference and possibilities, and enables learners to more effectively utilise their knowledge and skills (Flood, Hocking, Smythe, & Jones, 2019; Morgan, 2017). To be able to work collaboratively, learners must be able to navigate the complex relational world of practice (Crowley, 2014; WHO, 2016). Graduates require dispositional qualities and values that enable them to respond to and meet the relational demands inherent in the current health care landscape (Flood, Smythe, Hocking, & Jones, 2019). Central to interprofessional education is a practice and learning context that allows students to get to know other professions and develop dispositional qualities such as placing the patient at the heart of practice, trusting in others, being open, tactful and authentic, and engaging in genuine dialogue (Flood, Hocking, et al., 2019). Importantly, through engaging in genuine dialogue students learn to value and respect the contributions of both one's own and other health disciplines in providing comprehensive health care and support.

Context

The Auckland University of Technology (AUT) is one of the largest and most diverse health faculties in New Zealand. It offers Bachelor of Health Science (BHSc) programmes in a range of clinical disciplines (midwifery, nursing, podiatry, physiotherapy, oral health therapy, occupational therapy, paramedicine) and a number of other health disciplines (case management, counselling-psychology, health administration, managing care of the older person, psychotherapy, public and environmental health). Currently undergraduate students enrol in a 'common' first semester and then progress into specified health fields, where they have variable amounts and types of interaction between disciplines; a characteristic also seen in other New Zealand tertiary institutions offering health science education (Fouche, Kenealy, Mace, & Shaw, 2014). Although there are a number of longstanding successful interprofessional education initiatives that bring students from clinical study programmes together in either simulated or real time practice activities, none have offered structured, cumulative and, most importantly, embedded interprofessional programmes that students engage with over the duration of their undergraduate studies.

Vision

AUT has boldly addressed the need for embedding interprofessional education into existing clinical programmes through revisioning and explicitly positioning IPE as core business in the faculty. This has occurred in several ways, with a key aim of ensuring academic and clinical staff and students develop an intentional orientation towards and through interprofessional practice.

Aims

In 2016 the School of Clinical Sciences (SoCS) was established at AUT drawing together seven health professional programmes, with the co-location of teaching staff and an expectation of collaborative teamwork. Similarly, all BHSc students in the SoCS would participate in interprofessional learning activities throughout their undergraduate degrees. Learning with students from other disciplines in longer-term embedded interprofessional learning activities, in preference to short-term or add-on interprofessional learning, was an intentional decision to create an environment where commonalities in knowledge bases were made obvious, prompting perceptions of one's own and other health professions as equal in status (Floyd & Morrison, 2014). Pivotal to introducing interprofessional education across existing programmes was the establishment of an interprofessional steering committee, with members from each of the clinical programmes working together on all developmental, implementation and evaluation stages of an *Interprofessional Learning Zone* (IPLZ) at AUT.

Pedagogy

The AUT *Interprofessional Learning Zone* (IPLZ) is based on constructionist pedagogy, i.e. humans constructing meaning to their lives through their experiences, individually and socially (Biggs & Tang, 2011; Merriam, Caffarella, & Baumgartner, 2007). As social beings, individuals do not learn in isolation of their natural and bio-historical environment and thus continually draw on both past and present experiences and social engagement with others for purposeful intentional learning, viewed as highly relevant to interprofessional education (Hean, Craddock, Hammick, & Hammick, 2012). Educationalists, Biggs and Tang (2011), emphasise the 'doing' aspect of constructionist pedagogy, with the process of learning being foregrounded and teaching as 'not a matter of transmitting but of engaging students in active learning' (p. 22). Learning 'with, from and about each other' (CAIPE, 2016) is central to interprofessional education and the AUT IPLZ promotes this form of experiential learning in authentic collaborative practice contexts.

The SoCS have drawn on Transformative Learning Theory (Mezirow, 1991) and Social Theory of Learning through Communities of Practice (Wenger, 1998) to inform the IPLZ framework. Transformative Learning Theory provides a theoretical lens on the ontological process of integrating professional practice and interprofessional ways of being. In 'becoming' health professionals who are able to navigate through the complex relational world of practice, recognition and development of desirable dispositional qualities necessary for 'being' an interprofessional practitioner are required (Flood, Smythe, et al., 2019). Social Learning Theory provides a theoretical lens on contextual and human influences of practice communities on learning. These theories, combining both an ontological and social orientation, focus on the process of 'being' and 'becoming' a health professional and emphasise the importance of social interaction for learning to be intentional and meaningful. This contrasts with contemporary health professional curricula that remain focused on the acquisition and application of distinct knowledge and skills pertaining to specific health professions (Eraut, 1994; Fellenz, 2016).

Development of the Interprofessional Learning Zone

The SoCS established an interprofessional steering committee who were tasked with developing interprofessional learning that was relevant, logistically possible and responsive to the needs identified within practice contexts. However, for interprofessional learning to take hold and flourish a collaborative learning culture encompassing an ontological lens was fostered. Such a culture was viewed as espousing trust, respect and an openness toward one another, along with clear expectations, guidelines, and working relationships to support interprofessional learning. Before embarking on such a journey, it was critical to consider ways of building this culture. This started with the provision of space to unpack and discuss experiences and meanings of interprofessional learning in order to move toward a shared vision and collective understanding of what an interprofessionally capable graduate would look like.

The committee came together to develop an interprofessional vision and graduate profile statement with a number of related capabilities (dispositional qualities, knowledge and skills) central to preparing students for graduate practice as interprofessional practitioners (Flood, Hocking, et al., 2019). The interprofessional graduate profile identified key processes involved in becoming interprofessionally capable, namely interactions with others that were *intentional*, *collaborative*, and *purposeful*.

With this collective vision in view, the steering committee set to work on developing a framework of embedded interprofessional learning, which would focus on building capabilities to prepare students to become open, willing and equipped to engage with others in interprofessional health contexts. The committee realised that any framework developed would have to be sufficiently sensitive and responsive to both the needs of the existing health professional programmes represented and the organisational structures inherent in both the tertiary education and health sectors in Aotearoa New Zealand. The steering committee was informed by an existing interprofessional education model, underpinned by constructionist pedagogy (Charles, Bainbridge, & Gilbert, 2010). This model was adapted to better reflect the developmental levels for undergraduate AUT health students through providing opportunities for them to apply interprofessional learning to collaborative practice. The adapted model has allowed us to scaffold interprofessional learning to meet students' learning needs as they develop over time and through experience (Vygotsky, 1978).

Guiding principles were identified from which to build and embed interprofessional learning, to ensure its utility and sustainability. Included were:

- building on what already existed within the School and Faculty
- being open to new learning opportunities for a wider range of students
- prioritising interprofessional learning experiences that were likely to be transformational
- ensuring the interprofessional process and outcomes added to student and staff experiences
- providing a simple and streamlined process/platform and retaining programmes' discretionary judgement on interprofessional requirements for students.

Early consideration and ongoing incorporation of these guiding principles have enabled us to create momentum, a shift in thinking towards the incorporation of interprofessional learning into existing health professional programme curricula. This requires leaders, staff and students to develop ways of relating to one another that are consistent with the dispositional qualities identified for interprofessional collaborative practice. These guiding principles led to the development of the *Interprofessional Learning Zone* (IPLZ) that is a flexible 'space', providing an overarching construct that informs, shapes, develops and supports interprofessional learning for all students and staff. It comprises a combination of e-learning and face-to-face collaboration and is embedded throughout the curriculum of each health professional programme in the SoCS.

In the IPLZ, interprofessional learning units (IPL Units) have been developed to provide opportunities to integrate dispositional qualities, knowledge and skills, aligned with core professional learning, for interprofessional collaborative practice. In addition, each IPL Unit is informed by specified criteria at either the exposure, immersion or integration levels of increasingly more complex relational interprofessional learning (as shown in Fig. 10.1). An example of one IPL Unit within the IPLZ, *Moving and Handling*, provides a context at an exposure level (Fig. 10.1), for students to experience and develop interprofessional dispositional qualities through intentional interprofessional learning in practice with a number of professions. The dispositional qualities aligned with this IPL Unit are initially brought to the students' conscious awareness through targeted interactive interprofessional activities. This is followed by students actively demonstrating these dispositional qualities during the course of learning moving and handling techniques together.

In summary, the development of interprofessional learning embedded in and across a number of health programmes required the collaborative work of a team who journeyed together in all phases of the co-constructed process of developing an interprofessional learning zone. Creating an environment where the contributions of all those involved were respected and valued, while debated and discussed, was central to the innovation and advancement of interprofessional education. In addition, the modelling of collaborative practice by all members of the interprofessional steering committee, leaders, staff and students was viewed as a prerequisite for constructive interprofessional learning development. The process was further strengthened by a constructionist pedagogy that informed both theoretical and practice considerations, enabling the steering committee to develop a shared interprofessional vision, graduate profile and dispositional qualities that have been endorsed in the faculty and embedded into an interprofessional learning zone that all students and staff in the SoCS engage in. The interprofessional learning zone has been informed by, and continues to develop, an ontological approach and conceptual framework to guide and support the ongoing development of interprofessional learning and collaborative practice for students and staff across this diverse faculty.

<u>Exposure</u> is preparation for interprofessional practice, experienced among professions	**<u>Immersion</u> is simulated interprofessional practice, experienced among professions**	**<u>Integration</u> is 'real-time' interprofessional practice, experienced with clients and among professions**
• Health and environmental concerns	• Case based	• Real time practice
• Relevant to client-centred practice	• Focused on client but not physically present	• Working with clients – individual and/or groups
• Two or more professions	• Two or more professions	• Two or more professions
• Collaborative interactions	• Collaborative practice in simulated environments ○ Whole person/holistic approach	• Collaborative practice ○ Whole person/holistic approach ○ Mutually determined client-centred goals ○ Client integral to team ○ Collaborative planning ○ Collaborative interventions ○ Distributive leadership
• Focus of IPL on one or more dispositional qualities: ○ Hold the person/whānau at the centre of their practice ○ Empathically attend to the concerns of others ○ Engage in ongoing learning with, from and about others ○ Identify and critique their own prejudices/stereotypes and the possible impact on others ○ Build relationships through mutual respect and trust ○ Engage in genuine dialogue ○ Recognise and reflect on their own and contextual limitations ○ Value the perspectives and contributions of others	• Focus of IPL on one or more dispositional qualities: ○ Hold the person/whānau at the centre of their practice ○ Empathically attend to the concerns of others ○ Engage in ongoing learning with, from and about others ○ Identify and critique their own prejudices/stereotypes and the possible impact on others ○ Build relationships through mutual respect and trust ○ Engage in genuine dialogue ○ Recognise and reflect on their own and contextual limitations ○ Value the perspectives and contributions of others ○ Understand the health perspectives and roles of others ○ Attend to conflict in an open and respectful manner	• Focus of IPL on one or more dispositional qualities: ○ Hold the person/whānau at the centre of their practice ○ Empathically attend to the concerns of others ○ Engage in ongoing learning with, from and about others ○ Identify and critique their own prejudices/stereotypes and the possible impact on others ○ Build relationships through mutual respect and trust ○ Engage in genuine dialogue ○ Recognise and reflect on their own and contextual limitations ○ Value the perspectives and contributions of others ○ Understand the health perspectives and roles of others ○ Attend to conflict in an open and respectful manner ○ Adapt and respond to unpredictable health contexts and situations ○ Integrate professional knowledge and competence in interprofessional contexts

Fig. 10.1 Interprofessional learning unit levels

• Shared communication processes and structures to support interprofessional learning e.g. • Communication skills • Build relationships • Team work projects	• Shared communication processes and structures to support interprofessional learning <u>and</u> practice e.g. • Patient-as-person centred communication skills • Video simulations of patient-practitioner(s) interaction • Role modelling	• Shared communication processes and structures in practice e.g. ○ Case conference ○ Group sessions - debriefing ○ Conflict management
• Learning with, from, about and among	• Learning with, from, about and among	• Learning with, from, about and among
• Interprofessional awareness	• Interprofessional orientation	• Interprofessional engagement
• Responsiveness *(to student, context, location)*	• Responsiveness and flexibility	• Responsiveness, flexibility and adaptability
• Interprofessional learning outcome/s	• Interprofessional learning outcome/s	• Interprofessional learning outcome/s
• Completion of an assessment that meets interprofessional learning outcome/s (IPLO) and counts toward paper credits. *(This could be a specific IP assessment or existing assessment that meets the IPLO)*	• Completion of an assessment that meets interprofessional learning outcome/s (IPLO) and counts toward paper credits. *(This could be a specific IP assessment or existing assessment that meets the IPLO)*	• Completion of an assessment that meets interprofessional learning outcome/s (IPLO) and counts toward paper credits. *(This could be a specific IP assessment or existing assessment that meets the IPLO)*
• Opportunities for reflection on interprofessional learning	• Opportunities for reflection on <u>and</u> in interprofessional interactions	• Opportunities for reflection on <u>and</u> in interprofessional practice
• IPL unit has facilitator awareness of interprofessional pedagogy	• IPL unit has interprofessional facilitator/s implementing IP pedagogy	• IPL unit has interprofessional facilitator/s integrating IP pedagogy into practice
		Acknowledge the development work of Dr C. Jane Morgan, Dr Sue McNaughton, & Dr Brenda Flood (2017) AUT

Fig. 10.1 (continued)

References

AUT Interprofessional Steering Committee. (2018). *Interprofessional learning zone development plan.* Unpublished working document. Auckland, New Zealand: AUT.

Biggs, J., & Tang, C. (2011). *Teaching for quality learning at university* (4th ed.). New York, NY: Open University Press.

Centre for the Advancement of Interprofessional Education. (2016). *Statement of purpose.* Retrieved from http://www.caipe.org.

Charles, G., Bainbridge, L., & Gilbert, J. (2010). The University of British Columbia model of interprofessional education. *Journal of Interprofessional Care, 24*(1), 9–18. https://doi.org/10.3109/13561820903294549.

Crowley, S. (Ed.). (2014). *Challenging professional learning.* New York, NY: Routledge.

Eraut, M. (1994). *Developing professional knowledge and competence.* London, England: Routledge-Falmer.

Fellenz, M. R. (2016). Forming the professional self: Bildung and the ontological perspective on professional education and development. *Educational Philosophy and Theory, 48*(3), 267–283. https://doi.org/10.1080/00131857.2015.1006161.

Flood, B., Hocking, C., Smythe, L., & Jones, M. (2019). Working in a spirit of interprofessional practice: A hermeneutic phenomenological study. *Journal of Interprofessional Care, 33*(6), 744–752. https://doi.org/10.1080/13561820.2019.1577810.

Flood, B., Smythe, L., Hocking, C., & Jones, M. (2019). Interprofessional practice: Beyond competence. *Advances in Health Sciences Education.* https://doi.org/10.1007/s10459-019-09879-4.

Floyd, A., & Morrison, M. (2014). Exploring identities and cultures in interprofessional education and collaborative professional practice. *Studies in Continuing Education, 36*(1), 38–53. https://doi.org/10.1080/0158037X.2013.783472.

Fouche, C., Kenealy, T., Mace, J., & Shaw, J. (2014). Practitioner perspectives from seven health professional groups on core competencies in the context of chronic care. *Journal of Interprofessional Care, 28*(6), 534–540. http://dx.org/doi:10.3109/13561820.2014.915514.

Hean, S., Craddock, D., Hammick, M., & Hammick, M. (2012). Theoretical insights into interprofessional education: AMEE Guide No. 62, *Medical Teacher, 34*(2), e78–e101. https://dx.doi.org/10.3109/0142159X.2012.650740.

Institute of Medicine. (2015). *Measuring the impact of interprofessional education on collaborative practice and patient outcomes.* Washington, DC: National Academies Press.

Merriam, S. B., Caffarella, R. S., & Baumgartner, L. M. (2007). *Learning in adulthood: A comprehensive guide* (3rd ed.). San Francisco, CA: Wiley.

Mezirow, J. (1991). *Transformative dimensions of adult learning.* San Francisco, CA: Jossey-Bass.

Morgan, C. J. (2017). Graduates' development of interprofessional practice capability during their early socialisation into professional roles. *Journal of Interprofessional Care, 31*(4), 438–445. https://doi.org/10.1080/13561820.2017.1295029.

Pollard, K. C., Miers, M. E., & Rickaby, C. (2012). "Oh why didn't I take more notice?" Professionals' views and perceptions of pre-qualifying preparation for interprofessional working in practice. *Journal of Interprofessional Care, 26*(5), 355–361. https://doi.org/10.3109/13561820.2012.689785.

Reeves, S., Fletcher, S., Barr, H., Birch, I., Boet, S., Davies, N., ... Kitto, S. (2016). A BEME systematic review of the effects of interprofessional education: BEME Guide No. 39. *Medical Teacher, 38*(7), 1–13. http://dx.doi.org/10.3109/0142159X.2016.1173663.

Thompson, B. M., Bratzler, D. W., Fisher, M. J., Torres, A., & Sparks, R. A. (2016). Working together: Using a unique approach to evaluate an interactive and clinic-based longitudinal interprofessional education experience with 13 professions. *Journal of Interprofessional Care, 30*(6), 754–761. https://doi.org/10.1080/13561820.2016.1227962.

Vygotsky, L. S. (1978). *Mind in society: The development of higher psychological processes.* Cambridge, MA: Harvard University Press.

Wenger, E. (1998). *Communities of practice: Learning, meaning and identity.* Cambridge, England: Cambridge University Press.

World Health Organization. (2016). *Framework on integrated people-centred health services*. Retrieved from http://www.who.int/servicedeliverysafety.

11

The Linköping Journey

Johanna Dahlberg, Madeleine Abrandt Dahlgren, Mattias Ekstedt, Mats Hammar, and Annika Lindh Falk

In this chapter, we will outline how the curriculum for Interprofessional Education (IPE) at Linköping University was initiated, implemented and developed over the years, to become sustainable and valued by staff and students. A few years ago, a revision process was initiated to assure that the IPE curriculum was based on evidence and best practice (Lindh Falk, Dahlberg, Ekstedt, Heslyk, Whiss & Abrandr Dahlgren 2015). This process was, in hindsight, important regarding sustainability since it engaged faculty in a thorough investigation, especially bringing new teachers and students into the discussion about the core values and pedagogical challenges of IPE.

How Did It All Start?

In the late 1970s, the medical programme within the Faculty of Medicine and Health Sciences (FMHS) at Linköping University consisted of

J. Dahlberg (✉) · M. A. Dahlgren · M. Ekstedt · M. Hammar · A. L. Falk
Linköping University, Linkoping, Sweden
e-mail: johanna.dahlberg@liu.se

D. Forman et al. (eds.), *Sustainability and Interprofessional Collaboration*,
https://doi.org/10.1007/978-3-030-40281-5_11

the clinical part of the curriculum, following two years of preclinical studies at Uppsala University. Facing the threat of the government closing the Linköping campus, faculty and other stakeholders in the Linköping region initiated a project to establish a full medical programme with a new pedagogical approach at Linköping University. Interestingly, the external threat of losing the medical programme reduced internal tensions and conflicts, making way for new ideas and practices (Savage & Brommels, 2008). Additionally, the support and the shared general understanding between the County Council, the main health care provider in the region, and FMSH was important. It was evident very early on that the representatives of the healthcare provider understood the value of interprofessional collaborative practice, with improved patient safety and better use of available resources.

The project proposed the implementation of problem based learning (PBL) with early patient contact, vertical (between basic science and clinical studies) and horizontal integration (i.e. between disciplines and subjects), and to introduce interprofessional education involving all professional programmes at FMHS (Areskog, 1994; Bergdahl, Ludvigsson, Koch, & Wessman, 1991). The setting of IPE and PBL, with interprofessional tutorial groups, created a learning environment challenging the traditional hierarchies and bridging the silos between teachers and students from different professional programmes (Dahlgren, 2009; Wilhelmsson et al., 2009). In Sweden, all health professionals study at university level for three to five and a half years starting at undergraduate level, without other university courses required as a prerequisite. Therefore, the barrier of different educational levels, i.e. vocational versus university degrees, did not exist.

The IPE Curriculum at FMHS

Interprofessional education was introduced in 1986, as a ten-week compulsory course for all students in the first semester. The programmes involved were biomedical laboratory science, medicine, nursing, occupational therapy, and physiotherapy. Today speech and language pathology are also included. The content was, and still is, about health and disease, ethics, a holistic perspective in healthcare, and some fundamentals in epidemiology and scientific methods, with the purpose of building a common ground of values for healthcare work across professions. Over time, the IPE activity developed to a three-step curriculum. The interprofessional training ward (IPTW) was introduced in 1996, to be incorporated towards the end of the programmes involved. This made up the third step in the IPE curriculum once the second step was introduced in 2002. The, scope of the second step was initially sexual health but changed to quality improvement knowledge in 2011 (Fig. 11.1).

The initiative to start the IPTW was developed in collaboration between a group of students and teachers, who identified a demand for interprofessional education practice, immersed in a real setting for learning, towards the end of the programme when students typically have developed a professional identity (Wahlström, Sandén, & Hammar,

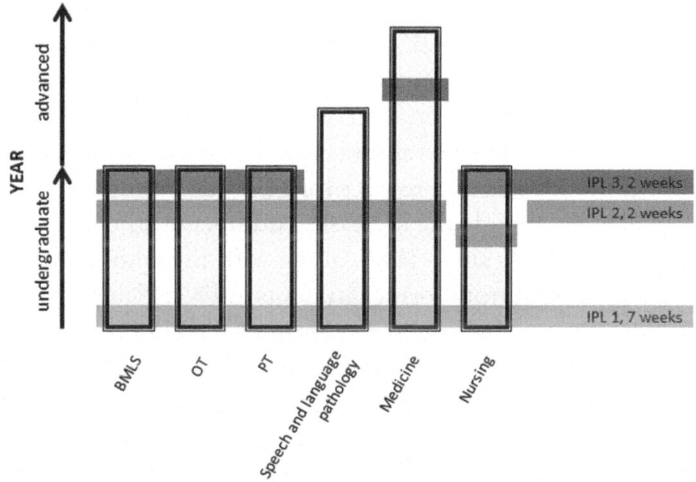

Fig. 11.1 Overview of the IPE curriculum at Faculty of Medicine and Health Sciences, Linköping University. Before the most recent revision, three steps of IPE were distributed over 11 weeks: IPL 1 is the introduction to regulation and ethics in health care; IPL 2 is about quality improvement work; and, IPL 3 is the placement at the interprofessional clinical training ward. Students are from Biomedicine and Laboratory Science (BMLS), Occupational Therapy (OT), Physiotherapy (PT), Speech and Language Pathology, Medicine, and Nursing. Following a revision in 2016, the IPE curriculum now encompasses a total of 8 weeks

1997). It is at this stage that both programme directors and clinical supervisors demonstrated leadership, building partnership with the students in the development and implementation process.

Sustainability and Resilience—Revision of the IPE Curriculum

Even though FMHS has incorporated IPE into their medical and health professional undergraduate programmes for more than 30 years, a group of students and faculty members have continuously voiced some concerns. One recurring issue is that IPE 'takes too much time'. However, the content of IPE is selected from what already existed in the different professional programmes; therefore IPE is not adding content but arranging learning activities in a different way benefitting from the interprofessional setting. Another common critique is that students in the very beginning of their professional education cannot benefit from IPE, since they have no references or experiences from a professional perspective. However, we argue that on the contrary, through an early IPE experience, a common ground of values is developed and established, along with life-long friendships and respect for other disciplines.

Other challenges include the increasing number of students, which has increased by 300–400% since 1986, along with the employment of new teachers recruited both from former students at FMHS and other universities. To address these challenges, the Dean of FMHS prompted a group of teachers representing the programmes involved, students and other stakeholders to inquire into and suggest changes for a revised IPE curriculum (Abrandt Dahlgren, 2015; Lindh Falk et al., 2015). The inquiry involved investigating global incentives, national and local policies, and the knowledge base of IPE; so it was not only an evaluation. The pedagogical discussions, which allowed all voices to be heard, subsequently created a renewed legitimacy for IPE, crucial for sustainability. The decision was to continue in line with the existing IPE curriculum, but change the length to a total of eight weeks instead of eleven, with the instruction to implement improvements based on the result of the inquiry. Specifically, the first step was scheduled over six weeks, and was carried out in parallel with programme-specific content. This step undertook to explore identical scenarios with added programme-specific triggers, thus making the IPE content intertwined with and relevant to the programme specifics. In addition, tutors were assigned to supervise both programme-specific and interprofessional tutorials, engaging more teachers in IPE.

The revised IPE curriculum (Dahlberg & Dahlgren, 2018) and how the development of student leadership capabilities is supported throughout the three steps will be described in the following section.

First Step: Professionalism in Healthcare

The IPE curriculum starts in the first semester with four weeks of full-time study scheduled into each of the six programmes in a way that students will experience how professional learning is tightly integrated with interprofessional learning. During this step, students recognize how their professional knowledge is to be executed in settings with other professionals. The rationale is 'learning together to enable working together'. At this early stage, the professional identification is primarily built upon expectations, rather than experiences from a professional perspective (Uhlin & Pelling, 2010). In addition, students become socially aware of any preconceived ideas of each other's professions and the traditional professional silo structure of the educational programmes and practices. The cohort of all first semester students consequently develops a common foundation of knowledge and values.

Leadership capabilities in this first stage are taught through the social structuring of the group work and the PBL pedagogy. One teacher is assigned as a tutor for each group of eight students, acting as a role model for the students. Gradually, the responsibility for facilitating the group is shifted over to the students. Students take turns in practising leadership concerning responsibility for frame factors and structural aspects, such as keeping to timeframes, pacing and scope of the discussion. Furthermore, the leadership skills also comprise a social and group dynamic aspect, as the tutor is expected to be attentive to the dynamics of the discussion, making sure that all members of the group are heard. Studying together in small groups encourages close discussions aimed at teaching leadership on an individual level, as the students are also prompted to take responsibility for, and leadership of, their own learning, in order to be able to contribute to the shared learning in the group.

Second Step: Quality Improvement and Learning

The second step of the interprofessional curriculum runs over two weeks in the last third of the undergraduate programmes. As in the first step, students from the six disciplines form interprofessional tutorial groups and use quality improvement projects from the clinical practice of the County Council (main provider of healthcare in the region) as scenarios or study objects while learning quality improvement knowledge. The purpose of the scenario is to enable students to inquire about the problems presented in the scenario, raise questions regarding what they need to learn and consequently develop their interprofessional understanding. During the learning process, the scenario is approached from the different professional perspectives of the participating students. In this process, new practical understandings and proposed solutions to the problem emerge. As the student groups are given the mandate of analysing and driving processes of change, they lower the boundaries between the academic and clinical contexts, as well as becoming 'leaders of change' in the professional context. Our experience is that students are fearless ambassadors of change, since they have no obligations to the culture of the working place they study. The assignment of executing a quality improvement project in a clinical setting provides a tool to negotiate practices between the student group and the health professionals; thus the whole team receives the opportunity to experience leadership in a clinical setting. While the purpose is to learn from, with and about each other to improve health and patient safety, the focus of the students is not purely their professional focus. Interestingly, interprofessional practice does not appear to be the only competence developed (Gjessing, Torgé, Hammar, Dahlberg, & Faresjö, 2014). Rather, the student teams act as united leaders for change based on their newly acquired general knowledge. Hence, there is a shift from the students' first experience during the first IPE step, where individual leadership is the primary focus, to jointly forming a team with a common interest in leading a process of change in the second step.

Third Step: Professional Perspectives in Collaboration

In the final step of the interprofessional curriculum the context involves a student-led training ward in one of the County Council hospitals (Fallsberg & Hammar, 2000). In Linköping, students from biomedical laboratory science, medicine, nursing, physiotherapy, occupational therapy and social work do placements together in one of four training wards during a two-week period. The student teams are supervised by a team supervisor and clinicians from their own profession. The learning objectives incorporate teamwork, communication, and ethics, while executing the skills of their own profession, with the goal of providing high quality care. The patients are highly involved and become partners within the learning environment. The students take joint responsibility for the total care of the patients while contributing their own professional perspective.

How Is Leadership Executed in This Setting?

In the early stages of the IPE curriculum, we suggest that students develop and practise leadership in their own tutorial groups and develop responsibility for their own and the group's learning. Recent research shows that this fundamental 'knowledge' is brought to the foreground of the placement in the clinical training ward towards the conclusion of the students' studies (Lindh Falk, Hult, Hammar, Hopwood, & Abrandt Dahlgren, 2013). Different professions enact different types of leadership and responsibilities, expected and unexpected, through the socio-material arrangements of IPTW, which is relevant for learning to occur. This creates an 'unexpected practice' that is unfamiliar to the students but a prerequisite for their interprofessional learning (Lindh Falk et al., 2013).

Proximity for Negotiations and Boundary Work

The socio-material arrangements of the ward signal a collaborative practice where all students share the responsibility of caring for the patients' basic needs, regardless of which professional programme they are studying. The proximity between the students in the enactments of these caring activities encourages negotiations and decision-making with respect to every specific task. The negotiations and decision-making are not only about specific professional activities but also involve a common set of values for professional healthcare work. The material arrangements at the ward also include the round room specially equipped with a round table and chairs for discussion, and a white board for daily notes, used for the analysis and reflection of the team together with the team supervisor at the end of the day. This room functions as a boundary zone (Edwards, Daniels, Gallagher, Leadbetter, & Warmington, 2009) where the students clarify how their respective professional roles and practical understandings of the caring situation contribute to the team and ultimately to the general understanding of the welfare of the patient.

Dealing with the 'Expected'

Organizing rounds in the IPTW involves a round table discussion, involving all the students, and is usually led by one of the medical students. This setting seems to be important for producing an execution of confident leadership. To understand and plan the treatment and care of the individual patients on the ward, the medical student interacts with the other students of the team, discussing their specific professional contributions. The team interaction requires that team members express their opinion regarding specific patients, in both what is said and done. To actively listen to and integrate the professional perspectives of others in decision-making are some of the 'doings' produced by the specific material arrangements. Therefore, the enactment of the rounds, from a leadership position, are an 'expected' professional responsibility of the medical students. From a pedagogical perspective, students from different professions could take turns leading the round table discussion; however, this is usually not practised.

On the other hand, for the nursing students, the organisation and administrative planning of daily work stands out as an important and 'expected' professional responsibility, such as a 'spider in the web', whereby one is responsible and oversees the activities, while people around you depend on your competence and type of leadership. The planning of caring tasks shared by all student members in relation to time for treatments provided by a specific profession requires liaising with other student team members and an awareness of their different competences. For both occupational therapy and physiotherapy students, the socio-material arrangements of the student team and the ward produce enactments of the 'expected' professional responsibility of being the only representative in a specific field of competence.

The socialisation process into a profession is challenging for the students and the experience from the IPTW is not sufficient to overcome the challenges of a traditional health care practice. A tentative conclusion is that the IPTW both predicts and thereby produces a practice where different professional responsibilities are performed in ways that produce expected and assumed roles.

Dealing with the 'Unexpected'

At the same time, the arrangement at the IPTW expects that all students, independently of professional training, are part of daily work which shapes practice, for instance caring for the basic needs of the patients, e.g. patients' morning routines. This arrangement seems to produce conflicting understandings. The 'unexpected' overall responsibility for and allocation of time for the basic care and needs of the patient clashes with the preparation for professions-specific work for the rest of the day and creates a conflict regarding the understanding of professional responsibility, a characteristic of a specific profession, and the general understanding of the tasks, roles and mobility of the professions in question.

The socio-material arrangements of the ward, requiring all students to be in the ward at all times, are an authentic feature of practice to the nursing students. Their practical understanding of tasks and general understanding of the role of the nurse is that of 'being stationary', in other words that the nurse's activities are confined within the ward. The nurse supervisor, usually the team supervisor too, reinforces this by being present in the ward. For the medical students, this 'practice' is not in harmony with their practical understanding of a doctor's practice. They have the general understanding that physicians are mobile, connected to different practices in the hospital throughout the day, e.g. the ward, outpatient clinic and operating theatre. This unforeseen conflict between the learning practice and the experience from earlier professional placements is also reinforced by the fact that the medical supervisor is only available in the ward for part of the day. The student team supervisor is usually a nurse who cannot compensate for the medical students' perceived need of professional supervision.

Capabilities for Leadership

As described, the IPE activities at FMHS are sequentially arranged and with increasing levels of demands, achieving progress to fulfil learning objectives defined from the core competency domains of the Interprofessional Education Collaborative Expert Panel (IPEC, 2011), including: (1) values/ethics for interprofessional practice, (2) roles/responsibilities, (3) interprofessional communication, and (4) teams and teamwork. These domains constitute and realise the socio-materiality of healthcare practice within the professional curriculum in a tangible way (Abrandt Dahlgren, Dahlgren, & Dahlberg, 2011). The domains cut across the practices of education and learning and are enacted within curriculum practice, with each step involving enactments of leadership activities in different social and material settings, progressing in the development of the competences described. Therefore, it is essential that an interprofessional curriculum is integrated from the outset through to the successful completion of a programme.

What Does It Take to Make IPE Sustainable?

Professor Nils-Holger Areskog was the leader and champion at FMSH in the early days (Areskog, 1994). He played a pivotal role in the development and implementation of IPE. At the time, as Dean of the faculty, he demonstrated courageous leadership and acted as a role model for many, both locally and internationally. Over time, the setup and the different activities within the IPE curriculum can be seen as a dynamic interplay between the policy level, the organisational level, the curriculum level, and the learning activity level. This is facilitated and made possible by the management structures within the faculty, where the Board of Education have a leading role. The Director of the IPE curriculum has a mandate in the Board of Education, possessing the responsibility and mandate from the Dean towards the programmes involved, for the planning and realisation of the educational activities, with interprofessional learning as a focus across the faculty. The Director is also a member of the Strategic Centre of Development and Research of IPE at FMHS, bringing a continuous reflexivity into the management of the IPE curriculum.

So, what makes the IPE curriculum sustainable? This question is difficult to answer. Over the years, barriers and challenges to IPE have arisen (Lawlis et al., 2014) but have been overcome due to robust organisation, committed leadership and dedicated teachers. Our impression is that the IPE curriculum per se has never been in question; the discussion has been about the length and content of the programme. Perhaps there is something in the Swedish academic culture, where the commitment from the leadership and the unquestionable value of an IPE learning experience bring stability and assertiveness to everyday work?

References

Abrandt Dahlgren, M. (2015). *I takt med framtiden: Utveckling av ett nytt interprofessionellt curriculum vid Hälsouniversitetet i Linköping.* Report from a new IPE curriculum development project at Linköping University. http://www.diva-portal.org/smash/get/diva2:808040/FULLTEXT01.pdf (In Swedish).

Abrandt Dahlgren, M., Dahlgren, L., & Dahlberg, J. (2011). Learning professional practice through education. In P. Hager, A. Lee, & A. Reich (Eds.), *Practice, learning and change: Practice-theory perspectives on professional learning*. Dordrecht: Springer.

Areskog, N. N. (1994). Multiprofessional education at the undergraduate level: The Linköping model. *Journal of Interprofessional Care, 8*, 279–282.

Bergdahl, B., Ludvigsson, J., Koch, M., & Wessman, J. (1991). Undergraduate medical education in Sweden: A case study of the Faculty of Health Sciences at Linköping University. *Teaching and Learning in Medicine, 3*, 203–209.

Dahlberg, J., & Dahlgren, M. A. (2018). *Interprofessional education at the Faculty of Medicine and Health Sciences of Linköping University, Sweden*. Linköping University. Retrieved 11 December, 2019, from https://liu.se/dfsmedia/dd35e243dfb7406993c1815aaf88a675/25588-source.

Dahlgren, L. O. (2009). Interprofessional learning and problem-based learning—A marriage made in heaven? *Journal of Interprofessional Care, 23*, 448–454.

Edwards, A., Daniels, H., Gallagher, T., Leadbetter, J., & Warmington, P. (2009). *Improving inter-professional collaborations: Multi-agency working for children's wellbeing*. Milton Park, Abingdon: Routledge.

Fallsberg, M., & Hammar, M. (2000). Strategies and focus at an integrated, interprofessional training ward. *Journal of Interprofessional Care, 14*(4), 337–350. https://doi.org/10.1080/13561820020003892.

Gjessing, K., Torgé, C. J., Hammar, M., Dahlberg, J., & Faresjö, T. (2014). Improvement of quality and safety in healthcare as a new interprofessional learning module—Evaluation from students. *Journal of Multidisciplinary Healthcare, 7*, 341–347. https://doi.org/10.2147/JMDH.S62619.

Interprofessional Education Collaborative Expert Panel. (2011). *Core competencies for interprofessional collaborative practice: Report of an expert panel*. Washington, DC: Interprofessional Education Collaborative. https://nebula.wsimg.com/3ee8a4b5b5f7ab794c742b14601d5f23?AccessKeyId=DC06780E69ED19E2B3A5&disposition=0&alloworigin=1.

Lawlis, T., Anson, J., & Greenfield, D. (2014). Barriers and enablers that influence sustainable interprofessional education: A literature review. *Journal of Interprofessional Care, 28*(4), 305–310. https://doi.org/10.3109/13561820.2014.895977.

Lindh Falk, A., Hult, H., Hammar, M., Hopwood, N., & Abrandt Dahlgren, M. (2013). One site fits all? A student ward as a learning practice for interprofessional development. *Journal of Interprofessional Care, 27*(6), 476–481. https://doi.org/10.3109/13561820.2013.807224.

Lindh Falk, A., Dahlberg, J., Ekstedt, M., Heslyk, A., Whiss, P., & Abrandt Dahlgren, M. (2015). Creating spaces for interprofessional learning: Strategic revision of a common IPL curriculum in undergraduate programmes. In A. Vyt, M. Pahor, & T. Tervaakanto-Maentausta (Eds.), *Interprofessional education in Europe: Policy and practice.* Garant: Antwerpen/Apeldoorn.

Savage, C., & Brommels, M. (2008). Innovation in medical education: How Linköping created a Blue Ocean for medical education in Sweden. *Medical Teacher, 30*(5), 501–507.

Uhlin, L., & Pelling, S. (2010). Inter-... what? About consolidating or changing perceptions about genus and power [Inter-... vadå? Om att befästa eller förändra föreställningar om genus och makt.]. In B. Wijma, G. Smirthwaite, & K. Swahnberg (Eds.), *Genus och kön inom medicin- och vårdutbildningar.* Lund: Studentlitteratur (In Swedish).

Wahlström, O., Sandén, I., & Hammar, M. (1997). Multiprofessional education in the medical curriculum. *Medical Education, 31,* 425–429.

Wilhelmsson, M., Pelling, S., Ludvigsson, J., Hammar, M., Dahlgren, L., & Faresjö, T. (2009). Twenty years' experiences of interprofessional education in Linköping—Ground-breaking and sustainable. *Journal of Interprofessional Care, 23*(2), 121–133.

12

Developing and Maintaining Interprofessional Teams in Rural and Remote Settings

Tony Smith, Simon Munro, and Monica Moran

Introduction

The authors of this chapter all live in rural Australia and work in what are known as University Departments of Rural Health (UDRHs), which are part of the multimillion dollar, Australian Government funded Rural Health Multidisciplinary Training (RHMT) Programme (Australian Government Department of Health, 2018a). The purpose of the RHMT programme is to '*improve the recruitment and retention of medical, nursing, dental and allied health professionals in rural and remote*

T. Smith (✉)
Department of Rural Health (UONDRH), The University of Newcastle, Taree, NSW, Australia
e-mail: tony.smith@newcastle.edu.au

S. Munro
Department of Rural Health (UONDRH), The University of Newcastle, Tamworth, NSW, Australia

M. Moran
Western Australian Centre for Rural Health, Geraldton, WA, Australia

D. Forman et al. (eds.), *Sustainability and Interprofessional Collaboration*,
https://doi.org/10.1007/978-3-030-40281-5_12

Australia', thus, in the longer term, improving the health status of the population living in those locations. As such, the objectives of the programme are to provide high quality rural health education experiences for health professional students, as well as to support existing rural and remote health professionals, engaging with the local community, including the local Indigenous population, and performing relevant research.

There are 16 UDRHs dotted across regional, rural and remote Australia and each is linked to one or more Australian universities that offer various health professional degrees. Supported by locally based interprofessional teams of educators and researchers, students undertake practice-based education with a real world, rural focus. As part of this approach and under their contractual obligations to the Australian Government Department of Health, all UDRHs are required provide opportunities for students to have interprofessional education experiences. Consequently, with co-located students and academic staff members from multiple health care disciplines, UDRHs have developed substantial expertise in interprofessional education and collaborative practice. This strategy promises to contribute to graduates' appreciation of sustaining existing models, as well as developing new models of interprofessional team-based care.

This chapter describes the features of rural and remote health service delivery and the numerous intersections with interprofessional education and collaborative team-based care. Rural and remote Australia encompasses multiple differing contexts including geographical, political, economic, cultural and spiritual variations. While the authors' personal experiences are grounded in the physical places and social spaces where we live, it is anticipated that there will be similarities with health care services and jurisdictions in other parts of the world, as well as contrasts that we hope will be informative.

Australia is a big country (some 7672,024 square kilometres) with a comparatively small population of 25 million people (Australian Bureau of Statistics, 2016a). Australia's total land area is larger than mainland Europe but with much lower population density. There are fewer than three persons per square kilometre in Australia compared to France with 117 people per square kilometre, Japan with 337 per square kilometre and even NZ with 15 people per square kilometre (http://alldownunder.

com/australian-facts/compare-size.htm). However, Australia's population is not spread across the entire land area. Figure 12.1 shows the Australian land mass shaded by degrees of remoteness, according to the Australian Standard Geographical Classification—Remoteness Area (ASGC-RA) (Australian Government Department of Health, 2018b). The vast, arid interior is sparsely populated, with most population concentrated along the Eastern and Southeast coast. The majority of Australians live less than 50 kilometres from coastal areas, which is where most large towns and major cities are located. There are, however, more than 1500 communities across Australia that are classified as rural or remote and

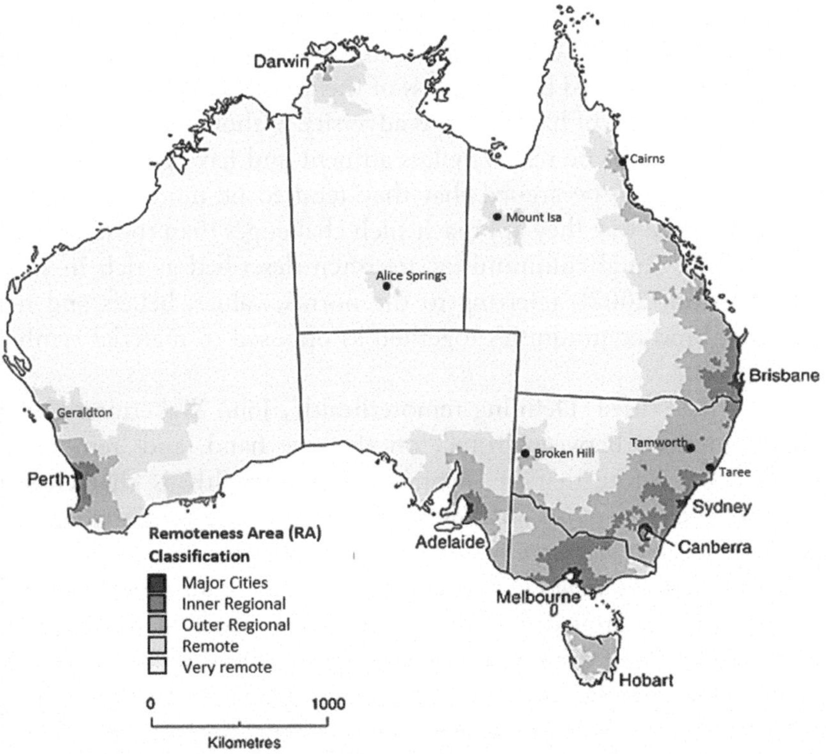

Fig. 12.1 Australian Standard Geographical Classification—Remoteness Area (ASGC-RA) (*Source* Australian Bureau of Statistics [ABS], 2016b)

over seven million people (almost one third of the population) live in those communities.

What Makes Rural and Remote Different?

While there are various ways of defining rural and remote and differentiating it from urban or metropolitan, there is a school of thought that it is not so much a matter of where people live, as the way they live that defines the difference. Geographical location and distance from the nearest large population centre are not the only defining characteristics. Rather, based on our observations, when people choose to live in smaller rural or remote communities they develop resilience and a sense independence, balanced by awareness of their dependence on each other, especially in the face of hardship and adversity. Although people who live outside the city may be relatively less affluent and have poorer access to services, it can also be argued that they tend to be more resilient and innovative in the way they approach such challenges than those who live in large cities. Rural communities are often described as rich in social capital (Alston, 2002), referring to the norms, values, beliefs and networks that bind communities together, as opposed to material symbols of wealth.

In an article titled 'Defining remote health', John Wakerman (2004) drew distinctions between 'rural', on the one hand, and 'remote' on the other. He wrote that in Australia 'remote health' is characterised by factors such as '*social isolation of practitioners*'; '*a strong multidisciplinary approach*'; '*overlapping and changing roles of team members*'; and, '*a relatively high degree of GP* [general practitioner] *substitution*' (p. 210). Consequently, he argued, in order to meet the needs of relatively less healthy, isolated and dispersed populations, a greater proportion of who are Indigenous, practitioners need particular capabilities, including being able to work across cultural, as well as professional boundaries.

The health needs and health disparities of Aboriginal and Torres Strait Islander people have been well documented. While they are intrinsically linked to intergenerational oppression since Australia was colonised, they also bear similarities to the needs of other First Nations populations around the world who have experienced dispossession of land, diminishment of cultural identity and loss of sovereign autonomy (Saggers, Walter, & Gray, 2011). Historical outcomes of colonisation in Australia continue to play out in the health and wellbeing of Aboriginal and Torres Strait Islander peoples and 'closing the gap' on the health disparity between Indigenous and non-Indigenous Australians is an ongoing national priority (Australian Government Department of the Prime Minister and Cabinet, 2019).

The need for health care and health professional education teams in rural and remote settings to include Aboriginal and Torres Strait Islander team members, as well as for all Australian health care workers to be able to practice in a culturally responsive framework, is well recognised (Indigenous Allied Health Australia [IAHA], 2015). The challenges of introducing interprofessional competencies in training programmes have also been well reported; however, much less has been written about the challenges of implementing culturally responsive interprofessional teaching and learning in health professional training programmes. Most health professional education and training focusses on attainment of technical skills, often at the expense of the inclusion of developing collaborative skills that are applicable to person, family and community-centred care, communication and shared decision-making, and cultural respect (Frenk et al., 2010; WHO, 2010).

In the next section, Simon Munro, one of this chapter's co-authors, himself a health professional educator and an Aboriginal man, explores the challenges health professionals may experience in developing collegial and culturally responsive relationships with Aboriginal colleagues. Informed by Aboriginal sources of knowledge, and particularly relevant to health care teams in rural and remote settings, these concepts also have broader relevance to the functioning of health care teams in general.

What We Can Learn from Indigenous Culture

Working with Aboriginal people as colleagues in a collaborative and understanding way seems to present as a mountain too high for many. It need not be so if we work collaboratively. For a non-Aboriginal health professional, engaging with the many unknowns associated with Aboriginal knowledge and ways of knowing and learning can be a daunting prospect. That is why there are Aboriginal identified positions in health care and health education teams. The Indigenous team members in those positions are often appointed for a dual purpose; primarily, to meet the standard requirements and duties of their position but also, importantly, to be available for everything else to do with Aboriginal culture, as required.

On the second point, speaking from personal experience, Aboriginal workers may be guarded about the role they play in the work environment when it comes to acting as a representative of their culture. Sometimes, for Aboriginal workers, local politics and cultural beliefs may preclude them from getting too involved in capacities outside their general professional roles and responsibilities. They must know and respect cultural, as well as professional boundaries and thus, practice in culturally safe, as well as physically, mentally and emotionally safe ways.

Cultural links in a collaborative sense are about being prepared to engage with knowledge systems to achieve understanding and then maintaining ongoing and meaningful systems of 'cultural praxis'. Cultural Praxis stems from general notions of praxis (distinct practices or customs) but with themes that relate specifically to Indigenous ways of knowing and learning. At the heart of cultural praxis is equity and parity of participation in decision making. Thus, 'cultural praxis' reflects the notions of Fraser (2008) that working towards greater equity involves holding together three interconnected social justice dimensions. Those dimensions are redistribution, recognition and representation, with close attention paid to the personal influences or embodied subjectivities (McNay, 2008) experienced by Aboriginal and Torres Strait Islander people, as well as the politics of emotion (Ahmed, 2004).

There is a vast interconnectedness of influences and established hegemonic biases affecting Aboriginal and Torres Strait Islander workers from the perspective of their non-Aboriginal colleagues. In the context of cultural praxis, these need to be identified, acknowledged, talked about, dismantled, reimagined, actioned and revisited. Martin Nakata (in McGloin, 2009) proposed locating oneself in both Indigenous (Aboriginal) and Western knowledge systems. In simple terms, it is about knowing where you are and where you stand; about a big 'knowledge map', the distinct features, the quicksand that might swallow you, the difficult areas that slow you down, the elements that obscure what is beyond, the blurred boundaries and the paths to negotiate. These concepts will be familiar to those who have attempted to find their way as part of an interprofessional health care team, especially in a rural and remote work environment with the added complexity of a cultural divide between team members, as well as with those needing care. When collaborating with Aboriginal co-workers and Aboriginal communities more broadly it is worthwhile to reflect on the numerous long-standing historical inequalities (Burke, Crozier, & Misiaszek, 2017) experienced directly and indirectly by Aboriginal and Torres Strait Islander people in an array of social, as well as professional domains.

It is important, therefore, to explore culturally sensitive strategies to support cross-cultural workplace collaboration. Indigenous Allied Health Australia (IAHA), an organisation that represents twenty-two different health professions, developed a culturally responsive framework based on six core capabilities embedded in a 'knowing, being, doing' context. The capabilities are: Respect for the centrality of cultures; Self-awareness; Proactivity; Inclusive engagement; Leadership; and, Responsibility and accountability (IAHA, 2015). These capabilities provide a structure and action plan for rural health care teams to work in a deeply collaborative and respectful way with Aboriginal health professionals for the benefit of all Australians. The IAHA framework has wider applicability, both within health care teams and for their engagement with communities more generally. Creating an environment that values diversity and welcomes Aboriginal and Torres Strait Islander health professionals has potential to increase the resilience of health care teams, with transformation of service delivery to meet the needs of individuals, families and communities.

Rural Practice Can Help Build Resilient Teams

There is a common perception that, because urban communities are more affluent and have greater access to resources and services, they are better than rural communities and, therefore, set the standard in health care. That perception can be challenged in terms of the inherent capacity of rural and remote people and communities to innovate in ways of delivering care, largely driven by necessity. Faced with a greater burden of disease and more limited health care resources, including workforce shortages, many rural practitioners and health care organisations explore creative solutions to ensure that their communities receive the care they need (Panagariya, 2014). This is in spite of, if not due to the unpredictable nature of rural life, including flood, fire, drought and, in the future, the ravages of climate change.

One of the greatest innovations in the delivery of health care to rural and remote Australians was the Royal Flying Doctor Service (RFDS). Pioneered by Reverend John Flynn in 1928 and first flying out of Cloncurry in Queensland, the service now covers virtually the entire continent. Interestingly, the RFDS was also the precursor to other fly-in fly-out (FIFO) models of care. The RFDS is highly regarded and provides an excellent service but FIFO has been referred to as a '*necessary evil*' (Hanley, 2012) and the question asked as to whether it is '*the panacea or the problem*' (Wakerman, Curry, & McEldowney, 2012). Flying specialised services into more remote population centres has obvious benefits in terms of access; however, the principal problem with FIFO, as well as with drive-in drive-out (DIDO) services, is that communities are reliant on a non-resident health workforce, so immediacy and continuity of care are still lacking. The further problem is that, although the FIFO and DIDO teams of health professionals may be effective, it is questionable whether they contribute to team-building and interprofessional leadership in the locations they visit. The valuable contributions of the FIFO and DIDO teams need to be backed-up with models of care that also support interprofessional team building and leadership development on the ground in relatively isolated, less well-served communities.

Rural practice is characterised by individuals with a common goal of ensuring sustainable local health service delivery, the withdrawal or absence of which can threaten the well-being of the entire community. In urban communities, if the hospital is closed or downgraded, or if the local general medical practice closes down, perhaps the worst outcome would be a longer journey by public transport to another hospital or general practice. In contrast, in rural and remote areas, the next nearest hospital may be hundreds of kilometres away, with no public transport available. Such challenges and potential threats build strong communities of resolute individuals, including committed health professionals who value each other's roles. Typically, rural health professionals practice in teams in which working and learning, as well as socialising together, often across professional boundaries, build a stronger sense of collegiality. When health professionals may be relatively isolated from their professional peers, the tendency is to rely on support or advice from those from another health profession. In the urban context, where there are more health professionals, each occupational group has great capacity and opportunity to form intra-professional rather than interprofessional relationships and teams.

Let us consider the style of leadership that might be appropriate to a situation where the workforce is transient and less permanent than in urban settings. While the team may share the common goal of providing health care to the community, as is the case in other contexts, individuals within the team may not share common professional attitudes, values and beliefs about how that goal might be best achieved. The leadership challenge, therefore, is how to bring disparate health professionals together so that common goals are represented in the way that the team works together. In real terms, consider how a rural or remote health service manager, who has their own particular professional affiliation and identity, might influence the performance of a team of rural health professionals, many of who are from a discipline other than their own.

In the late 1960s and early 1970s, Paul Hersey and Ken Blanchard developed a theory referred to as *situational leadership* (Hersey & Blanchard, 1969), the fundamental principle of which is that no single leadership style can be successfully applied in all circumstances. Leaders and managers need to be responsive to situations and being effective requires flexibility and a willingness to change style as needed. Hersey and Blanchard categorised leadership styles or behaviours as:

- *Telling*, where the leader or manager instructs the team with a unidirectional flow of information, the aim being to complete the task at hand safely and in a timely manner;

- *Selling*, where the idea is to open a two way communication aimed at convincing the team of the need to achieve the goal or complete the task;
- *Participation*, where decision-making is shared, with a more democratic approach and greater emphasis on relationship-building; and lastly,
- *Delegating*, where the manager or leader allocates tasks or duties, overseeing or monitoring activities, making sure the targeted outcomes are achieved.

According to Hersey and Blanchard, one behaviour is no better than the others; it is entirely situationally dependent. However, in a diverse interprofessional team in a small rural or remote health service, where team members may have considerable clinical experience, as well as competence and strong commitment, the more collegial and consultative leadership styles (*Participation* and *Delegation*) are perhaps likely to be more effective than the more authoritarian approaches (*Telling* or *Selling*). The particular situation is one where the capabilities of individual team members must be acknowledged and guided accordingly. The manager or leader is like the conductor of an orchestra, trusting in the ability of each member to deliver when called upon, even if their services are not always required. Thus, the situationally dependent challenge is to ensure that when those more transient practitioners are present, such as FIFO or DIDO service providers, they are integrated into the team effectively and are thus 'playing the same tune' as more permanent, locally-based team members.

Sustaining a Culture of Rural Collaborative Practice

The culture of an organisation, such as a health service, speaks to the way that things are done within that organisation. The development of a culture that values diversity and change is an essential element of leadership of interprofessional rural health care teams. Champions of interprofessional practice may come and go within a rural health organisation; however, individuals do not sustain teams that genuinely embody a culture of interprofessionalism. The culture needs to be embedded and enshrined in the vision and mission statement within the strategic plan of the organisation, so that even if the champion or champions move on, the culture of interprofessional collaboration is supported and sustained within a reconstituted team. Careful consideration should be given to how the vision and mission of the organisation are framed in order to represent the key elements of interprofessional collaborative practice. Although it is possible to tease-out generic aspects, it is also important to appreciate that each organisation is different and these differences also need to be acknowledged and represented among the team if the vision is to be sustained.

The World Health Organization (WHO) published a *Framework for Action on Interprofessional Education and Collaborative Practice* in 2010. In that document, collaborative practice is defined as '*when multiple health workers from different professional backgrounds provide comprehensive services by working with patients, their families, carers and communities to deliver the highest quality care across settings*' (WHO, 2010, p. 7). Part of the argument in the framework is that collaborative practice is most effective where care addresses and is organised around the target population's needs. Effective leadership of interprofessional rural health teams needs to value the uniqueness of the community it serves and respond according to defined community need.

It is sometimes said that, 'if you have seen *one* rural community, you have seen *one* rural community', meaning that they are all different in various ways. The generic aim is to create a 'collaborative practice-ready' health care team, while at the same time recognising that all rural communities are not the same and so the population needs may differ substantially from one community to another. For example, a coastal rural community with a high retiree population will have greatly different health care needs compared with an inland mining community. In a similar sense, no two teams are the same, whether because of the different disciplines represented within the team or because of the different individuals involved at different times. While diversity and change may be assured elements of rural practice, it is nevertheless possible to distil certain core components that contribute to the development of a sustainable culture of collaborative practice. These are summarised in Table 12.1, as informed by and formulated from multiple sources. Though perhaps not uniquely rural, they are certainly fundamental considerations in the rural

Table 12.1 Key elements, features and characteristics that support development and maintenance of interprofessional collaborative rural practice (D'Amour, Ferrada-Videla, San Martin Rodriguez, & Beaulieu, 2009; Lindeke & Block, 1998; Morris & Matthews, 2014; Norsen, Opladen, & Quinn, 1995; San Martín-Rodríguez, Beaulieu, D'Amour, & Ferrada-Videla, 2009; WHO, 2010)

Key elements	Features and characteristics
Defined community needs	• Familiarity with patient, family and carer populations and locally-relevant health care needs • Deep appreciation of local Indigenous health • Evidence-based indicators and predictors of need • Evaluation of health care outcomes
Staff education and training	• Sound foundational profession-specific knowledge and skills • Continuing development of interprofessional and cross-cultural competencies • Awareness and appreciation of practice roles and boundaries
Shared goals, attitudes, values and beliefs	• Valuing diversity and potential for change • Respect and trust between team members • Interpersonal communication and relationships • Welcoming environment for new, part-time and casual staff
Responsive situational leadership	• Participatory governance, with shared decision-making • Delineation of authority and accountability • Champions of, and advocacy for interprofessional collaborative practice • Awareness of organisational policies and politics
Targeted resourcing and built environment	• Adequate available resources and information technology • Alignment of resources with organisational and human needs • Physical representation of local Indigenous art and culture • Efficient use and equitable allocation of resources and funding • Shared, negotiated space and time

and remote context and are a useful guide to leaders of rural interprofessional health care teams.

Case Study—What to Do About Macaloo?

The following case study of the fictional town of Macaloo reflects our shared experiences of health service delivery in remote communities. While Macaloo does not really exist, the challenges and the joys of working in rural and remote locations such as Macaloo are very real. We invite you to make use of the comments at the end of the case study to help you contemplate how we as educators, managers, clinicians, planners and health policy makers can support the sustainability and resilience of rural health services and the communities they serve.

Macaloo is a small remote town 800 kilometres inland from the nearest metropolitan city on the Australian East coast. It has a population of 1300 people, approximately 60% of whom are of Aboriginal heritage and are a collective of several different Aboriginal nations in that area. The town was once prosperous in wool, cattle and cotton production. The effects of drought and advent of mechanised mega-farming has resulted in business closures, unemployment and families relocating to find work. The main land use is now large-scale cattle farming and open-cut coal mining. The mines have a mostly FIFO workforce accommodated on the mine site, so the town sees little of the financial benefit from the Macaloo mine.

The town still has one medical centre, with a sole doctor who trained in India and moved to Australia eight years ago. There is also an Aboriginal practice nurse and an Aboriginal Health Worker, both of whom grew up locally, a part-time physiotherapist who is married to a local farmer, and an Egyptian-born pharmacist who runs the chemist shop and works closely with the local doctor.

The Macaloo health services are supplemented by a DIDO chronic disease management team, which visits once per month to support people living with a range of metabolic and cardio-vascular conditions. This team includes a dietitian, exercise physiologist, diabetic educator and nurse coordinator. Because of the way their funding works, they are not able to see people with anything other than chronic diseases. There is also a FIFO paediatric team, which provides occupational therapy, speech pathology, psychology and audiology services for one week every three months. Children who are referred to this service must first been seen by the regional consultant paediatrician who flies in once every six months.

The medical centre is the hub for all health service delivery in the district and operates five and half days each week. Otherwise, afterhours, there is a telehealth service but, unfortunately, the technology is unreliable. There are no hospital beds in the town and no residential aged care or mental health services. For all in-patient care, local people must travel to the nearest rural hospital, which has 40 acute care and 24 aged care beds. It is over 200 kilometres away by road. For more complex inpatient care, patients must be evacuated to one of several metropolitan hospitals, the nearest of which is 850 kilometres away. The Royal Flying Doctors service operates an air transport service for urgent transfers.

For most of the Aboriginal population in the Macaloo district, barriers restricting timely engagement with health services in the larger centres are financial, suitable transport, concerns about being away from home and family, accommodation and the cultural insensitivity and judgemental attitudes of unfamiliar health service providers and other staff. For those health professionals who do work in the region, living in a rural or remote community and providing wrap around primary health services also comes with a range of challenges and barriers, so few stay for very long and recruitment is always ongoing. Their challenges include differing funding streams that make service integration difficult, a transient health workforce, with the exception of a few locals who experience 'change fatigue' due to the frequent personnel changes on the visiting teams, and difficulty accessing continuing professional development.

Therefore, it is important to remember that:

- Teams must actively intersect and engage to provide support to one another.
- The local population can be engaged in and become part of the team-based care in remote communities to minimise fragmentation of service delivery.

- Personnel changes provide challenges for collaboration. Visiting and resident teams must actively connect in order to provide high quality care in a high-need community like Macaloo.

Summary and Conclusion

Living and working in a rural and remote location presents health care challenges that have potential to strengthen the resilience of both individuals and teams. The construct of resilience, or the ability to successfully adapt to life's demands has moved beyond being considered a fixed personality trait to be re-conceptualised as a developmental pathway that can be enhanced via experience and over time (Luthar, Cicchetti, & Becker, 2000). Resilience is an important capability for the successful transition into practice for new graduates and, therefore, for sustaining the rural and remote health professional workforce. Indeed, this is why strategies such as the Australian Government's funding of the RHMT programme are important for future workforce development. However challenging, rural and remote health care provides a broad variety of professional development opportunities, including interprofessional collaborative practice and the development of cross-cultural competencies, which helps create highly capable and resilient practitioners.

References

Ahmed, S. (2004). *The cultural politics of emotion.* Edinburgh: Edinburgh University Press.

Alston, M. (2002). Social capital in rural Australia. *Rural Society, 12*(2), 93–104.

Australian Bureau of Statistics. (2016a). *Community profiles.* Retrieved June 16, 2019, from https://www.abs.gov.au/websitedbs/D3310114.nsf/Home/2016%20Census%20Community%20Profiles.

Australian Bureau of Statistics. (2016b). *The Australian Statistical Geography Standard (ASGS) Remoteness structure map of 2016 remoteness areas.* Retrieved April 10, 2018, from https://www.abs.gov.au/websitedbs/d3310114.nsf/home/remoteness+structure.

Australian Government Department of Health. (2018a). *Rural Health Multidisciplinary Training (RHMT) 2016–2018—Program framework.* Canberra: Department of Health. Accessed August 6, 2019. https://www1.health.gov.au/internet/main/publishing.nsf/content/rural-health-multidisciplinary-training-program-framework.

Australian Government Department of Health. (2018b). *Australian Statistical Geographical Classification—Remoteness Area (ASGC-RA).* Retrieved August 7, 2019, from https://www.health.gov.au/health-workforce/health-workforce-classifications/australian-statistical-geographical-classification-remoteness-area.

Australian Government Department of Prime Minister and Cabinet. (2019). *Closing the gap report 2019.* Canberra. Retrieved August 15, 2019, from https://ctgreport.pmc.gov.au/sites/default/files/ctg-report-2019.pdf?a=1.

Burke, P. J., Crozier, G., & Misiaszek, L. I. (2017). *Changing pedagogical spaces in higher education: Diversity, inequalities and misrecognition* (Kindle edition). London: Routledge.

D'Amour, D., Ferrada-Videla, M., San Martin Rodriguez, L., & Beaulieu, M.-D. (2009). The conceptual basis for interprofessional collaboration: Core concepts and theoretical frameworks. *Journal of Interprofessional Care, 19*(Sup1), 116–131.

Fraser, N. (2008). *Scales of justice: Reimagining political space in a globalizing world* (Kindle edition). Chichester: Wiley.

Frenk, J., Chen, L., Bhutta, Z. A., Cohen, J., Crisp, N., Evans, T., et al. (2010). Health professionals for a new century: Transforming education to strengthen health systems in an interdependent world. *Lancet 4, 376*(9756), 1923–1958. https://doi.org/10.1016/s0140-6736(10)61854-5.

Hanley, P. (2012). The FIFO conundrum. *Australian Journal of Rural Health, 20,* 48.

Hersey, P., & Blanchard, K. H. (1969). *Management of organisational behaviour: Utilising human resources.* Englewood Cliffs, NJ: Prentice-Hall.

Indigenous Allied Health Australia (IAHA). (2015). *Cultural responsiveness in action: An IAHA framework.* Canberra: IAHA.

Lindeke, L. L., & Block, D. E. (1998). Maintaining professional integrity in the midst of interdisciplinary collaboration. *Nursing Outlook, 46*(5), 213–218.

Luthar, S. S., Ciccheti, D., & Becker, B. (2000). The construct of resilience: Acritical evaluation of guidelines for future work. *Child Development, 71*(3), 543–562.

McGloin, C. (2009). Considering the work of Martin Nakata's 'cultural interface': A reflection on theory and practice by a non-indigenous academic. *Australian Journal of Indigenous Education, 38,* 36–41.

McNay, L. (2008). The trouble with recognition: Subjectivity, suffering and agency. *Sociological Theory, 26*(3), 271–296.

Morris, D., & Matthews, J. (2014). Communication, respect, and leadership: Interprofessional collaboration in hospitals of rural Ontario. *Canadian Journal of Dietetic Practice & Research, 75*(4), 173–179.

Norsen, L., Opladen, J., & Quinn, J. (1995). Practice model: Collaborative practice. *Critical Care Nursing Clinics of North America, 7*(1), 43–52.

Panagariya, A. (2014). The challenges and innovative solutions to rural health dilemma. *Annals of Neuroscience, 21*(4), 125–127.

Saggers, S., Walter, M., & Gray, D. (2011). Culture, history and health. In R. Thackrah & K. Scott (Eds.), *Indigenous Australian health and cultures* (pp. 1–21). Sydney, Australia: Pearson Australia.

San Martín-Rodríguez, L., Beaulieu, M.-D., D'Amour, D., & Ferrada-Videla, M. (2009). The determinants of successful collaboration: A review of theoretical and empirical studies. *Journal of Interprofessional Care, 19*(Sup1), 132–147.

Wakerman, J. (2004). Defining remote health. *Australian Journal of Rural Health, 12*(5), 210–214.

Wakerman, J., Curry, R., & McEldowney, R. (2012). Fly in/fly out health services: The panacea or the problem. *Rural and Remote Health, 12*(2), 2268.

World Health Organization (WHO). (2010). *Framework for action in interprofessional education and collaborative practice.* Geneva, Switzerland: WHO. Retrieved August 15, 2019, from https://www.who.int/hrh/resources/framework_action/en/.

13

Sustaining Interprofessional Collaboration in Brazil

José Rodrigues Freire Filho and Aldaísa Cassanho Forster

Introduction

This chapter presents the trajectory of interprofessional collaboration in health care in Brazil and discusses the most successful practices and challenges for promoting the sustainability of the model.

Universal health systems, which focus on comprehensive care, face the challenge of adopting strategies to improve interaction among professionals, with a view to providing care that is centred on the needs of patients and communities.

J. R. Freire Filho (✉)
Department of Social Medicine, University of São Paulo (USP); Regional Network for Interprofessional Education in the Americas (REIP), Ribeirão Preto, São Paulo, Brazil

A. C. Forster
Department of Social Medicine, University of São Paulo, Ribeirão Preto, São Paulo, Brazil
e-mail: acforste@fmrp.usp.br

D. Forman et al. (eds.), *Sustainability and Interprofessional Collaboration*,
https://doi.org/10.1007/978-3-030-40281-5_13

The debate on initiatives for enhancing interaction among health professionals began in the twentieth century, gaining visibility in the late 1970s through publications focused on multiprofessional approaches and proposals for implementing interdisciplinary education to promote collaboration among health professionals (D'Amour & Oandasan, 2004; Matuda, Aguiar, & Frazão, 2013).

Interprofessional collaboration is a way of working that involves professionals from different areas/specialties/professions who act in an interdependent, integrated manner with clearly defined functions, sharing a sense of teamwork, objectives, values, and responsibilities to meet the health needs of users, families, and communities, with the aim of providing patient-centred comprehensive care (D'Amour, Goulet, Labadie, San Martín-Rodriguez, & Pineault, 2008; Morgan, Pullon, & McKinlay, 2015; Reeves, Perrier, Goldman, Freeth, & Zwarenstein, 2013; West & Lyubovnikova, 2012; World Health Organization [WHO], 2010).

There is a set of core elements that health professionals must incorporate into their work dynamic in order to implement interprofessional collaboration. These are: sharing, partnership, power, and interdependence (D'Amour & Oandasan, 2005). Collaboration occurs only when professionals recognise that their work and practice is incomplete by its very nature and that collaboration through horizontal relationships geared towards users' needs will promote better health actions (D'Amour & Oandasan, 2005).

To obtain the desired health outcomes, interprofessional collaboration must extend beyond the team in a given sector; in other words, it must occur between different teams in a specific service or sector and between different services in the health care network and across sectors, to facilitate patient-centred comprehensive care (Agreli, Peduzzi, & Bailey, 2017; Agreli, Peduzzi, & Silva, 2016; Reeves et al., 2013).

Some authors identify two potential levels of collaboration among professionals: interprofessional collaborative practice, which occurs when collaboration is incorporated into health services' practice; and interprofessional teamwork, which is a deeper level of interprofessional work, with strong interdependence (Morgan et al., 2015). In this chapter, interprofessional collaboration will be discussed along with the achievements through mutual effort, dialogue, information-sharing, and joint action, resulting from training processes based on Interprofessional Education (IPE), all focused on solving the population's health problems (WHO, 2010) (Fig. 13.1).

Interprofessional collaboration and education are integrated and mutually influential in providing comprehensive care, as called for in universal health systems. In Brazil, an understanding of IPE and primary health care (PHC) practices provides input for implementing and consolidating the interprofessional collaboration model.

The framework of the structural model of interprofessional collaboration that approximates the Brazilian reality emphasises that collective actions can be analysed in respect of four dimensions and ten associated indicators involving relationships between individuals and the organisational settings which influence collective action. The four dimensions of this model that allow us to analyse interprofessional collaborative action are:

1. shared goals and vision;
2. internalisation;

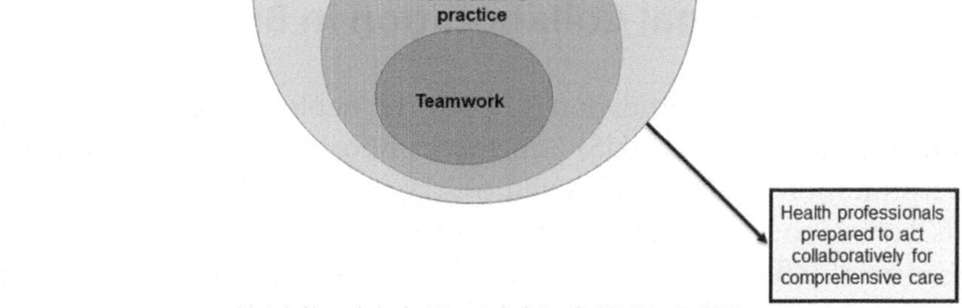

Adapted with permission from Morgan, S., Pullon, S., & McKinlay, E. (2015). Observation of interprofessional collaborative practice in primary care teams: An integrative literature review. International Journal of Nursing Studies, 52, 1217–1230

Fig. 13.1 Relationship between interprofessional collaboration, collaborative practice, and teamwork

3. formalisation and
4. governance.

To measure the shared goals and vision, which refers to the existence of common goals and their appropriation by the team, the predicted indicators are goals achieved and client-centred orientation vs. other allegiances.

For the internalisation dimension, which represents the awareness of professionals about their interdependencies and the importance of managing them, use indicators related to obtaining of mutual acquaintanceship and establishing trust.

The third dimension that refers to formalisation clarifies expectations and responsibilities and its indicators are the ability to establish formalisation tools and information exchange.

Finally, the fourth dimension, Governance, aims to guide and support professionals toward collaborative interprofessional and interorganisational practices with the indicators being centrality, leadership, support for innovation, and connectivity (D'Amour et al., 2008).

This model has viable characteristics for sustaining interprofessional collaboration, since it allows the development of educational activities through the use of IPE being established in a curriculum, making it permanent, as well as the governance function, which plays a strategic role in ensuring the sustainability of interprofessional collaboration.

Interprofessional Collaboration in Brazil

The constitutional foundation for Brazil's public health system—the Unified Health System (SUS)—includes important elements that favour interprofessional collaboration and education in health care, such as universal access to health, comprehensive care, social participation and team-based work (Barr, 2015; Ceccim, 2004; Costa, 2016). Based on the premise that 'SUS is interprofessional', its principles are recognised to be closely aligned with the theoretical and methodological frameworks of interprofessional collaboration and education, particularly with the advent of PHC, which has various health professions and social services work together on teams in the service delivery structure and in the daily tasks (Peduzzi, 2016; Starfield & Shi, 2002).

In Brazil, PHC is guided by the Family Health Strategy, which was first instituted in 1994 as the Family Health Programme. The strategy focuses on collaboration to reorient health care by increasing its response capacity (Costa, 2016; Pinto & Giovanella, 2018). Important aspects that sustained this strategy were the political and social movements to ensure its implementation in the national health model (Pinto & Giovanella, 2018). The Family Health Strategy has worked because it contributes to the expansion of PHC, along with institutionalisation of evaluation and promotion of equity and expansion of service provision, being a sustained model in Brazil. At a minimum, PHC includes a physician, nurse, technician or nursing auxiliary and community health workers, supported by other multidisciplinary teams, such as oral health, dental surgeons, auxiliaries, oral health technicians, and the Expanded Family Health Nucleus teams. These teams include social workers, pharmacists, physical therapists, speech pathologists, occupational therapists, physical educators, and psychologists, among others (Freire Filho, Forster, Magnago, Caccia, & Rivas, 2015; Matuda et al., 2013; Peduzzi, 2016; Starfield & Shi, 2002).

Therefore, Brazil has a PHC-focused health care model with interprofessional teams, in which users and their needs guide health promotion, disease prevention, and health recovery work. PHC is therefore the locus of best practice initiatives for sustainable interprofessional collaboration. In Brazil, PHC is still recent, as is the inclusion of interprofessional initiatives. However, PHC in the country is expected to support an interprofessional model, as this is the opportune space for the development of health collaboration (Giovanella & Mendonça, 2014; Starfield & Shi, 2002). Beyond PHC, there are other initiatives in mental health services and public hospitals (Câmara et al., 2016), which are also focusing on IPP.

Brazil has a tradition of implementing relatively advanced public policies for health and health education that are consistent with the needs of the population. These policies address important problems such as: hospital-centric and technician-focused teaching; proposed curricula based on the transmission of knowledge, with little incentive for critical and reflexive thinking; and training institutions distanced from the real issues in people's lives and health (Costa & Borges, 2015; Haddad et al., 2010, 2012). However, this tradition favours IPC because of initiatives that the country has historically had to transform its health and education model, such as the publication of the National Policy on Continuing Health Education, the implementation of interprofessional collaboration and education in the country, and the operationalisation of changes in health practices aimed at enhancing care (Peduzzi, Norman, Germani, Silva, & Souza, 2013).

One noteworthy event for introducing interprofessional collaboration and education in Brazil was the establishment of the National Policy on Continuing Education in Health, through the Minister's office of the Minister of Health Decree number 198/2004, which consolidated key elements for implementing health education from the perspective of teaching/health service/community integration. It recognises the national health system as a privileged space for shared learning by health professionals and students from the various areas of health, managers, and users of the services (Brasil Ministério da Saúde, 2018; Peduzzi et al., 2013).

Pursuant to the National Policy on Continuing Education in Health, different initiatives were created to ensure that the education and development of workers and health professionals is aligned with SUS principles of universality, comprehensiveness and equity in the health care system and, therefore, are suitable for teamwork. Two such examples are the Multiprofessional Health Care Residency Programme for Education through Labor for Health (PET-Saúde), both established through partnerships between the Ministry of Education and the Ministry of Health (Câmara & Pinho, 2015; Costa & Borges, 2015).

Multiprofessional residencies, formally established in 2005, are geared towards local and regional needs and situations and involve various health care professions in a single training process, with teaching activities carried out in the health services. PET-Saúde, a programme for education through work for health in turn, was established in 2008 to strengthen teaching/health service/community integration with the direct involvement of health care students in SUS services, through the formation of learning groups made up of students, professionals, and educators from different health care professions. Both initiatives provide an enabling environment for building interprofessional competencies (Brasil Ministério da Saúde, 2018; Câmara & Pinho, 2015). These IPE models in Brazil are expected to be sustainable, as they are being incorporated into the whole process of professional health education, being institutionalised by the country's government and applied at the institutional level, and included in the country's national plan to continue. The current edition of PET Saúde began in April 2019 and will end in 2021. The periodicity of the programme is biennial and there is a Brazilian network of education and interprofessional work (ReBETIS) that maintains the country's strong desire for change so that the IPC is sustainable, besides promoting champions in the theme.

Another significant move was the incorporation of IPE into an important legal framework: the National Curriculum Guidelines for undergraduate studies in medicine, published in 2014. The Guidelines explicitly state that the teaching-learning process for future medical professionals must include building competencies for teamwork, centred on integration and interprofessionality (Freire Filho, Costa, Forster, & Reeves, 2017). However, the expectation is that, starting with doctors, the IPE can be incorporated for all health professionals.

IPE-based initiatives for all health professions are found in the curricula of institutions of higher education in the states of Ceará, Rio Grande do Sul, Rio Grande do Norte, Rio de Janeiro, Minas Gerais, and São Paulo and in the Federal District, with most of the initiatives focused on teaching/health service/community integration processes, in connection with PHC. These experiences, have sparked a change in the health professionals' education for making shared learning spaces viable, demonstrating how it has been possible to strengthen teaching based on interprofessionality at the undergraduate and postgraduate levels in Brazil (Barr, 2015).

Interprofessional Collaboration Strategies Underway in Brazil

Brazil is striving to guarantee the sustainability of collaboration at the national level through the health care and the education systems since the SUS implementation to trigger processes of change and strength the SUS. Many of its efforts are the result of Brazil's track record, but they also respond to calls made by international health agencies.

The year 2016 marked a milestone in interprofessional collaboration and education in the Region of the Americas, through the active work done by the Pan American Health Organization (PAHO), which called on its Member States to study and discuss IPE at a technical meeting in Bogota, Colombia, where it encouraged countries to prepare a national action plan for implementing this approach (Pan American Health Organization [PAHO], 2017).

Starting in 2017, motivated by the agenda put forward by PAHO, Brazil's Ministry of Health gave priority to including guidelines on IPE in its health care professional training policies and education. It immediately promoted linkages with the Ministry of Education, institutions of higher education, and the ReBETIS to prepare Brazil's action plan for 2017 and 2018 (Brasil Ministério da Saúde, 2018).

The plan formalises the incorporation of IPE within the Secretariat of Management of Work and Education in Health agenda to strengthen the continuing education in health professions for practices that promote reflection on the work process and the construction of collaborative and meaningful learning activities. It was structured based on a compilation of the main educational initiatives underway in Brazil, to which the theoretical and methodological premises of IPE could be applied (taking into account the organisational structure of SUS) in order to strengthen interprofessional collaboration.

The plan made headway on strategic points for strengthening interprofessional collaboration and education in the context of health care education, training and work. This included professional development for teachers in IPE, mapping IPE initiatives in Brazil's institutions of higher education in health professions, dissemination and production of knowledge on IPE and collaborative practice. Along with this, encouragement of interprofessional collaboration and education in forums, where health professionals at both undergraduate and post-graduate level, receive continuing and permanent education (Silva, Cassiani, & Freire Filho, 2018).

The plan's developments include: publication of Resolution the National Health Council 569, of 8 December 2017, adopting Technical Opinion number 300/2017, which presents general principles including diversity of interdisciplinary practices and interprofessional teamwork in health care among others to be incorporated into the National Curriculum Guidelines for all undergraduate health care courses, to guide the development of curricula and teaching activities with an IPE approach; and publication of an edition of the journal *Interface-Comunicação, Saúde, Educação* [Interface: Communication, Health, Education] focusing on interprofessional collaboration and education in health (Brasil Ministério da Saúde, 2018; Costa, Freire Filho, Brandão, & Silva, 2018).

The framework for action to implement the IPE plan in Brazil was structured according to five action lines: strengthening IPE for the reorientation of undergraduate health care courses, analysis of IPE initiatives currently underway in the country, faculty development for IPE, enrichment of spaces for dissemination and production of knowledge on IPE, and including IPE within the context of health professional continuous education (Brasil Ministério da Saúde, 2018). The implementation process already has many advances, nevertheless, it is important to continue monitoring and evaluating the planning activities and status of the planned actions. Also, investing in processes that can approximate the relations between Ministry of Health and Ministry of Education is crucial for this process (Brasil Ministério da Saúde, 2018; Freire Filho & Silva, 2017).

Noteworthy was the Second Regional Technical Meeting on Interprofessional Health Education: Building the Capacity of Human Resources to Move Towards Universal Health, held from 5 to 6 December 2017, in Brasilia, DF. The event, organised by the Ministry of Health, together with PAHO/WHO, set a broad agenda for incorporating the subject into health education policies in the countries of the Region of the Americas and formalised the Regional IPE Network of the Americas (REIP), aiming to promote IPE and collaborative practice in health care in the Region of the Americas, with Brazil serving as representative of the executive secretariat for 2018–2021, together with Argentina and Chile (Silva et al., 2018).

With the development of Brazil's action plan, there was also the launch of the Health Education Innovation Laboratory in September 2017. This was a strategy that aimed to provide a flexible, useful and collaborative tool for information and knowledge exchange that will enable a descriptive analysis and evidence of successful and innovative experiences. The first round of this focused on continuing education in health and included IPE and practices as one of its themes. This initiative stemmed from the need to strengthen the links between IPE and the National Policy on Continuing Education in Health, which serves as the mechanism for dialogue with the base level of Brazil's educational and health systems. The aim of the Health Education Innovation Laboratory was to highlight national experiences in interprofessional practices currently underway and encourage their replication elsewhere.

Another major step forward in 2018 in terms of promoting the alignment of undergraduate courses in health with the theoretical-conceptual and methodological frameworks of IPE was the PET-Saúde/Interprofessionality decree, which states that the IPE should be incorporated into the curricula of all undergraduate courses in the health area, with activities of interactive learning with the community, targeting public and private non-profit institutions for higher education throughout Brazil (Oandasan & Reeves, 2005). This alignment occurs through the articulation between the educational institutions and the SUS. In this sense, it can be stated that the PET-Saúde/Interprofessionality initiative and the whole process for its implementation is considered as successful practices in Brazil for the establishment of a resilient health system that can generate sustainable public value, capable of supporting complex transformations in health through the establishment of effective collaborative practices. The Ministry of Health has provided technical and financial support to projects, programmes and public policies aimed at qualifying and adapting the workers' profile to social health needs, having as an axis the teaching-service integration to maintain the development of IPE in the country (França, Magnago, Santos, Belisário, & Silva, 2018).

Challenges for Interprofessional Collaboration in Brazil

In the Brazilian context, since the creation of SUS, there have been many initiatives to reorient the education of health professionals and the health care model. All have been aimed at enhancing health care work processes, through interprofessional collaboration, to provide comprehensive care consistent with users' needs. Nevertheless, to move this process forward in a more consolidated manner, interprofessional collaboration and education must be implemented in all entities involved in patient care. To sustain interprofessional collaboration in Brazil it is necessary to make it an integral part of the competencies of health professionals. Also, it is essential to make every profession recognise the role of the other, mitigating conflicts among them. And it is having the clarity that through interprofessional activities it is possible to improve resilience in the area of health (França et al., 2018; Ministério da Saúde, 2018). This process is still in the implementation level in the whole country.

The challenges to effectively implement interprofessional collaboration through IPE in Brazil can be analysed at three levels: macro, which demands sustainable policies for reorienting professional education, such as the National Curriculum Guidelines and PET-Saúde, and maintenance of the care model organised around interprofessional teams; mezzo, which includes implementation of curriculum designs, programmes, and components and proposes continuing education initiatives focused on building competencies for collaboration; and micro, which considers interpersonal and interprofessional relationships and interactions The success of interprofessional actions in the micro context and their systematisation will depend on coordination among the three levels, of which there are initiatives for the development of interprofessional competences among health professionals (Oandasan & Reeves, 2005).

The Ministry of Health, together with the Ministry of Education, pledges to coordinate, monitor, and support the measures taken at the mezzo and micro levels, taking into account the policies established at the macro level. However, despite the gains made, investment is still needed in a fundamental component of the macro dimension: regulation of health care work, which is still under development in the country. In this area, mechanisms for regulating scopes of practice need to be discussed and adopted by the ministries and professional boards, in order to move beyond traditional models of self-regulation and a strict biomedical approach, as well as isolated and independent professional work (Peduzzi, 2016).

Brazil has seen comparatively greater progress in interprofessional collaboration and practice in health services and in the daily work of professionals than in the area of teaching (Batista, 2012; Peduzzi et al., 2013; Silva et al., 2018). As a result, greater investment is needed today in initiatives that promote IPE in undergraduate and graduate programmes that educate health professionals, as has been done with the launch of strategic programmes of the Ministry of Health, such as PET- Saúde. In the coming years, this will guarantee that interprofessional collaboration in Brazil is sustained. It is important to mention that in interprofessional practice, initiatives sustained through the reality of work are those from permanent health education actions, such as those proposed with the inclusion of students and health professionals from different professions learning and practicing interprofessionality together. These interprofessional characteristics within Brazil's health system will facilitate the sustaining of interprofessional practice.

PET-Saúde, launched more than a decade ago, is one of Brazil's great innovations to sustain the interprofessional practice in the country. This programme presents evidence that the SUS is a health system that enables the development of sustainable interprofessional teams, due to its own conformation that involves different health professionals in practice. Besides this it allows the socialisation of students in the context of interprofessional health teams, as well as with patients, bringing benefits to the population. Research shows that having a team-friendly health system is essential to sustain interprofessional teamwork, and this is present in Brazil (Nuffer, Gilliam, McDermott, & Turner, 2015; Peduzzi, 2016; van Dijk-de Vries, van Dongen, & van Bokhoven, 2017).

To sustain the interprofessional activities in practice it is necessary to provide incentives for continuing education for the entire team. Therefore, it is crucial to provide excellent communication experience, conflict resolution, and shared decision-making with students, to maintain an ongoing relationship with interprofessional collaborative teams, and recognise sites and professionals who demonstrate exceptional performance in interprofessionally team-based care (Nester, 2016).

References

Agreli, H. F., Peduzzi, M., & Bailey, C. (2017). The relationship between team climate and interprofessional collaboration: Preliminary results of a mixed methods study. *Journal of Interprofessional Care, 31*(2), 184–186.

Agreli, H. F., Peduzzi, M., & Silva, M. C. (2016). Atenção centrada no paciente na prática interprofissional colaborativa. *Interface: Comunicação Saúde Educação, 20*, 905–916.

Barr, H. (2015). *Interprofessional education: The genesis of a global movement* (pp. 1511–1523). London: Centre for Advancement of Interprofessional Education.

Batista, N. A. (2012). Educação interprofissional em saúde: concepções e práticas. *Cad Fnepas, 2*(1), 25–28.

Brasil Ministério da Saúde. (2018). *Política Nacional de Educação Permanente em Saúde: o que se tem produzido para o seu fortalecimento?* Brasília: Secretaria de Gestão do Trabalho e da Educação na Saúde. Departamento de Gestão da Educação na Saúde, Ministério da Saúde.

Câmara, A. M. C. S., Cyrino, A. P., Cyrino, E. G., Azevedo, G. D., Costa, M. V. D., Bellini, M. I. B., ... Reeves, S. (2016). Interprofessional education in Brazil: Building synergic networks of educational and healthcare processes. *Interface: Comunicação Saúd, Educação, 20*(56), 5–8.

Câmara, A. M. C. S., & Pinho, D. L. M. (2015). A educação interprofissional no PET-Saúde: uma experiência de educação transformadora. *Cadernos de Educação, Saúde e Fisioterapia, 2*(3).

Ceccim, R. B. (2004). Equipe de saúde: a perspectiva entre-disciplinar na produção dos atos terapêuticos. In R. Pinheiro & R. A. Mattos (Eds.), *Cuidado: as fronteiras da integralidade* (pp. 259–278). Rio de Janiero: IMS-UERJ.

Costa, M. V. D. (2016). The interprofessional education in Brazilian context: Some reflections. *Interface: Comunicação Saúde Educação, 20*(56), 197–198.

Costa, M. V. D., & Borges, F. A. (2015). O Pró-PET-Saúde frente aos desafios do processo de formação profissional em saúde. *Interface: Comunicação Saúd. Educação, 19,* 753–763.

Costa, M. V. D., Freire Filho, J. R., Brandão, C., & Silva, J. A. M. D. (2018). A Educação e o trabalho interprofissional alinhados ao compromisso histórico de fortalecimento e consolidação do Sistema Único de Saúde (SUS). *Interface: Comunicação Saúd, Educação, 22*(Suppl. 2): 1507–1510.

D'Amour, D., & Oandasan, I. (2004). *Interdisciplinary education for collaborative, patient-centred practice: Research and findings* (Report) (pp. 64–98). Ottawa, ON: Health Canada.

D'Amour, D., & Oandasan, I. (2005). Interprofessionality as the field of interprofessional practice and interprofessional education: An emerging concept. *Journal of Interprofessional Care, 19*(Suppl. 1), 8–20.

D'Amour, D., Goulet, L., Labadie, J. F., San Martín-Rodriguez, L., & Pineault, R. (2008). A model and typology of collaboration between professionals in healthcare organizations. *BMC Health Services Research, 8*(1), 188.

França, T., Magnago, C., Santos, M. R. D., Belisário, S. A., & Silva, C. B. G. (2018). PET-Saúde/GraduaSUS: retrospectiva, diferenciais e panorama de distribuição dos projetos. *Saúde Em Debate, 42,* 286–301.

Freire Filho, J. R., Costa, M. V. D., Forster, A. C., & Reeves, S. (2017). New national curricula guidelines that support the use of interprofessional education in the Brazilian context: An analysis of key documents. *Journal of Interprofessional Care, 31*(6), 754–760.

Freire Filho, J. R., Forster, A. C., Magnago, C., Caccia Bava, M. C. G. C., & Rivas, N. P. P. (2015). Trabalho em equipe: uma análise a partir dos Núcleos de Apoio à Saúde da Família da microrregião de saúde de Passos/Piumhi. *MG. Revista Cereus, 7*(2), 169.

Freire Filho, J. R., & Silva, C. B. G. (2017). Educação e prática interprofissional no SUS: o que se tem e o que está previsto na política nacional de saúde. In R. R. C. Toassi (Ed.), *Interprofissionalidade e formação na saúde: onde estamos?* (pp. 28–39). Porto Alegre: Rede Unida.

Giovanella, L., & Mendonça, M. H. M. D. (2014). Atenção primária à saúde. In L. Giovanella, S. Escorel, L. V. C., Lobato, J. C., Noronha, & A. I. Carvalho (Eds.), *Políticas e sistema de saúde no Brasil* (pp. 493–545). Rio de Janeiro: Editora Fiocruz.

Haddad, A. E., Brenelli, S. L., Cury, G. C., Puccini, R. F., Martins, M. D. A., Ferreira, J. R., & Campos, F. E. D. (2012). Pró-Saúde e PET-Saúde: a construção da política brasileira de reorientação da formação profissional em saúde. *Revista Brasileira de Educação Médica, 36*(1, Suppl. 1), 3–4.

Haddad, A. E., Morita, M. C., Pierantoni, C. R., Brenelli, S. L., Passarella, T., & Campos, F. E. (2010). Formação de profissionais de saúde no Brasil: uma análise no período de 1991 a 2008. *Revista de Saúde Pública, 44,* 383–393.

Matuda, C. G., Aguiar, D. M. D. L., & Frazão, P. (2013). Cooperação interprofissional e a Reforma Sanitária no Brasil: implicações para o modelo de atenção à saúde. *Saúde E Sociedade, 22,* 173–186.

Ministério da Saúde. Secretaria de Gestão do Trabalho e da Educação na Saúde. (2018, October 31). *PET-Saúde divulga resultado final dos projetos selecionados.* Retrieved from http://portalms.saude.gov.br/noticias/sgtes/44588-pet-saude-divulga-resultado-final-dos-projetos-selecionados.

Morgan, S., Pullon, S., & McKinlay, E. (2015). Observation of interprofessional collaborative practice in primary care teams: An integrative literature review. *International Journal of Nursing Studies, 52*(7), 1217–1230.

Nester, J. (2016). The importance of interprofessional practice and education in the era of accountable care. *North Carolina Medical Journal, 77*(2), 128–132.

Nuffer, W., Gilliam, E., McDermott, M., & Turner, C. J. (2015). Sustainability of a practice-based interprofessional introductory pharmacy practice experience course. *American Journal of Pharmaceutical Education, 79*(5), 62.

Oandasan, I., & Reeves, S. (2005). Key elements of interprofessional education. Part 2: Factors, processes and outcomes. *Journal of Interprofessional Care, 19*(Suppl. 1), 39–48.

Pan American Health Organization. (2017). *Interprofessional education in health care: Improving human resource capacity to achieve universal health report of the meeting*. Bogota, Colombia, December 7–9, 2016. Washington, DC: PAHO.

Peduzzi, M. (2016, March). O SUS é interprofissional. *Interface: Comunicação Saúde Educação* (Botucatu), *20*(56), 199–201.

Peduzzi, M., Norman, I. J., Germani, A. C. C. G., Silva, J. A. M. D., & Souza, G. C. D. (2013). Interprofessional education: Training of health professionals for teamwork focused on users. *Revista Da Escola de Enfermagem Da USP, 47*(4), 977–983.

Pinto, L. F., & Giovanella, L. (2018). Do Programa à Estratégia Saúde da Família: expansão do acesso e redução das internações por condições sensíveis à atenção básica (ICSAB). *Ciência & Saúde Coletiva, 23,* 1903–1914.

Reeves, S., Perrier, L., Goldman, J., Freeth, D., & Zwarenstein, M. (2013). Interprofessional education: Effects on professional practice and healthcare outcomes. *Cochrane Database of Systematic Reviews, 28*(3), CD002213.

Silva, F. A. M. D., Cassiani, S. H. D. B., & Freire Filho, J. R. (2018). A Educação Interprofissional em saúde na Região das Américas. *Revista Latino-Americana de Enfermagem, 26,* e3013.

Starfield, B., & Shi, L. (2002). Policy relevant determinants of health: An international perspective. *Health Policy, 60*(3), 201–218.

van Dijk-de Vries, A., van Dongen, J. J. J., & van Bokhoven, M. A. (2017). Sustainable interprofessional teamwork needs a team-friendly healthcare system: Experiences from a collaborative Dutch programme. *Journal of Interprofessional Care, 31*(2), 167–169.

West, M. A., & Lyubovnikova, J. (2012). Real teams or pseudo teams? The changing landscape needs a better map. *Industrial and Organizational Psychology, 5*(1), 25–28.

World Health Organization. (2010). *Framework for action on interprofessional education and collaborative practice.* Geneva: WHO.

14

Building and Sustaining Student Leadership in IPE: Experience with the Knowledge and Skills Exchange

Emily Audet, Christine Hirsch, Kalyaani Vickneswaran, Mehmuna Ayub, Mahisa Arain, Travis Norton, and Sharon Buckley

Introduction

Student-led IPE occurs when healthcare students:

> *design, deliver and evaluate events and activities that bring their peers together to "learn about, from and with each other" to enable effective collaboration and improve health outcomes.* (adapted from Hoffman, Rosenfield, Gilbert, & Oandasan, 2008; World Health Organization, 2010)

E. Audet
Shrewsbury and Telford Hospitals NHS Trust, Shrewsbury, UK

C. Hirsch · M. Ayub · M. Arain · S. Buckley (✉)
University of Birmingham, Birmingham, UK
e-mail: S.G.Buckley@bham.ac.uk

K. Vickneswaran
Royal Wolverhampton NHS Trust, Wolverhampton, UK

T. Norton
University Hospitals NHS Foundation Trust, Birmingham, UK

D. Forman et al. (eds.), *Sustainability and Interprofessional Collaboration*,
https://doi.org/10.1007/978-3-030-40281-5_14

IPE societies are an important component of student-led IPE and can range in scope from the institutional to the national (Aberdeen IPE Society, 2018; Global Health Workforce Alliance, 2019). Since 2015, we have worked to build and sustain the Knowledge and Skills Exchange (KASE), an IPE society for health professions students at our own institution. The University of Birmingham offers pre-registration training for a range of health professions, including dentistry, dental hygiene and therapy, medicine, nursing, physiotherapy, pharmacy, clinical psychology and, relatively new to the UK context, physician associate. Via the University Guild of Students, trainee health professionals can access many different academic, sporting and recreational societies. Whilst many of these attract members from different faculties and programmes across the university, KASE is the first student society to focus on enabling its members to understand their and others' professional roles, to communicate across boundaries and to learn from each other's skills.

The last five years have been an exciting and, occasionally, frustrating journey for us, as we have sought to establish, grow and sustain KASE. We hope that our experience and insights, illustrated throughout this chapter by our individual comments and reflections, will inspire you to start your own dynamic society for the benefit of trainees and the patients they will care for.

Establishing the Knowledge and Skills Exchange (KASE)

In June 2015, the University of Birmingham hosted a national student conference for the UK Centre for the Advancement of Interprofessional Education (CAIPE). Inspired by this event, medical student, Emily Audet, and nursing student, Hayley Lawley, shared their desire to expand IPE opportunities for Birmingham students with Sharon Buckley, Chair of the university Interprofessional Education steering group:

> *I was saddened by the modest number of medical students attending interprofessional events and dismayed at hearing inaccurate assumptions about doctors and medical students from other healthcare professions. I wanted to*

> *bring healthcare students together to help overcome the cultural barriers that were becoming apparent to me as I gained more clinical experience. I believed that introducing IPE at a student level would prepare us for better multi-disciplinary working once qualified.* (Emily, medical student, founder and KASE president 2015–17)

Sharon acted as a catalyst for discussion by introducing Emily and Hayley to a pharmacy student completing an IPE-related final year project and to a dental student active in a group working to promote the United Nations Sustainable Development Goals (United Nations Department of Public Information, 2015); and the founding committee was born:

> *Together we (four) formed the nucleus of the new student society. A varied group with diverse experience and ideas of how the society could work, our first challenge was to agree aims and common goals, then develop a name and mission statement that encompassed these.* (Emily)

After two lively brainstorming sessions, the group agreed that the Knowledge and Skills Exchange (*KASE*) captured their mission to '*bring healthcare students together for better patient care*'; and that KASE's goals were to provide opportunities for all Birmingham healthcare students to share experiences, whilst improving their understanding of each other's professional roles. KASE would also aim to promote good cross-profession communication and relationships, to enhance collaborative practice and patient safety, and to generate ideas for projects for the betterment of the local community and advancement of IPE. The group held an 'Introduction to Birmingham's Healthcare courses' presentation and 'Question and Answer' session, at which they publicised their work and elicited student views on these aims. Attendees were enthusiastic about the society's direction and several students from programmes not previously represented joined the group (Fig. 14.1).

Growing the Knowledge and Skills Exchange

Once established, the founding group worked hard to build the society by holding themed clinical workshops, arranging regular volunteering

Task	Students	Faculty
Engage an enthusiastic nucleus of students	• Discuss ideas with course colleagues and friends • 4-6 students representing different health professions	• Run events that expose students to IPE concepts • Students may self-select themselves as advocates of IPE • Approach likely students and encourage involvement
Engage faculty support	• Identify and contact institutional IPE champion(s)	• Suggest/facilitate resources and opportunities through external events
Generate initial aims and identity	• Brainstorm and draft aims in writing • Research other student societies	• Review and comment on draft aims if invited
Refine the group and its function	• Hold an initial event for students to introduce society and gain feedback	• Assist students with funding for snacks and consumables, publicity and rooming

Fig. 14.1 Summarises practical steps for students and faculty to establish a student IPE society

opportunities in the community and organising an interprofessional team-building weekend away, together with the University's first Healthcare Team Challenge. They created a formal committee with defined structure and roles and worked with the Guild of Students to establish KASE as a recognised student society.

Capitalising on members' strengths, interests and networks, the committee offered a variety of educational and fun activities that appealed to students across healthcare programmes:

> *With the University of Birmingham United Nations Sustainable Development Goals Society, I organised regular volunteering with the Midland Langar Seva Society (MLSS). Interprofessional teams of students helped to distribute food to homeless people in the city, after which volunteers socialised together. These events were always oversubscribed and have run regularly since the establishment of KASE.* (Mehmuna, dental student and KASE Volunteering and Communications Lead 2016–19)

The group often used topical themes as the basis for activities, timing them to coincide with national events:

> *I organised a KASE event to coincide with World Tuberculosis Day 2018. Participants learned about TB and explored the patient experience of having the illness; and different KASE members contributed their professional expertise to the discussion.* (Travis, nursing student and KASE President 2017–18)

Previous experience of IPE events also informed activity choice, particularly the weekend away and Healthcare Team Challenge, which proved to be a major success for the society; and which resulted in a significant increase in KASE membership (see Box 14.1).

As leaders of an official Guild society, KASE committee members had access to a bank account, insurance, university-wide publicity channels and other facilities that enabled the society to grow. Meeting Guild requirements proved to be a challenge, but one that the committee considered worthwhile:

> *Complying with Guild regulations proved challenging, as committee members were often away from campus on clinical placement. Despite this, the benefits outweighed the difficulties and linking with an institutional body is something that I recommend wholeheartedly.* (Kalyaani, medical student and KASE secretary 2016–19)

Faculty supported KASE enthusiastically from its inception, attending committee meetings as needed and inviting members of the committee to join the University's IPE steering group. This proved to be a collaboration with major advantages for both parties:

As members of the IPE steering group, we can promote KASE events to all healthcare programmes and have better access to event space, funding, staff support and resources. We give student input, opinion and feedback to faculty-led IPE initiatives. KASE members have co-facilitated IPE events with staff, including a series of half day interprofessional simulations, and a 'Health-care, teams and IPE' introductory event for all incoming health professional students. (Travis) (Fig. 14.2)

Box 14.1 The KASE weekend away and healthcare team challenge 2017

The KASE leadership applied to the university Alumni Impact Fund, which supports student projects on a competitive basis; and used their £2000 award to arrange a team-building weekend away and Healthcare Team Challenge at the University outdoor activity centre in the Lake District, a UK national park. The event attracted students not previously involved with the society and brought together twenty-six students from eight different professions.

Over three days, four interprofessional teams worked together to problem solve, attempt physical challenges and complete domestic chores. Organisers challenged teams to generate and present a holistic care plan for a patient with complex needs in readiness for a HealthCare Team Challenge to be held on campus 10 days later. In evaluation, participants reported that their understanding of the challenges that other health-care professionals face had increased, as had their respect for other professions; that they had learned more about themselves and others and planned to continue their interprofessional learning. Organisers reported benefits to committee cohesion and team working; and increased confidence in their own leadership and resilience:

> *As a final year medical student with clinical exams looming, leading the weekend away and Team Challenge was sometimes hard for me. The very positive feedback from participants and my own enjoyment in juggling the competing demands on my time, gave me confidence in my ability to cope that has transferred into my clinical work.* (Emily)

Task	Students	Faculty
Create a programme of events	• Include a variety of educational and social activities, taking into account student availability and interests • Consider a high profile event e.g. Team-building Weekend Away, Healthcare Team Challenge • Make full use of committee's strengths, interests and networks • Look for funding opportunities	• Offer expertise in organising and running events • Suggest options in the university or affiliated organisations e.g. sporting and outdoor pursuits venues • Suggest sources of funding and assist with preparation of applications
Work with others	• Learn from other student societies; consider joint events • Link to national events e.g. health awareness days • Work with local societies to offer interprofessional volunteering opportunities	• Suggest societies and organisations of interest, and broker introductions
Contribute to faculty-led events	• Facilitate teaching sessions, simulations, ethical dilemma workshops, conferences, patient safety events	• Integrate student-led IPE into formal IPE teaching and events • Advocate with faculty on behalf of the group
Advertise events widely	• Establish a society identity and branding • Use all available channels for publicity	• Assist distribution of promotional materials • Promote the society to other faculty

Fig. 14.2 Summarises practical steps for students and faculty to grow their nascent student IPE society

	• Set-up and use society social media e.g. Twitter, Facebook, Apps etc.	
Build formal committee structures	• Join the institutional union or guild • Hold team-building events to build cohesion and skills • Role model collaborative working • Learn each other's strengths	• Offer expertise in organising and running events • Offer constructive feedback on activities and events

Fig. 14.2 (continued)

Sustaining the Knowledge and Skills Exchange

The founding group worked to ensure society sustainability in various ways, the most influential of which was continuing to offer an exciting programme of activities, particularly the ever popular community volunteering. KASE publicised events as enjoyable opportunities for development and provided certificates of participation for professional portfolios. Assisted by faculty, KASE members contributed to a UNESCO funded project to develop bioethics scenarios (University of Birmingham, 2017) and, in 2018, had the opportunity to share their KASE experience at All Together Better Health IX IPE conference (Powell et al., 2018). Participant feedback and suggestions for new events informed choice of activities; being mindful of the capacity and limitations of committee members was essential:

> *Our guiding principle was to do a few events, but do them well so that, over time, the reputation of KASE as a lively and effective society would grow.* (Mahisa Arain, dental student and KASE events co-ordinator 2016–19)

More prosaically, two committee members recruited from each programme helped to provide the continuity so essential to sustainability:

We planned always to have two representatives (from each programme) on the committee, one junior and one senior. This improved representation at meetings and meant that, for example, when one nursing student graduated, there would still be a nursing student on the committee whilst we recruited another, more junior, individual. The bigger committee also allowed us to develop additional roles, sharing work and opportunities with a larger group. (Emily)

The Guild of Students requirement to have a minimum number of paying members also supports sustainability:

We offered paying members free access to events and also prioritised them for events with limited space. This encouraged attendance and contribution. (Mahisa)

Sustaining a student IPE society is an ongoing challenge and cyclical levels of interest and activity are to be expected. Our experience is a powerful example of the importance of teamwork and leadership for continued survival and growth:

KASE has now existed for over four years, long enough for us to see fluctuations in its vibrancy as the interest, enthusiasm and capabilities of student organisers wax and wane; and to witness the importance of committee teamwork and leadership in building a resilient society: teamwork to avoid 'single point of failure' and leadership to harness the enthusiasm and energy of members to good effect. (Sharon Buckley, IPE lead and KASE faculty support) (Fig. 14.3)

What Have We Learned?

Through reflecting on our experiences (Driscoll, 1994) and in the context of others who have followed the same journey, we have articulated the benefits and challenges of IPE societies as a vehicle for student leadership of IPE; and considered how such societies might grow and develop in the future.

Task	Students	Faculty
Plan for succession	• Include one junior and one senior committee member from each programme • Establish annual budget and funds by: membership, affiliation to Student guild etc.	• Promote the society opportunities to programmes • Advise on formal tasks • Expect fluctuations in activity, support as needed
Promote membership	• Attend institutional student fairs/inductions • Consider a membership fee • Offer members' benefits: free events, priority etc.	• Establish and maintain communication channels with programmes
Build local reputation	• Establish popular events in a society calendar • Consider fewer events, done well • Advertise activities as opportunities for professional development • Generate certificates for participation • Vibrant social media presence • Link with local charities and organisations • Gain and act on event feedback	• Advocate for the society • Offer opportunities for curriculum development projects, research and evaluation • Recognise student engagement • Help maintain student energy
Build wider reputation	• Link to organisations with student chapters e.g. CAIPE • Attend conferences and events to share experience and ideas	• Support student conference attendance and events • Share information about upcoming interprofessional events • Suggest and support participation in curriculum development

Fig. 14.3 Offers practical ways to build a sustainable student IPE society

We have found that the relaxed learning and social environments that KASE offers, away from the rigours of professional programmes, foster IPE outcomes well, including open communication, appreciation of the value of teamwork and collaboration and commitment to culture change:

> *Great opportunity for discussion and sharing ideas, learning from one another's ideas and experiences.* (Participant, End of Life Care event)

> *I want to break the barriers between different healthcare professionals.* (Participant, weekend away and Healthcare Team challenge)

Not only have participants reported skills development from KASE events, but naturally, as committee members took ownership of different roles and events, they too developed a multitude of professional, personal and team-work skills. They acquired competence and confidence in leadership:

> *I have been impressed at the transformative effect that leading IPE had upon those individuals involved – seeing students grow in confidence and insight.* (Sharon)

> *I developed skills in writing funding applications, presenting to large dynamic groups of people, teaching, events organising, chairing a committee, writing and creating academic presentations and submitting work to international conferences. I have learned that I am most comfortable with leading in a collaborative way, that taking into account the perspectives of my colleagues is very important to me and that my approach is completely different to that of the traditional 'heroic' leader.* (Emily)

And in their ability to build their own resilience and that of the society:

> *Volunteering is a regular event and, as volunteering lead, I have learned to delegate tasks through simple, reproducible instructions so that others can lead these outings when I am unavailable. Following a spate of last-minute*

cancellations, I discussed with the committee ways of improving student commitment and of managing an event with reduced numbers. I generated a waiting-list system and began to contact students who missed events without sending apologies. Through tackling these issues with committee and students, I have gained confidence in problem-solving and in having difficult conversations with my peers. (Mehmuna)

It is evident that these benefits are starting to carry forward into practice, particularly for the founding group, who are now early career clinicians:

With *KASE*, *I developed better understanding of other healthcare roles in the care of my patients, whilst gaining confidence in how my own professional role complements others delivering care.* (Mahisa)

Being part of KASE improved my understanding of other healthcare roles, and thus my confidence in communicating within the multidisciplinary team, facilitating more appropriate and timely patient referrals. (Travis)

I am now more comfortable approaching different healthcare professionals for help in the clinical environment, which increases the pool of knowledge and experience that I can draw from to provide good patient care. My experience has motivated me to look for opportunities in clinical education as I progress through my career. (Kalyaani)

I saw the enthusiasm and collaboration among the group; witnessed the skill and leadership of Emily and Travis and the commitment and expertise of other committee members. I watched a small group of students turn into 30+ students, all committed to the cause of progressing IPE and collaborative practice; who I felt sure would be standard bearers for culture change in their organisations when they qualified. (Sharon)

And, for some, has led to unexpected opportunities:

This experience has given me the confidence, motivation and skills to take on big team and leadership challenges within healthcare. I now Chair the interprofessional expert advisory board of a national charity. (Emily)

> *We worked with Sharon and Christine to represent the University of Birmingham and present our work at the All Together Better Health IX conference in New Zealand. This gave us experience in the team-work and collaboration involved in co-production of presentations and papers.* (Kalyaani)

Witnessing the work of KASE has influenced faculty perceptions too:

> *Working with a group of enthusiastic students who shared our ideals and aspirations for IPE at Birmingham was a great motivator for staff involvement. It fosters a stronger IPE team-working approach when developing our programme of IPE activities and provides a level of vibrant energy that connects with the student body and sustains and motivates the supporting faculty.* (Christine Hirsch, IPE pharmacy programme lead)

> *Through working with KASE, I have greater awareness of the importance of integrating students into IPE development and implementation. I was very positive about the society and keen to support in any way that I could. I felt that some suggested ideas were rather over ambitious – I was proved wrong on several occasions.* (Sharon)

Our experiences resonate with those of others, including the value of informal environments offered by student led IPE (Rosenfield, Oandasan, & Reeves, 2011; VanderWielen, Do, et al., 2014; VanderWielen, Enurah, Osburn, LaCoe, & Vanderbilt, 2013) and opportunities to overcome curricular, financial and attitudinal barriers that often limit faculty-led initiatives (Chicorelli et al., 2016; Curran, Deacon, & Fleet, 2005; Hoffman et al., 2008; Sunguya, Hinthong, Jimba, & Yasuoka, 2014); by generating IPE advocates, a source of student-feedback and collaboration, and student volunteers (Bridges, Davidson, Odegard, Maki, & Tomkowiak, 2011; Hoffman et al., 2008; Sunguya et al., 2014). We agree that student-led activities may allow students to challenge assumptions more effectively, whilst also promoting more socialisation and peer-respect than institutional-led initiatives (Cooper, MacMillan, Beck, & Paterson, 2009; Hoffman et al., 2008; VanderWielen, Do, et al., 2014); we echo the experience of Hoffman and colleagues that student-led IPE provides early exposure to multidisciplinary team working, a powerful preparation for future practice (Hoffman et al.,

2008). It will be interesting and instructive to witness how student attitudes change with time as their practice and acculturation into their professional careers progress.

The challenges we experienced also reflect those of others (Chicorelli et al., 2016; Cooper et al., 2009; Hoffman et al., 2008), with the exception of lack of faculty support and difficulties in appealing to culturally diverse student groups (Chicorelli et al., 2016; Hoffman et al., 2008), which were not problems that KASE experienced. Timetabling, placement and assessment differences across programmes skewed profession participation in events to an extent that the committee did not anticipate; and complying with Guild regulations for student societies, though it gave valuable support, was unexpectedly time consuming for students who were often away from the campus on clinical placement. Over time, faculty and students came to appreciate the reserves of energy, commitment and time needed to ensure that KASE remained a lively and vibrant society, resonating with the experience of Sunguya and colleagues (2014). We have found that, through coping with these challenges, committee members have developed better resilience.

> *Organising committee, planning events and encouraging participation to a level where KASE was a continuously active group was a task that I worked on for 2 years alongside working towards my medical degree. It took persistence and stamina, and taught me the importance of delegation. As a Foundation Doctor I have felt better prepared in managing my time and energy: performing my clinical duties, ensuring a strong training portfolio and then taking on extra opportunities to further support my personal and professional development.* (Emily)

> *As KASE secretary I was constantly ensuring that I was up to date with paperwork and deadlines, this required regular communication with the KASE committee and the Student Guild. I learnt to organise and prioritise my time between my degree course requirements and outstanding KASE tasks. I feel I am now in a better position to cope efficiently with the demands of working and training as a Junior Doctor.* (Kalyaani)

Whilst the society has achieved many of its aims, some remain an aspiration:

We hoped to establish the weekend away and Healthcare Team Challenge as a recognised KASE annual event. However the alumni fund was a 'one-off' and we continue to look for other funding to support the establishment of a legacy event. (Travis and Christine)

Since the society's inception, collaboration with faculty has provided a valuable network of support for meeting the challenges associated with establishing, growing and sustaining KASE:

Early identification of challenges was essential for KASE to establish itself as a successful student-led society that could withstand an ever changing student population. This has been achieved through the close collaboration between students and staff, who facilitated and shared expertise, offered guidance on events and mentored us through the process from developing an identity to advising us on funding applications and abstract submissions. (Kalyaani)

The success of collaborative student and faculty IPE projects has been highlighted by Bridges et al. (2011). We have found that support from faculty staff has been essential in enabling the process of establishing, growing and sustaining KASE, and helping overcome barriers. Other literature also emphasises the importance of faculty support for student-led IPE, to help overcome challenges such as resource location, funding, recruitment and sustainability (Hoffman et al., 2008; Sunguya et al., 2014; VanderWielen, Do, et al., 2014; VanderWielen, Vanderbilt, et al., 2014).

KASE in the Future

We anticipate that sustainability for KASE will be an ongoing challenge, funding being a major issue in today's climate of competition for resources to support extracurricular activities. Campaigning by faculty to gain top-down support will need to be matched by creativity from the society to overcome this inevitable hurdle:

Through widening participation in student-led IPE, there could be greater incentive for institutional financial support. We are exploring giving formal accreditation for time spent delivering or participating in interprofessional events, and supporting the development of formal leadership skills for the KASE committee. We hope that this will improve incentive for those considering participating in IPE and further encourage KASE membership and recruitment to the committee supporting sustainability. (Sharon)

Individuals representing views of patients, carers and other users of the healthcare services have recently started working with the IPE steering group to provide additional perspectives on care, and we hope that these representatives will start to work with KASE.

At present, KASE stands alongside a wide range of traditional uniprofessional student societies offering activities for students from specific healthcare programmes and fostering a sense of professional identity. Whilst there will always be a place for these societies, we look to a future in which a society for healthcare students from all programmes is predominant, so that collaborative learning is seen as the norm, within which particular professional specialisms flourish. A national Healthcare Student Society, with chapters in different universities, as in Canada (Global Health Workforce Alliance, 2019) is a model to which we aspire and we hope that, in the long term, KASE makes a contribution towards realising this vision.

As our experience grows, so will our understanding of how to overcome challenges. We will continue to learn, develop and adapt to achieve KASE's goals and to facilitate culture change in healthcare for the benefit of all:

It is essential to support students in their autonomous IPE activity. It is today's students who will be the change agents of the future and they will be more effective in this if they themselves are convinced not only of the importance of collaborative practice, but also how to do it. (Sharon)

Acknowledgements We would like to thank Hayley Lawley (nursing), Rajdeep Banga (dentistry), Ekra Gul (pharmacy) and Alice Warner (physician associate), founders and committee members of KASE for their commitment and expertise in making the society a success; the UK Centre for the Advancement of Interprofessional Education (CAIPE) for a travel scholarship for Kalyaani Vickneswaran to attend All Together Better Health IX; and the faculty of the University of Birmingham for its support and encouragement of KASE events and conference attendance.

References

Bridges, D., Davidson, R, Odegard, P. S., Maki, I., & Tomkowiak, J. (2011). Interprofessional collaboration: Three best practice models of interprofessional education. *Medical Education Online, 16,* 6035. https://doi.org/10.3402/meo.v16i0.6035.

Chicorelli, J., Dennie, A., Heinrich, C., Hinchey, B., Honarparvar, F., Jennings, M., ... Livingston, L. A. (2016). Canadian student leaders' perspective on interprofessional education: A consensus statement. *Journal of Interprofessional Care, 30*(4), 545–547. https://doi.org/10.3109/13561820.2016.1159187.

Cooper, B., MacMillan, B., Beck, R., & Paterson, M. (2009). Facilitating and evaluating a student-led seminar series on global health issues as an opportunity for interprofessional learning for health science students. *Learning in Health and Social Care, 8*(3), 210–222. https://doi.org/10.1111/j.1473-6861.2008.00212x.

Curran, V., Deacon, D., & Fleet, L. (2005). Academic administrators' attitudes towards interprofessional education in Canadian schools of health professional education. *Journal of Interprofessional Care, 19*(1), 76–86. https://doi.org/10.1080/13561820500081802.

Driscoll, J. (1994). Reflective practice for practise. *Senior Nurse, 13,* 47–50.

Hoffman, S., Rosenfield, D., Gilbert, J., & Oandasan, I. (2008). Student leadership in interprofessional education: Benefits, challenges and implications for educators, researchers and policymakers. *Medical Education, 42,* 654–661. https://doi.org/10.1111/j.1365-2923.2008.03042.x.

Powell, E., Norton, T., Vickneswaran, K., Ayub, M., Arain, M., Hirsch, C., & Buckley, S. (2018, September). *Building an interprofessional society using a team-building weekend away and student-led healthcare team challenge: Experience and lessons learned.* Abstract ID: 1173 All Together Better Health IX, Auckland.

Rosenfield, D., Oandasan, I., & Reeves, S. (2011). Perceptions versus reality: A qualitative study of students' expectations and experiences of interprofessional education. *Medical Education, 45*(5), 471–477. https://doi.org/10.1111/j.1365-2923.2010.03883.x.

Sunguya, B., Hinthong, W., Jimba, M., & Yasuoka, J. (2014). Interprofessional education for whom?—Challenges and lessons learned from its implementation in developed countries and their application to developing countries: A systematic review. *PLOS One, 9*(5), e96724. https://doi.org/10.1371/journal.pone.0096724.

VanderWielen, L., Do, E., Diallo, H., LaCoe, K., Nguyen, N., Parikh, S., ... Dow, A. (2014). Interprofessional collaboration by health professional students: A case study of the inter health professionals alliance at Virginia Commonwealth University. *Journal of Research in Interprofessional Practice and Education, 3*(3). https://doi.org/10.22230/jripe.2014v3n3a132.

VanderWielen, L., Enurah, A., Osburn, I., LaCoe, K., & Vanderbilt, A. (2013). The development of student-led interprofessional education and collaboration. *The Journal of Interprofessional Care, 27*(5), 422–423.

VanderWielen, L., Vanderbilt, A., Dumke, E., Do,. E., Isringhausen, K., Wright, M., ... Bradne, M. (2014). Improving public health through student-led interprofessional extracurricular education and collaboration: A conceptual framework. *Journal of Multidisciplinary Healthcare, 7,* 105–110.

World Health Organization. (2010). *Framework for action on interprofessional education and collaborative practice.* World Health Organization. https://apps.who.int/iris/handle/10665/70185.

Websites

Aberdeen IPE Society. (2018). *About us.* Available at https://aberdeenipesociety.webs.com/about-us [Accessed 1/8/19].

Global Health Workforce Alliance. (2019). National health sciences students' association. Vancouver, Canada: World Health Organization. Available at www.who.int/workforcealliance/members_partners/member_list/nhssa/en [Accessed 1/8/19].

United Nations Department of Public Information. (2015). Sustainable development goals knowledge platform. *Sustainable Development Goals.*

United Nations. Available at https://sustainabledevelopment.un.org/sdgs [Accessed 1/8/19].
University of Birmingham. (2017). *UNESCO bioethics cases.* Available at https://www.birmingham.ac.uk/research/activity/unesco-bioethics/projects/Interprofessional-Bioethics-Cases.aspx [Accessed 7/19].

15

Building and Sustaining Patient and Community Partnerships in Interprofessional Education

Angela Towle, William Godolphin, Cathy Kline, and Darren Lauscher

Introduction

Trends in health care such as consumerism, the increased need for chronic care, and more involvement of patients in decision-making, provide powerful reasons to involve patients[1] in the education of health professionals (Towle et al., 2010). In order for students to acquire the knowledge, skills, and especially the attitudes and behaviours, to put

A. Towle (✉) · C. Kline
Patient & Community Partnership for Education & Department of Medicine, University of British Columbia, Vancouver, BC, Canada
e-mail: angela.towle@ubc.ca

W. Godolphin
Patient & Community Partnership for Education & Department of Pathology & Laboratory Medicine, University of British Columbia, Vancouver, BC, Canada

D. Lauscher
Patient & Public Member, UBC Health Council, University of British Columbia, Vancouver, BC, Canada

D. Forman et al. (eds.), *Sustainability and Interprofessional Collaboration*,
https://doi.org/10.1007/978-3-030-40281-5_15

collaborative patient-centred care into practice, patients must become a core part of interprofessional education (IPE). Although examples of patient involvement in IPE have appeared in the literature (Brault et al., 2016) most innovations and initiatives are described only in their initial stages (Towle et al., 2010). We do not know whether the effort expended in their implementation results in long-term programmes or what the key factors are that promote sustainability. In this chapter we describe factors that have sustained the work of the Patient and Community Partnership for Education (PCPE) unit at the University of British Columbia (UBC), Canada, from university and community perspectives. For 15 years we have designed, implemented and evaluated multiprofessional and interprofessional educational initiatives that aim to give patients and community members the power to educate students without the mediation and control of faculty and to put patients at the centre of the education process in a way that enhances their authentic and autonomous voices (Towle & Godolphin, 2015).

A Model of Sustainability

Our conceptual framework is derived from that developed by Shediac-Rizkallah and Bone (1998) for community-based health programmes, and subsequently modified by Vogel (2009) for her study on sustainability of service-learning programmes. Although there are some important differences between community-based health programmes and educational programmes, such as the involvement of learners, Shediac-Rizkallah and Bone's (1998) framework is the most referenced, inclusive framework for summarising empirical studies on sustainability. Vogel defined three degrees of sustainability: durability; routinisation/institutionalisation; and adaptability (see Fig. 15.1). Both Shediac-Rizkallah and Bone (1998) and Vogel (2009) found three major groups of factors to be influential in sustainability: factors in the broader community environment; programme design and implementation factors; factors within the organisational setting. We use these groupings to categorise facilitating factors and barriers to sustainability for our work (see Fig. 15.2).

Durability: programme continues without additional sources of support at an institutional level; it survives but has not grown and may have shrunk.

Routinization / institutionalization: programme continues within an organizational structure. Routinization occurs when a programme has become a stable and regular part of an organization's routine activities; institutionalization has the characteristics of routinization but also includes policy and infrastructure support.

Adaptability: programme has led to other initiatives within the institution and beyond.

Fig. 15.1 Definitions of degrees of sustainability

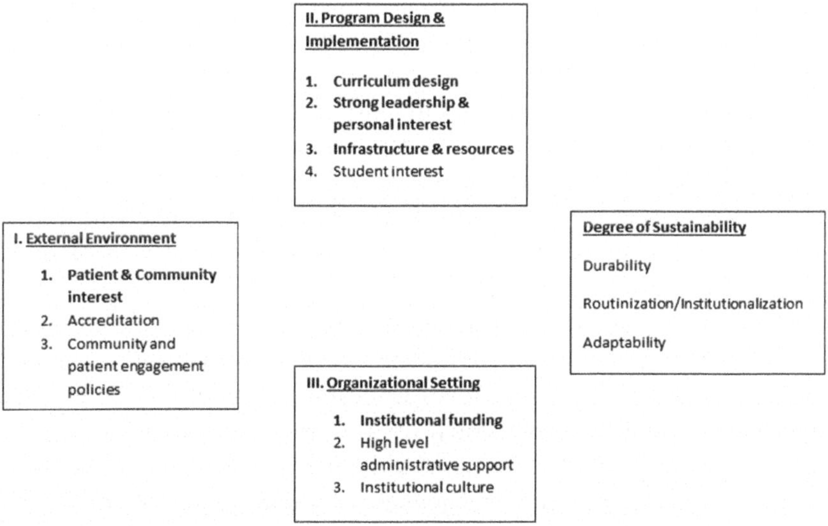

Fig. 15.2 Factors of most importance in our work according to the conceptual framework for sustainability (*Note* These are factors that others have found to be important. The ones most important in our work are bolded)

Our Work in Patient/Community Involvement from 2005 to 2019

Our first patient and community involvement in education initiative arose out of research we conducted into the difficulties that Indigenous people have with health care communications, with funding from the Ministry of Health targeted at 'special', i.e. underserved, populations. When we asked Indigenous informants for a solution, they said that health professionals should 'come and spend time with us'. Our first community pilots were in summer 2005, and a long-term partnership with Sto:lo First Nation started in 2006 (Kline, Chhina, Godolphin, & Towle, 2013). In what we call the 'Community as Teacher' programme students learn alongside Aboriginal youth at summer camps led by Elders, youth workers and cultural leaders. These continue despite several changes in leadership at the community level. Since the programme began over 200 students from 13 different health professional programmes have participated.

In 2005 we organised an international conference: 'Where's the patient's voice in health professional education?' At that time, we were beginning to realise that patient involvement in education is key to promoting truly patient-centred care and shared decision-making. This entails changing attitudes towards patients so that they are viewed as experts with experiential knowledge and partners in care. The conference, in Vancouver, brought together many isolated pioneers in moving from patient as passive to active participant in the education of health professionals (Farrell, Towle, & Godolphin, 2006).

At the conference we heard about a number of successful models of 'Patient Centres' that led us to explore the concept of a Community Centre for Health Professional Education that would address challenges faced by health professional programmes such as facilitating and strengthening patient involvement and interprofessional collaboration. The project resulted in the engagement of a core group of community organisations, students and faculty to contribute to and support a vision for community-campus partnerships and guiding principles.

This initiative laid the foundations for a three-year project funded by the UBC Teaching and Learning Enhancement Fund (TLEF) that resulted in the Patient and Community Voices (PCV) workshop series and the Patient & Community Fair. The PCV workshops are designed by community members, with input from faculty and students, and are led by a panel of patients/caregivers who share with students their unique medical experiences and health care expertise (Towle & Godolphin, 2013). Learning outcomes depend on the workshop topic (e.g. mental health peer support, stigma and HIV, communicating with people with aphasia or hearing loss). Each workshop has 20–30 students from multiple programmes. The initial four workshop topics have now expanded to eight and new ones continue to be developed, some as student projects. From offering workshops on an ad hoc one-off basis we now offer a series that has become integrated into the occupational therapy curriculum. The Fair was an annual one-day event that ran from 2009 to 2014 attended by students between, or instead of, classes. Between 20 and 40 community organisations had a booth to display information, and several one-hour patient panels were held on various topics throughout the day (Towle, Godolphin, & Kline, 2015).

In 2010 we began planning our interprofessional Health Mentors Programme (HMP) and admitted the first cohort of 90 students in 2011. The HMP is a longitudinal programme in which teams of four students from different health professions learn from and with a mentor who has a chronic condition or disability, or is a caregiver (Towle et al., 2014). The goals of the programme are to learn about living with a chronic condition from the patient's perspective and to develop interprofessional competencies. Since 2011, over 200 mentors have taught over 1500 students from 12 different professions; 50 mentors have taught three or more cohorts.

In 2012 the 'Special Populations' fund changed parameters to focus on postgraduate medical education. This opportunity led us to develop a programme of activities to involve patients and community organisations in teaching health advocacy. Initial research led to a grant-funded project to develop, implement and evaluate a workshop for postgraduate trainees. The workshop is currently being adapted for students in physiotherapy, occupational therapy and pharmacy with a TLEF grant.

Not all health professional students are able to participate in the programmes described above. A two-year TLEF grant (2017–2019) allowed us to expand opportunities for student experiential learning from patients. One result has been the creation of a Living Library, a flexible on-line resource consisting of video-vignettes of patients and caregivers talking about their health care experiences that can be integrated into existing curriculum. We are also responding to increasing requests for patient involvement in curricula in different health professional programmes.

Examples of Factors Important for the Sustainability of Our Work

External Environment

Patient and Community Interest

Initial and ongoing interest and commitment from individual patients and community organisations has been critical. Without that none of our work would have been possible. From our early community consultations about a Community Centre, it was clear that the public want to see a shift in training so that health professionals work in partnership with patients and other health professionals. Partnership requires health professionals to recognise the expertise of others, understand patients' lived experiences, take a holistic approach, be non-judgmental, and be more sensitive to cultural and language barriers (Kline, Asadian, Godolphin, Hewitt, & Towle, 2018). Being able to shape the hearts and minds of the next generation of health professionals is an intrinsically attractive idea to patients and community members.

Individual patients value and want to strengthen the Canadian health care system that provides universal access to publicly funded health services. Patients are motivated by their desire to give back and the internal gratification of 'knowing you are making a difference'. Feedback from students provided to patients directly through conversations, through unsolicited personal acknowledgement from students in private e-mails and thank-you notes, or through PCPE (e.g. at support meetings) shows them how they influence the students' thinking. In turn the patients' own thinking is broadened as they learn. Recognising the accumulated knowledge a patient holds and building on intrinsic motivation is more sustainable than creating a fee-based, transactional service in which a patient is hired to stand in front of students and tell their story. Involvement in education can be a 'foot in the door' of the university: with long-term involvement other doors open, new opportunities arise.

The mission statement of many patient advocacy organisations includes reference to the education of health professionals, citizens, board members, policy makers and funders. For community organisations, engaging with the university is seen as a good thing to do and offers both short and long-term benefits. In the short-term such community-university partnerships validate the work of organisations, are viewed favourably by funders and have direct benefits to their members (e.g. personal growth, empowerment). It allows organisations to involve their volunteers outside of the agency to keep them engaged while taking them out of their disease and reconnecting them with the world.

In the long-term there is the promise of better health care provided by health professionals who are more responsive to community needs. Sustained partnerships provide an opportunity for community agencies to garner further contacts in the university for other collaborative activities (e.g. summer student placements, or research partners). Although there is recognition of the value of combining expertise and incentives to foster relationships with the university that may lead to other opportunities, maintaining these relationships requires commitment and is taxing for community organisations. Many are under-funded and under-resourced when it comes to participating in large-scale, ongoing educational activity. It requires capacity to keep these relationships alive and build new ones and they have to decide how much effort to put in—is it a one off or has it long term potential that needs to be built into work plans?

Accreditation

An external factor that has been useful in our context is the introduction of requirements for IPE in Canadian accreditation standards for health professional programmes. This imperative has prompted faculty to increase IPE and provides an opening to promote/include our patient engagement interprofessional activities in the opportunities they offer students in otherwise over-full curricula.

However, there are tensions associated with playing the IPE accreditation card. To meet requirements programmes want to offer all students the same opportunities. We do not have the capacity to deliver high quality patient-centred learning experiences for all students, nor is it desirable for these experiences to be mandatory. It is critical that we offer a variety of options.

Community and Patient Engagement Policies

National and international movements to involve patients in health services and research affect sustainability indirectly, providing a rationale for the importance of patient engagement in education (Towle et al., 2016). Many patients involved in our work also participate in multiple health-related engagement activities through different organisations and projects. Because of their long-term engagement in building knowledge around their condition, patients are often better informed than some of their providers. They have networks of peers they can draw from, not just their own lived experience, and can bridge silos between service delivery, research and education. We hear that workplaces value students with these patient-centred experiences that set them apart from the many good candidates they are able to choose from.

A parallel movement of relevance to our work has been the increased public scrutiny of higher education, leading universities to reaffirm their dedication to preparing students for engaged citizenship, to changing social and economic inequalities, and to contributing to their communities as place-based institutions (Fitzgerald, Bruns, Sonka, Furco, & Swanson, 2012). In many universities community engagement has become integrated into the core mission of teaching and research, and institutional commitment is manifest through their strategic plans. Such has been the case in the last two UBC strategic plans.

Programme Design and Implementation

Curriculum Design

Various aspects of curriculum design have been key factors in ensuring the sustainability of our work. We categorise them into: purpose and philosophy; design and governance principles; variety and flexibility; and quality assurance. Some of these aspects are not only important for sustainability of programmes within the academy but for sustainability of patient and community interest.

Purpose and Philosophy

Our work is underpinned by the intent to educate students to practice shared decision-making with their patients in a multiprofessional and interprofessional context (Brault et al., 2016). We focus on the patient as a uniting lens for IPE, reinforcing collaborative practice via real life experience. Unlike most IPE that is competency based, the nature of learning in our programmes is cognitively ill-defined, not prescriptive; most is in the affective domain and transformative. Because our work is based on principles and values, it allows flexibility with respect to educational activity and promotes sustainability in the face of circumstances beyond our control (e.g. if funding is reduced, or curricula change).

Design and Governance Principles

Putting shared decision-making into practice we follow the principle of involving students, faculty, and patients/community in everything we do, though we are flexible in the ways of getting input. Co-creation of the educational design ensures relevance and buy-in. Another principle is that learning experiences that involve relationship development are elective. In-depth longitudinal relationships with patients such as occur in the HMP are not for all students—they are at different stages in readiness to learn in the affective domain. A requirement to participate by reluctant students would be disruptive and the kiss-of-death for sustainability. A third design principle is the autonomous and authentic voice of the patient as teacher with students in small groups to facilitate discovery, with faculty in a supporting role to ensure genuine patient-centred learning, consistent with our philosophy.

Variety and Flexibility

Students have a wide variety of interests and ways they want to learn, hence the importance of providing a variety of learning opportunities from one-off workshops, to an immersive three days (cultural camps), to a longitudinal experience (HMP). Grounding the offerings in a common purpose means that students learn similar things even though delivery is different. Variety in patient mentors is also important for rich student learning, e.g. having a large mix of chronic illnesses, and a diverse range of persons across culture, ethnicities and sexual identities.

In our experience, flexibility is important for sustainability from the perspective of patients and students. It allows for different levels of commitment depending on patient interests, availability, life or health circumstances. Flexibility in curriculum design provides freedom for exploration on the part of patients and students and promotes ownership of learning. For example, a success of the HMP is the generous time frame for meetings and reflective journaling and the flexibility to accommodate scheduling problems incurred by students or mentors. The HMP manual is non-prescriptive; it provides a starting point for further discussion.

Quality Assurance

Quality programmes lead to positive experiences and increase the likelihood that students, faculty and patients will want to keep them going. We take a scholarly, evidence-informed approach to curriculum design that leads to rigour and quality. We look at other models of active learning, conduct needs assessments, and evaluate both short and longer term outcomes. We innovate and learn through small-scale pilots. All our programmes have ongoing mechanisms to obtain feedback from students, faculty and patients so that we can monitor and maintain quality. Our connections with the community (relationships and conversations) are structured so we already have a vetting process before people become involved in our programmes since organisations know their volunteers and they and peers can make recommendations. The staff of organisations are best suited to recruit and support patients as they know their members' skills and abilities, special needs, individual circumstances, and readiness to participate. We have a rigorous selection process for the HMP that has resulted in high quality mentors who have impressed faculty with their enthusiasm and wealth of expertise. As a consequence the HMP has been our 'flagship success' and marked a turning point in the sustainability of our work. Students were enthusiastic, and when faculty read the honest and authentic student reflections they became champions. It raised our profile and credibility. The publications and presentations that result are also important for recognition of our work locally and beyond (e.g. Cheng & Towle, 2017; Towle et al., 2016; Ruitenberg & Towle, 2015).

Strong Leadership and Personal Interest

Strong leadership has been identified as an important factor in implementing all educational innovation, including partnering with patients (Brault et al., 2016). In our case leadership came from two faculty members who were recognised leaders in the field of shared decision-making. Between them they had different but vast experience in educational design, delivery, innovation, grant writing and scholarship. Through previous leadership roles they had forged many connections with faculty in the different health programmes and earned credibility in their own institution (social capital). Their leadership was based on a clear vision of patients as educators, underpinned by a set of guiding principles. The solid goal/philosophy (informed, shared decision-making) allowed them to talk to others about our rationale and use as a lens for others and ourselves (touchstone).

Infrastructure and Resources

Of critical importance to the sustainability of university-community engagement is the broker or boundary spanning role (Weerts & Sandmann, 2010) to manage and maintain connections with both the community (individual patients and organisations) and the academy. Our unit (consisting of two faculty co-directors, two full-time staff and one or two student staff) plays this role and is the holder of many relationships. We have adopted a number of approaches to build and maintain community relationships that foster long-term commitment for sustainability. Regular community consultations and dialogues, and the Patient and Community Fair (made possible because of community interest) have resulted in large and growing number of community contacts (patient groups, non-profits). A monthly newsletter has created a sense of being part of an active community even though an individual's involvement may be episodic. The continuity role our unit plays maintains relationships with organisations when staff turn over.

We have developed over time a pool of experienced patient educators and provided acknowledgement of their contributions in the form of certificates, photos, awards, and support meetings, as well as immediately accessible support when things are not working. The relationships we have with patients allow us to be sensitive to their cycles of wellness and know when they are interested in deeper involvement or unable to meet commitments to the programme. We manage difficult situations such as when mentors become too ill to continue or die, supporting their students and also honouring those who have died. Sharing one's story takes a toll and we need to be mindful of the burnout factor and/or life getting in the way. We recruit new mentors each year to replenish the pool as well as increase diversity, and we find alternative roles that patients may play if they are unable to be a health mentor. We go to great lengths to involve patients/community in co-presenting (e.g. at conferences, research rounds) and co-authoring publications. Sharing power deepens their investment in us and creates deeper levels of commitment from community.

Our wide community connections and engagement expertise is available as a central resource to the health professions faculty, reducing the burden for faculty who are trying to involve patients on their own but do not have, or only have restricted, relationships with the community.

Student Interest

Students play important roles in sustainability through their interest, motivation and feedback on positive experiences. Students recognise the limits to textbook and classroom learning; patients are able to tie in the current real-world events that affect their lives, bring out-of-the-box thinking into the mix of textbook learning or provide a 'real case study'. They reinforce the classroom teachings but also highlight that there are sometimes different perspectives. Students are inspired when they learn about the lived experience of health and health care from patients in a setting where they are not responsible for their care or providing a service, and in a safe environment where they can ask sensitive questions and explore difficult topics. They contrast it to drier ways of learning IPE such as contrived case-based learning or on-line modules. They also want opportunities that set them apart from peers and better prepare them for the workplace. Through reading student reflections (that are not defined or scored according to a rubric but simply provide a basis for conversation) faculty recognise and value the power of these experiences with patients and how it results in learning at the affective level. In patient-led IPE, students are focused on the patient and the contributions of their profession to their care, rather than on professional identities or hierarchies. The patient experience thus unites students in ways that are meaningful and constructive rather than competitive.

Organisational Setting

Institutional Funding

Sustainability would be impossible without institutional funding. We took advantage of small amounts of money available on a regular basis for educational innovation through the university. For example, the Teaching and Learning Enhancement Fund, a low-barrier fund for educational innovation, and the Equity Enhancement Fund for community-based initiatives that enhance equity, diversity, and inclusion at UBC. Although short-term, these funds forced us to be nimble and do pilots, to be continually innovating. The challenge has been to find funding to sustain these successful innovations when project funding ends. The Ministry of Health Special Populations fund gave us stable funding over a number of years for our work with indigenous communities and other marginalised populations. Over the past few years we have received institutional funding from UBC Health on an annual basis to partially cover the costs of our patient engagement activities because we have been able to demonstrate the benefit. However, we have not yet secured permanent ongoing funding for our work. We have made several unsuccessful attempts to work with university fund raisers to find support from corporate or alumni donors, though we still believe there are missed opportunities.

High Level Administrative Support

There is a central body that provides coordination across all the health and human service programmes at UBC and that is the home for IPE. Although the institutional identity of this body has changed over the years it has given us a permanent home and infrastructure and some financial support. Its leaders have supported and encouraged us, and facilitated relationships with health professional programmes. However, turnover of leadership and key faculty resulted in loss of champions at several levels and the need to re-make the case for our work every few years. High level support and institutional funding are critical to community organisations because it signals how much effort will likely be put into maintaining this outside relationship.

Institutional Culture

Institutional culture is made manifest through university policy. UBC has made commitments through its strategic plan to Community Engagement and Student Transformative/Experiential Learning. Both these commitments are relevant to our work and legitimise what we do. In demonstrating its commitment the institution provides opportunities for us to present our work, through news stories and presentations at showcase events. Sustainability is enhanced if you are able to hitch your wagon to whatever relevant institutional policies there are, including re-using the same words as appear in strategic plans. We have also shaped policy, for example by facilitating development of the UBC Health Patient Engagement Framework that generated recommendations approved by the UBC Health Council (leaders from all the health professional programmes). We have subsequently used these recommendations to legitimise our work, so setting the path for future sustainability. In another example, establishment of a named award (the Kerston award) in 2014 to honour outstanding patient and community educators who have made a difference to student learning at UBC, triggered an institutional change when it became included in the work of the central awards committee. Recognition of need for patient/community members on that committee to judge the award led to patient/community membership on other committees.

Conclusions

The strengths of our work that contributed to sustainability were: building trust between university and community; high quality programmes; strong relationships with leaders /significant champions in the university and community; student evaluations; culture of safety; constant efforts to evaluate, disseminate and publish. Adaptability was essential to sustainability, not just an outcome. Working with the community drives ways of adapting (few people in the community can afford to provide long-term commitment like the HMP but more people can show up for a one-off interview with a student). Sustainability has also been due to the resilience of the volunteer patients who had the strength and support to live with their chronic conditions and are dedicated to helping students learn despite their own health problems. Their resilience is matched by that of PCPE members who have persisted in their vision and found creative ways to overcome challenges, and who have had the fall-back of regular jobs and/or tenure if their experiments were unsuccessful.

Overall the barriers to the sustainability of our work came from inside the institution; environmental factors were facilitating. Barriers included: competing institutional priorities; systemic problems with IPE such as scheduling, funding, assigning credit and extra workload; curriculum changes; turnover of faculty. We had to work continually to raise and maintain the profile of our work, but it was hard to find time for marketing and engaging with faculty when we were busy innovating and seeking funding.

In conclusion, our key messages for the sustainability of patient and community involvement in IPE are: the importance of relationships at different levels (student-patient; PCPE-organisation); long term commitment leading to other opportunities for involvement of the community and academy; reciprocity (mutual benefits); and the importance of creating positive experiences.

Note

1. We use the word 'patient' as an umbrella term to include people with health conditions (service user, client, consumer, etc.), their caregivers (including carers, parents and family members) and others with relevant lived experience (community member, citizen or lay person).

References

Brault, I., Vanier, M.-C., Dumez, V., Towle, A., Godolphin, W., Pittenger, A. L., ... Collins, L. (2016). Partnering with patients in interprofessional education in Canada and the USA: Challenges and strategies. In D. Forman, M. Jones, & J. Thistlethwaite (Eds.), *Leading research and evaluation in interprofessional education and collaborative practice* (pp. 329–353, Chapter 16). Basingstoke, Hampshire, UK: Palgrave Macmillan.

Cheng, P. T. M., & Towle, A. (2017). How patient educators help students to learn: An exploratory study. *Medical Teacher, 39,* 308–314.

Farrell, C., Towle, A., & Godolphin, W. (2006). *Where's the patient's voice in health professional education?* Vancouver: Division of Health Care Communication, University of British Columbia. ISBN 0-9782028-0-5.

Fitzgerald, H. E., Bruns, K., Sonka, S. T., Furco, A., & Swanson, L. (2012). The centrality of engagement in higher education. *Journal of Higher Education Outreach and Engagement, 16,* 7–27.

Kline, C., Asadian, W., Godolphin, S., Hewitt, C., & Towle, A. (2018). From "academic projectitis" to partnership: Community perspectives for authentic community engagement in health professional education. *Engaged Scholar Journal, 4,* 79–96.

Kline, C. C., Chhina, G. S., Godolphin, W. J., & Towle, A. (2013). Community as teacher model: Health profession students learn cultural safety from an Aboriginal community. *Michigan Journal of Community Service Learning, 20,* 5–17.

Ruitenberg, C. W., & Towle, A. (2015). "How to do things with words" in health professions education. *Advances in Health Sciences Education, 20,* 857–872.

Shediac-Rizkallah, M. C., & Bone, L. R. (1998). Planning for the sustainability of community-based health programmes: Conceptual frameworks and future directions for research, practice and policy. *Health Education Research, 13,* 87–108.

Towle, A., Bainbridge, L., Godolphin, W., Katz, A., Kline, C., Madularu, I., ... Thistlethwaite, J. (2010). Patient involvement in medical education. *Medical Education, 44,* 64–74.

Towle, A., Brown, H., Kerston, R. P., Hofley, C., Lyons, H., & Walsh, C. (2014). The expert patient as teacher: An interprofessional health mentors programme. *Clinical Teacher, 11,* 301–306.

Towle, A., Farrell, C., Gaines, M.E., Godolphin, W., John, G., Kline, C., … Thistlethwaite, J. (2016). The patient's voice in health and social care professional education. The Vancouver Statement. *International Journal of Health Governance, 21,* 18–25.

Towle, A., & Godolphin, W. (2013). Patients as educators: Interprofessional learning for patient-centred care. *Medical Teacher, 35,* 219–225.

Towle, A., & Godolphin, W. (2015). Patient involvement in health professional education: Promoting their authentic and autonomous voices. *Clinical Teacher, 12,* 149–154.

Towle, A., Godolphin, W., & Kline, C. (2015). The community comes to campus: The Patient and Community Fair. *Clinical Teacher, 12,* 1–7.

Vogel, A. (2009). *Advancing service-learning in health professions education: Maximizing sustainability, quality and co-leadership.* Ph.D. thesis, Johns Hopkins University, Baltimore, Maryland, USA.

Weerts, D. J., & Sandmann, L. R. (2010). Community engagement and boundary-spanning roles at research universities. *Journal of Higher Education, 81,* 702–727.

Part V

Updates on Previous Developments

16

Interprofessional Collaborative Leadership in Health Care Teams: From Theorising to Measurement

Carole Orchard, Margot Rykhoff, and Erin Sinclair

Background

It has long been presented that leadership roles in health care are held by individuals who have a formal title and responsibility to hire, to monitor, and to evaluate those under their direct supervision. Theories of leadership have usually considered describing a leader as an individual who has some characteristics that are associated with leading or using skills to guide others. More recently, leadership scholars have challenged this view in light of the shifting trends towards team based

C. Orchard (✉)
Arthur Labatt Family School of Nursing, Western University, London, ON, Canada
e-mail: corchard@uwo.ca

M. Rykhoff
Faculty of Health Sciences and Wellness, Humber College ITAL Collaborative Nursing Programme, University of New Brunswick, Saint John, NB, Canada

E. Sinclair
Guelph General Hospital, Guelph, ON, Canada

D. Forman et al. (eds.), *Sustainability and Interprofessional Collaboration*,
https://doi.org/10.1007/978-3-030-40281-5_16

practice in organisations and in particular health care settings. Since the early twenty-first century a shift in viewing the leader as working with followers through a relational perspective is being proposed.

While a number of books have been published with a focus on Collaborative Leadership many view this form of leadership between a focus on organisations, (Archer & Cameron, 2009) or as part of communities of practice (Frydman, Wilson, & Wyler, 2000). The latter seems to be more related to collaborative leadership within health care teams. At the same time, rarely is there consideration given to the traditional organisational leader and their workers whom they supervise within even newer models of leadership. One example of this is the focus on authentic leadership (Avolio & Gardner, 2005) which begins to focus on followership or leadership within the context of the leader's role. There is an emerging scholarship within organisational management leadership beginning to explore team leadership focusing on 'shared leadership' (Bligh, Pearce, & Kholes, 2006; D'Innocenzo, Mathieu, & Kukenberger, 2016; Hoch, 2012; Klein, Ziiegert, Knight, & Xiao, 2006; Muethel & Hoegl, 2013; Nicolaides et al., 2014; Wang, Waldman, & Zhang, 2014), leadership structures and processes (Morgenson, DeRue, & Karam, 2010); and distributed leadership (Mehra, Smith, Dixon, & Robertson, 2006). Rarely is the combination of formal organisational and team leadership addressed with the exception of the work by Ensley, Hmieleski, and Pearce (2006), Pearce (2004) and Pearce and Sims (2002). Thus while there is a growing attention to the process of leadership which according to Northouse is 'a process whereby an individual influences a group of individuals to achieve a common goal' (Northouse, 2019, p. 5) rarely is it envisioned within the context of health care team collaboration.

The implementation of the Canadian Interprofessional Health Collaborative's Interprofessional Collaborative Competency Framework (CIHC) in 2010 identified collaborative leadership as a competency domain for health providers who share the leader role as collaborators within their teams. Collaborative leadership is described as: 'learners/practitioners work[ing] together with all participants including patients/clients/families, to formulate, implementation and evaluate care/services to enhance health outcomes' (CIHC, 2010, p. 15).

There has been some work done in the area of clinical leadership. Patrick, Laschinger, Wong, and Finegan (2011) published a measure for staff nurses providing direct care that utilised Kouzes and Posner's Leadership Elements (2007) but did not focus on the attributes being used related to team working and their collaborative leadership. Edmonstone (2009) also discussed the importance of focusing on clinical leadership as a part of sharing the leading with health providers in direct care, but no measure for this form of practice was presented. Thus there is a gap in the literature that fully explores the conceptualisation and measurement of Interprofessional Collaborative Leadership within the health care team context. The purpose of this chapter is to address this gap.

Literature Review

A growing number of authors have published papers focusing their scholarship and research specifically on forms of team leadership (Chen, Kanfer, Kirkman, & Allen, 2007; Pearce, 2004; Pearce & Sims, 2002; Raelin, 2006; Salas, Cooke, & Rosen, 2008) with each providing more clarity around how team leadership could be enacted.

Raelin (2006, 2011) is a strong proponent of new ways of addressing team leadership. He states 'the dominant Western tradition of centering leadership within the individual, [there is a need for] replacing this orientation with a focus on practice including the social interaction among the practitioners to the activity in question' (2011, p. 199). Raelin puts forward what he terms leaderful practice (2011) as a collaborative agency in teams (2017). He identifies this form of practice leadership as 'collective action emerging from mutual, discursive, sometimes recurring and sometimes evolving patterns in the moment and over time among those engaged in the practice' (2017, p. 216). In contrast Pearce and colleagues have focused on the intersection between formal leaders in an organisation and their interface with those within their areas of responsibility who function in teams. Pearce (2004) presents the view that both are relevant but vertical leaders need to be able to assess when shared versus directive leadership is required; how to prepare teams to enact this shared leadership within their work group; and how shared leadership can utilise the best capabilities within knowledge workers. Pearce and Sims (2002) also studied vertical versus shared leadership associated with change management and found **vertical and shared leadership** is significantly related to team effectiveness. They also found that **shared leadership is a predictor to team effectiveness and concluded** that vertical leaders need to enact transformative, transactional, and empowering leadership practices to support team effectiveness (2002).

A number of papers were found that are beginning to study associations between shared leadership and both team effectiveness and team performance (D'Innocenzo et al., 2016; Ensley et al., 2006; Mehra et al., 2006; Wang et al., 2014). Most of the authors have focused on structural elements within team leadership with limited attention to relational and social dynamics within the teams. Only one of the articles found focused on professionals in a team and identified a variance between professionals within a team who due to their professionalisation seek for autonomy (Muethel & Hoegl, 2013). When one professional asserts a position within the team their ability to influence acceptance of the viewpoint is more readily challenged by another professional who holds a divergence to that position (Muethel & Hoegl, 2013). Given that health care teams are comprised of a number of professionals from different disciplines, the above dynamic is likely consistently at play and needs to be considered within the context of health care practice. Bligh et al. (2006) provided an interesting perspective that may have some credence to professionals and their functioning within teams. They suggest that each member needs to have developed self-leadership in order to have effective team based leadership. They suggest that self-leadership is comprised of their sense of individual trust, self-efficacy, and commitment to the work which then influences how they share in leadership which is further moderated by team interdependence and task complexity evolving into knowledge creation (Bligh et al., 2006). In further papers Wang et al. (2014) and D'Innocenzo et al. (2016) identified complexity of work as impacting on team effectiveness. Wang et al. (2014) assert that what is shared between team members influences their team effectiveness and improves when the work is more complex, while D'Innocenzo suggests that while team tasks are significantly moderated by complexity, there is a point when the level of complexity can impact negatively on performance. What this balance is needs to be further studied. Given that health care teams deal with new patients having increasing complexity and uncertainty for their care needs, rarely do individual professionals have the required knowledge, skills, and expertise needed to deal alone with their total care. Thus what might be the maximum level of complexity in health care teams to work effectively together to achieve shared goal outcomes is beyond simply attending to team performance issues. This is particularly relevant within the strong ethos of many health care systems pressuring for higher levels of performance as a means to contain costs within a care environment comprising increasingly complex patients (Hunter, 2008).

A further challenge in understanding collaborative leadership within client-centred collaborative practice in health care is the inclusion of each patient into their health care team's collaborative care. A dimension that has not been addressed as yet in literature found.

While there is growing literature on shared leadership in teams, in most cases this form of leadership does not address the uniqueness of health care teams. Team leadership that allows for the dynamic shifting in teamwork within each patient's care coupled with dealing with groups of diverse health professionals representing varying disciplinary foci coming together in such new models of leadership. Hence, while shared leadership and the studies and theorising associated with this form of leadership have been helpful, it required a deeper understanding of the meaning of interprofessional collaborative leadership. Leadership that addresses the fundamental understanding of what is this form of and how might it be enacted, and measured. In the remainder of this chapter we will re-introduce our theorised model of leadership, provide a synopsis of a concept analysis of interprofessional collaborative leadership leading to the development of an instrument to test for this form of leadership within health care teams and finally the initial testing of the new measure.

Theorised Model of Leadership

What then are the unique elements in interprofessional collaborative leadership? Orchard, Sonibare, Morse, Collins, and Al-Hamad (2017) proposed that within such health care teams there is: an interdependency in their work, a sharing in responsibilities for patients' care leading to effective outcomes, viewing themselves members of a cohesive partnership, and having the capacity to manage their relationships with each other. If we then apply the conceptualisation of both Raelin's leadership practice to the team itself along with Pearce's view of vertical and shared leadership, a theorised model was proposed by Orchard and Rykhoff (2014). In this model an inter-relationship between vertical (formal) leaders proposed by Pearce and Sims (2002) discussed above and a collaborative team with linkage between both through relational coordination as proposed by Gittell, Godfrey, and Thistlethwaite (2013) is presented. Relational coordination as theorised by Gittell (2002) comprises working relationships that integrate shared goals, shared knowledge, and mutual respect. Support for the interface of relational coordination between formal (vertical) and collaborative leadership in health care relates to the three mediators of intergroup contact theory found by Pettigrew and Tropp (2008). These being: reduction of anxiety in coming into a team, with the team members showing both empathy and respect for the new member, and then clarification of others' roles at both a contextual level (focal role) and at a team functioning level (functional role) (Fig. 16.1).

If we relate back to Gitell's constructs of relational coordination one can see an interface with shared knowledge and mutual respect. This interface then focuses teamwork being on shared goals in addressing each patient's needs. While the literature cited does present other concepts to consider that might descript the elements associated with collaborative leadership, at the present time the theorised model integrates Kouzes and Posner Leadership practices (2006). These being: challenging the process, inspiring a shared vision, enabling others to act, modelling the way, and encouraging the heart. In Table 16.1 is shown how both a vertical leader and a team using collaborative leadership would demonstrate these elements.

Studies are now needed to test this theorised model to determine its relevance to interprofessional collaborative practice. While measures were available to assess vertical leadership, relational coordination and leadership practices there were no validated instruments located related specifically to the application of collaborative leadership to team-based collaborative leadership. Thus the need is to learn whether the constructs of collaborative leadership accurately measure this form of leadership.

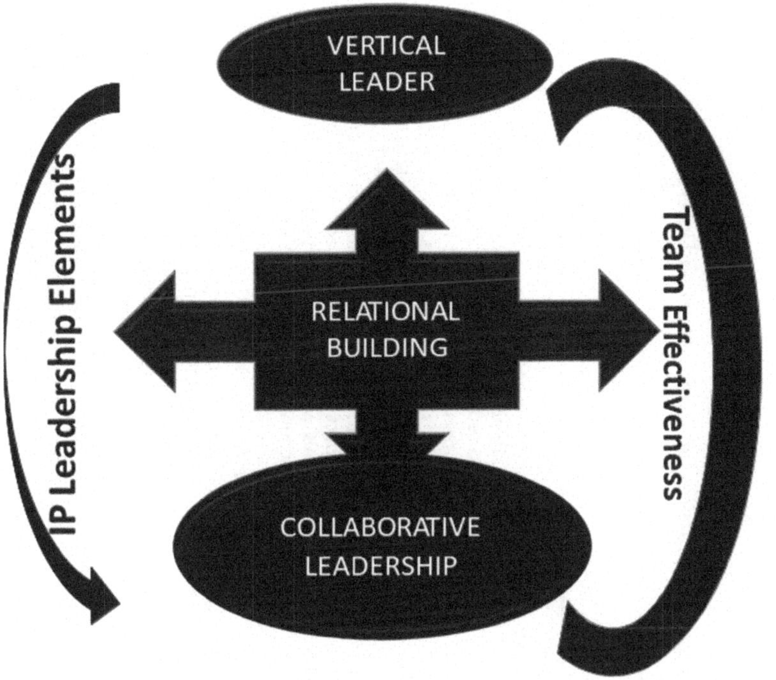

Fig. 16.1 Framework for integration of vertical and collaborative leadership (*Source* Orchard & Rykhoff, 2014)

This resulted in Rykoff, Orchard, and Wong (2015) conducting a concept analysis of collaborative leadership as applied to interprofessional health care teams.

Table 16.1 Comparison for enacting Kouzes and Posner Leadership practices between vertical and interprofessional team leaders

Leadership practice (Posner & Kouzes, 1993)	Vertical leader	Interprofessional team leadership
'Model the way'	Clarifying own values and validating and connecting actions to the group's shared values	Team members know their own personal values and how these may enhance or interfere in working with others; helping the team to stay focused on patient care and their own well-being
'Inspire a shared vision'	Helping group to see a desired future	Members focus on patient-specified goals and when the team considers how to get there; help each other to bring their ideas together in an agreed-upon plan with the patient
'Enable others to act'	Fostering collaboration and striving to create an atmosphere of trust and human dignity by strengthening each person's capabilities	Members help to guide the team in promoting respect for all members and in arriving at shared goals with patients and team members; encourage other members to take on the leadership role and support clients in their decision-making with the team
'Challenge the process'	Searching for opportunities to change the status quo and look for innovative ways to improve the organisation	Carrying out on-going reflection on how the team works together with patients and based on feedback make necessary changes; related to their provider roles with an interprofessional patient-centred context
'Encourage the heart'	Recognising contributions of others	Recognising the positive work of all team members, including the patient towards achieving shared goals; celebrating achievements of steps towards patient-set goals of care and well-being

Source Adapted from Orchard and Rykhoff (2014)

Concept Analysis

A concept analysis of 'collaborative leadership' was undertaken using the strategy proposed by Walker and Avant (2011). For the purposes of this chapter the meaning of the concept, a literature review on the current use of the concept, the identification of the attributes, antecedents and consequences leading to a definition will be provided. An independent article on the total process is in review for publication.

Meaning of the Collaborative Leadership

> Although there are definitions for terms that include 'collaborative', 'collaboration', and 'leadership' as single concepts, the combined words 'collaborative leadership' were not found in either of the online dictionaries (i.e. online Lexico English Dictionary or online Merriam-Webster). Likewise, none of the medical, nursing, or allied health dictionaries provided a definition of 'collaborative leadership'. The CIHC collaborative leadership domain as stated earlier in this chapter describes this domain as 'Leaders/practitioners understand[ing] and can apply leadership principles that support a collaborative practice model by supporting the following collaborative functions: promoting patient outcomes, facilitating working relationships, team processes, decision making, positive climates, shared leadership, and principles of quality improvements' (p. 15). A culture of collaborative leadership seems to require teams to contribute their combined knowledge, skills and expertise in transforming patients' care (Nickitas, 2012).

Literature Search

An in depth literature review was carried out searching several databases including: Academic Search Complete, Business Source Complete, Cumulative Index to Nursing and Allied Health Literature, Medline, PubMed, Proquest, and Google Scholar. The search applied keywords of:

'collaborative leadership,' 'shared leadership,' 'shared governance,' 'shared decision making,' 'interprofessional collaborative practice,' and 'health care teams'. A further search of books on shared or collaborative leadership was also undertaken. Finally grey literature from organisations, such as the CIHC, and Institute of Medicine (IOM) was reviewed resulting in a total of 14,638 citations. Next a narrowing of the search focusing on 'collaborative leadership', 'shared leadership', 'interprofessional collaboration' (IPC), and 'frontline health care teams' reduced the total to 1092 articles. The titles and abstracts of these articles were reviewed using the CIHC working definition of collaborative leadership that reduced the articles to 116. Finally the full paper of this latter group of articles was carried out and a further 80 were eliminated due to their lack of relevance to team based practice in health care. Thus the final literature used for this review included 36 papers (Fig. 16.2).

The literature reviewed is more focused on shared rather than collaborative leadership within teams and is most frequently associated with project work. Only in health care is the role of the patient within the team discussed as part of collaborative team leadership. At the same time discussion related to collaborative or shared leadership has been found in several disciplinary fields including: arts (Kramer & Crespy, 2011); business (Archer & Cameron, 2009; Carson, Tesluk, & Marrone, 2007; Chrislip & Larson, 1994), psychology (Bligh et al., 2006; Drescher, Korsgaard, Welpe, Picot, & Wigand, 2014), education (Morrison & Arthur, 2013; Raelin, 2006), and military studies (Lindsay, Day, & Halpin, 2011). Within these fields the focus has been on collaborative leadership within the context of team effectiveness as an outcome of shared leadership processes. Collaborative leadership has also been reported as a predictor of organisational success (Archer & Cameron, 2009).

Elements associated with shared leadership include: common shared goals, knowledge and work alignment, and a shared agreement to integrate members' own interests within those of the teams (Drath et al., 2008). Overall, there is consistency in viewing shared or collaborative leadership as a form of leadership within a group of individuals who share a common goal to reach an agreed upon outcome. However, within health care an added unique feature of this form of leadership

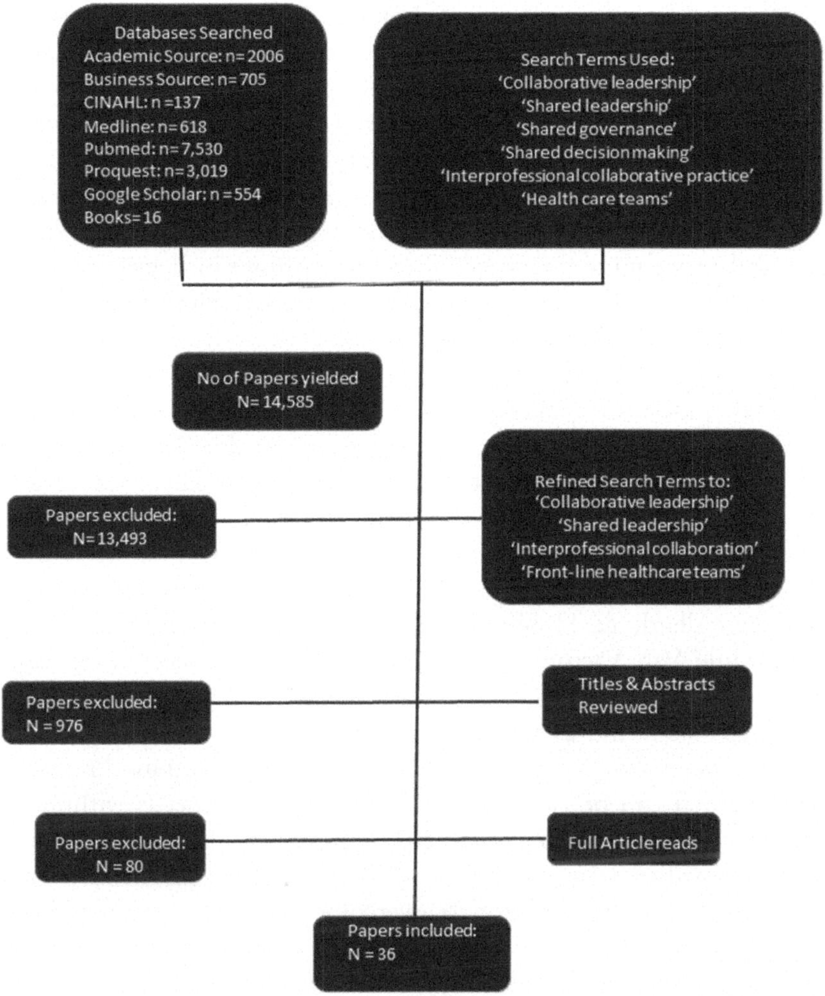

Fig. 16.2 Literature research refinement process

is the inclusion of the patient as a member of the collaborative team (CIHC, 2010; Kneibel & Greiner, 2003; WHO, 2010). Thus collaborative leadership within health care settings is seen as having elements that are both convergent and divergent from those discussed in the literature reviewed. Thus there does not seem to be a consistent understanding of the conceptual clarity around collaborative leadership that necessitated an exploration of its relevant attributes, antecedents and consequences. And how this will fit into the previously presented theorised model of collaborative leadership. While the literature reviewed was helpful in understanding the elements that comprise the structure of collaborative leadership, it was somewhat limited in exploring the relational aspects such as what comprises how teams arrive at shared goals, shared knowledge, and enact mutual respect. Therefore, a more in depth analysis of the literature related to relational aspects associated with the meaning of collaborative leadership was undertaken.

According to McCallin (2007) interdisciplinary leadership is a form of shared leadership applied within a specific situation where all team members are prepared to assume responsibility for their shared care planning and goal setting. In a patient care situation shared care planning is dependent on unique needs of each patient. Other authors have focused more fully on specific situations and those aspects that need to be addressed within a team. One aspect presented is situational awareness (Bleakley, Allard, & Hobbs, 2013; Mackintosh, Berridge, & Freeth, 2009) while Van Vactor suggested situational awareness also incorporates a mindfulness around how team members share their combined knowledge, skills and expertise (2012). Situational awareness is defined as a process in which team members present their unique knowledge and skills that can be considered to address specific needs within each goal setting event (Bleakley et al., 2013). Being mindful seems to relates to how individual team members consider how the team identify a plan of care that has the capacity to overcome patients' identified health and social challenges (Van Vactor, 2012). Casimiro, Hall, Kuziemsky, O'Connor, and Varpio (2015) suggest that when a team uses situational awareness there is a greater opportunity for engaging patients in their own care (i.e. a fundamental aspect associated with interprofessional collaborative patient-centred care). For example, in any patient encounter with health professionals the care interface is not directed by a vertical leader but by the team of health professionals working together to develop interventions for a specific patient in addressing the means to overcome health issues for which they are seeking help (Pearce, Manz, & Sims, 2014). In contrast, mindfulness focuses on how each team member focuses his/her attention to the context (situation) and to its variability needed to be attended to (Langer, 2014). Langer further asserts that when a person is attending to its variability there is an allowance to ensuring we are not being judgmental of others and being respectful to others views (Langer, 2014). Mindful people allow openness to others that can encourage innovation through new ways of thinking from the sharing of differing perspectives (Langer, 2014). Thus both *situational awareness* and *mindfulness* appear to be two relational aspects that need to be present for team members to enact collaborative leadership.

How team members then work together is dependent on their ability as a team to have shared purposes, and vision about their teamworking and how it will be applied to each patient situation (Chong, Aslani, & Chen, 2013; Weller, Barrow, & Gasquoine, 2011). Hence, collaborative leadership is about how team members agree to work interdependently with each other to achieve shared goals (van Schaik, O'Brien, Almeida, & Adler, 2014). Weingardt (1996) suggested that when professionals work 'across each other's' professions (e.g. in his paper engineers working with architects) there needs to be a partnering between these two professions to achieve a shared outcome. He termed this partnership as needing a *symbiotic relationship*. This approach was in response to ongoing disagreements between the two professions that impeded their shared work. In health care Li (2004) presented a slightly different dimension to a relationship between patients and nurses as being about what she termed as *symbiotic niceness* that she defined as 'the sharedness of patients and nurses' experiences and a reciprocal notion of therapeutic help' (p. 2571). If we expand this thinking into teamwork, it can relate to how team members work together in a reciprocal relationship in which there is respect for each other's contributions to their teamworking. These contributions then can result in achieving set goals for the team and for their patients' care (Anonson et al., 2009; D'Amour, Ferrada-Videla, Martin-Rodriguez, & Beaulieu, 2005; Henneman, Lee, & Cohen, 1995).

Therefore, while collaborative leadership requires a situational awareness and mindfulness it also needs to comprise a willingness of team members to enter into symbiotic relationships that allow for reciprocal sharing between its members for the purpose of achieving team goals

(Anonson et al., 2009; van Schaik et al., 2014; Weller et al., 2011). To achieve the above necessitates a team as a whole, utilising shared assets that individual team members bring into their collaborative work (Bethea, Holland, & Reddick, 2014; Thompson, Navarra, & Antonson, 2005; Van Vactor, 2012). Costa's (2003) conceptualisation of trust in teams is comprised of two dimensions—cognition and affect-based that is helpful in understanding team trust. In health care teams when a new member enters into a relationship with other team members that person's competence in professional practice is first assessed (cognition) and then the person's ability to 'fit into' the team follows (affective-based) (Costa, 2003). It then seems that the capability of each member to competently contribute his/her skills and expertise to the team's work is a requirement for IP collaborative leadership. Weller et al. (2011) suggests this sharing also needs to include known information, and their understanding of mental models associated with care (Weller et al., 2011), along with each member's contribution to team decision making, and willingness to share power with each other (Bohmer, 2013; Jabbar, 2011).

When power is shared within a team and collective trust exists within the membership it opens opportunities for any of the members to participate in leading the team. The 'leading' role is more associated with a coordination and follow up across the membership related to each agreed upon plan of care, rather than as a traditional 'directing role' enacted through vertical leading (Orchard & Rykhoff, 2014). In the competency domain for IP collaborative leadership all team members are expected to be willing to lead the team with the support and cooperation of their fellow team members (CIHC, 2010). Hence in a health care team all members demonstrate a willingness to assume a collaborative leadership role and in so doing contribute to the team's credibility (Frenk et al., 2010; IOM, 2010). Collaborative leadership necessitates interdependent working relationships; effective team processes; shared decision making, shared expectations; and focusing on continuous quality improvement (Adams, Greiner, & Corrigan, 2001; IOM, 2003; Markle-Reid et al., 2017; Saint et al., 2010).

In summary, the literature reviewed and the concept analysis process applied resulted in the following definition of 'collaborative leadership' as a dynamic process with four critical attributes that constitute the phenomenon—(a) situational interactive process (mindfulness, complexity of care required, facilitating patient-engaged care), (b) collaborative interdependence (symbiotic relationship, respect, trust for each other's expertise, shared capacities to achieve goals), (c) shared assets (information, mental models, decision making and power), and (d) capacity to lead (professional competence, knowledge, skills, expertise, credibility in the team) (Rykhoff, Orchard, & Wong, 2019). Each of these attributes was then explored within further literature to gain a depth of understanding of their meaning within collaborative leadership (Fig. 16.3).

Next the attributes were reviewed to consider which antecedents are needed to ensure they can be enacted (Walker & Avant, 2011). Personal factors such as professional role awareness and competence (Baker, Egan-Lee, Martimianakis, & Reeves, 2011) are foundational to allow for the attribute of *situational awareness* to be present. Environmental factors may also influence a team member's personal factors such as complexity of patient care (Casimiro et al., 2015), team members' perception of their psychological safety at both team and organisational levels (Nembhard & Edmonson, 2006; van Schaik et al., 2014), team

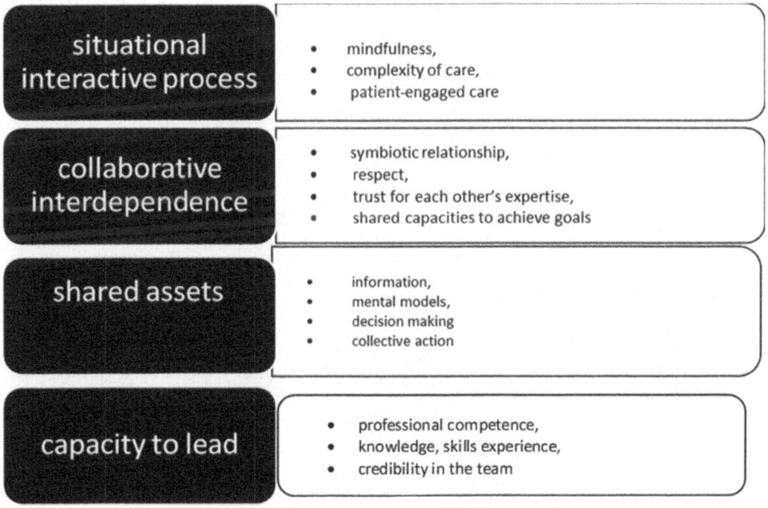

Fig. 16.3 Collaborative leadership attributes with sub concepts (*Source* Rykoff et al., 2015)

trust (Barczak, Lassk, & Mulki, 2010; Costa, 2003; McAllister, 1995) and structures within an institution or agency that are perceived to support team work (Nembrand & Edmonson, 2006).

Finally each attribute was considered as to what would be the consequences if both the antecedents and attributes were present. Consequences then are the outcomes of a concepts attributes to goal achievement within a team (Walker & Avant, 2011). Overall when the attributes are present the outcomes can be considered at the patient, health care team, and institution/agency levels. For the patient there is a likelihood of enhanced health outcomes resulting from decreased potential patient safety issues and care fragmentation (CIHC, 2010; Adams et al., 2001; IOM, 2003; Markle-Reid et al., 2017; Saint et al., 2010). For the health care team members, it has been reported that collaborative teamwork results in enhanced job satisfaction through a sense of empowerment (Boyle & Kochinda, 2004; Houghton, Pearce, Manz, Courtright, & Stewart, 2015; Nembhard & Edmondson, 2006). Benefits for health care institutions/agencies could be through reductions in staff turnover, shortened patient lengths of stays (for inpatients), fewer patient untoward events from the impact of effective teamwork from IP collaborative team leadership (Poulton & West, 1993; West et al. 2015). Figure 16.4 outlines the attributes, their antecedents and consequences of IP collaborative leadership.

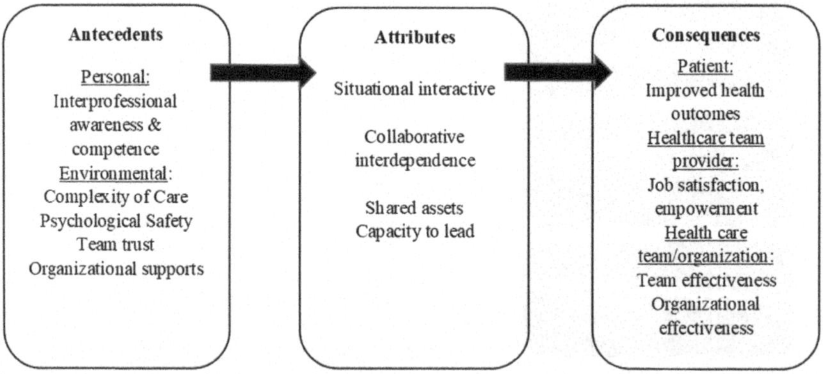

Fig. 16.4 Antecedents, attributes and consequences of collaborative leadership in interprofessional teams (*Source* Rykoff et al., 2015)

Development and Testing of the Assessment of Interprofessional Collaborative Leadership Scale (AICLS)

To lay the ground work for the Assessment of Interprofessional Collaborative Leadership Scale (AICLS) instrument development the attributes emerging from the concept analysis developed by Rykoff et al. (2015) were studied further to identify attributes that could be measured including: situational interactive process, collaborative interdependence, shared assets and capacity to lead. A literature review for each was further carried out to determine what constructs could be used to create items for measuring the attributes. This process resulted in selecting sub-constructs for the generation of items that impacted both *situational awareness* and *collaborative interdependence.* A transformation from the stated attribute for situational awareness became the construct for *symbiotic relationship* and *mindfulness* for collaborative interdependence. Care was taken to ensure all the intents from the concept analysis and meanings of each attribute were captured in the item generation. Both *shared assets* and *capacity to lead* were retained as identified in the analysis.

An operational definition for each of the constructs for the AICLS was then generated.

Symbiotic relationship: is a collaboration in which team members have their own well-established roles and also mutually adapt to changing demands of the dynamic

Mindfulness: is a thoughtful and extended focusing of one's attention on immediate experiences as they transpire

Shared assets: are environments that encourage an openness to distribute knowledge, skill and expertise within a team and

Capacity to lead: is a willingness to both lead and accept accountability for the position of leadership (Sinclair & Orchard, 2018).

Finally an **operational definition** for collaborative leadership reflecting the instrument constructs was arrived at, this being 'Collaborative leadership occurs when all members of a team, including the patient/family, ***symbiotically*** accept their ***capacity to lead*** the group by demonstrating ***mindfulness*** of the value in working together, and using their ***shared assets*** to assist patients to reach achievable and desired health outcomes' (Sinclair & Orchard, 2018).

Item Generation

In the next phase of the AICLS item generation was carried out. A total of 28 items that were believed to reflect each of the concepts within the four attributes were generated. Symbiotic Relationships comprised 5-items; mindfulness 9-items; and both shared assets and capacity to lead each contained—7 items. The initial items generated are provided below.

Following the item generation a Content Validity Assessment was carried out (Table 16.2).

CVI Review

A group of 12 international interprofessional experts (from Canada, US, UK, Australia, New Zealand and Germany) were contacted and requested to rate each of the AICLS' 28 items using a 5 point rating scale (1 = never to 5 = always) and a content validity index (Lynn, 1986) using a 4 point relevancy scale with 1 = completely irrelevant to 4 = extremely relevant was provided in an online Qualtric Platform (Turning Point National Program, 2017). Six of the experts completed both the instrument and CVI index. The overall CVI mean was 15.32 (SD = .65); all of the subscales were rated from 3.66 to 3.96 out of 4.00 (symbolic relationships M = 3.96, SD = .08; mindfulness M = 3.84, SD = .13; shared assets M = 3.86, SD = .23; and capacity to lead M = 3.66, SD = .21). Of the 28 items, only one item received a score of 2 from one respondent—which seemed to be wording related. A revision in the wording was carried out to finalise the instrument for stage 2 testing. Thus, based on the CVI the instrument was rated to be very relevant by the experts.

Table 16.2 AICLS items by construct

Symbiotic relationships
1. Help the members to appreciate their contributions to the group's teamwork
2. Encourage team members to value each other's individual expertise
3. Encourage team members to harness their complementary capabilities (shared knowledge, skills & expertise) to address care plans
4. Allow all team members to have a chance to voice their opinions
5. Promote the team members' seeing their shared outcomes as meaningful and valuable
Mindfulness
6. Encourages team members to develop processes to lead to creating a shared decision-making environment
7. Encourages team members to focus beyond the status quo (i.e. normal way of doing things) on relevant key issues
8. Encourages team members to consider creative solutions to complex patient/client care planning
9. Encourages team members to re-evaluate traditional ways of dealing with similar situations
10. Encourages open discussions amongst all team members around patient care issues
11. Is receptive to supporting team member suggested changes
12. Encourages team members to adapt to varying situations
13. Encourages team members questioning of things that do not make sense
14. Supports team members' creative innovation in solutions where there is uncertainty to patient/client care planning
Shared assets
15. Ensure there are opportunities for all team members to share their perspectives around patient/client care planning issues
16. Encourage team members to establish shared goals around their teamwork
17. Facilitate team members' adjustments to situational role needs
18. Encourage team members to participate in accepting responsibility for their contributions within team decision-making processes
19. The decision-making process focuses on shared goals of all team members
20. There is attention to encouraging integrated perspectives to facilitate shared decision-making processes within patient/client care plan development

(continued)

Table 16.2 (continued)

Shared assets
21. When plans of care are implemented the work is distributed across the team members depending on members' capabilities
Capacity to lead
22. Team members support patients/clients being the collaborative leader
23. Team members are willing to serve in a team leading capacity when asked
24. All team members accept ownership and accountability for their shared teamwork
25. All team members contribute to common goals shared by the team
26. Team mentor one another to be able to lead the team effectively
27. There is support for the leader of the team rotating depending on the needs for our developing care planning
28. Together we select the leader for our team

Initial Testing of the AICLS

Ethics approval for the next stage of testing was obtained by both the Ethics Board at Western University and also from the practice site used for the testing.

Study Design

A cross sectional validation of the AICLS was planned to be carried out using both an exploratory factor analysis (EFA) and a confirmatory factor analysis (CFA) to determine the final subscales' evidence of its dimensional structure and reliability. To carry this out a two staged analysis process for validation of the instrument was planned.

Sample/sampling frame: Health providers working within a Southwestern Ontario hospital were approached through the Vice President of Patient Services and Chief Nursing Executive (VP & CNE) at the health care setting. There was a planned sample size of 400 to allow for both an EFA and a CFA of the instrument. This sample size would allow for random separation of equal numbers of respondents into two groups (Group A data would be analysed for the EFA and group B for the CFA.

Data Collection

Once ethics approval was received the setting's VP & CNE sent an email (short summary of the study and URL to access the survey) invitation via their settings' intranet system to all staff. The survey contained both the letter of information and the 28-item instrument located on the university's Qualtrics Platform (Turning Point National Program, 2017) was accessed online by respondents. Respondents were asked to read the letter of information and if they agreed to then complete the instrument by rating each item on a 5-point rating scale (1 = never to 5 = always) as well as entering their demographic information (gender, age, employment status, educational preparation and health provider role; years in practice and years in current teams). Respondents' implied consent was obtained by completing the survey. All staff received reminders one week after the initial invitation and a further reminder at the beginning of the 3rd week.

Data Analysis

Analysis of data was carried out using SPSS v. 26. A total of 101 responses were obtained which was far less than the 400 planned for. Thus the plan for both an EFA and CFA was not feasible. We were able to provide only a descriptive analysis of the data obtained and evidence of reliability for the instrument.

Characteristics of the Respondents

Female respondents represented slightly more than three-quarters of the pool ($n = 74$, 77.9%) while males were slightly less than one-quarter (22.1%). The mean age of respondents was 43.22 years (SD = 12.395) with a range from 21 to 66 years of age. Sixty-eight percent of the respondents were employed full-time ($n = 65$) with one-quarter ($n = 24$, 25.3%) employed part-time and only 6.3% ($n = 6$) reporting they worked on a casual or other basis. Slightly more of the respondents reported their professional educational preparation as a bachelor degree

Table 16.3 Characteristics of respondents to survey

Variable	*n*	Male	Female	Missing
Gender	101	20 (22.1%)	74 (77.9%)	7 (6.9%)
		M	SD	Range
Age	83	43.22	12.395	21–66 years
Employment status	*n*	%		
Full time	65	68.4		
Part time	24	25.3		
Casual/other	6	6.3		
Educational preparation				
Certificate/diploma	31	33.0		
Bachelor degree	33	35.1		
Master's degree	11	11.7		
Ph.D.	3	3.2		
Other	16	17.0		

($n = 33$, 35.1%) than those with certificate or diplomas in their practice fields ($n = 31$, 33.0%). Almost 16% of the respondents reported graduate preparation in their professions ($n = 14$). A further 16 respondents selected other (Table 16.3).

When the respondents' professional designations were analysed the largest number of respondents reported being a registered nurse/clinical nurse specialist ($n = 47$, 49.5%) followed by physicians ($n = 17$, 17.9%), practical nurses ($n = 9$, 9.5%), then respiratory therapists ($n = 4$, 4.2%) with equal numbers of both nurse practitioners and pharmacy technicians ($n = 5$, 3.2%), and finally physical therapists ($n = 2$, 2.1%. A further 7.4% of respondents selected other ($n = 7$) (Table 16.4).

Table 16.4 Distribution of respondents across health professional roles by percentage of total

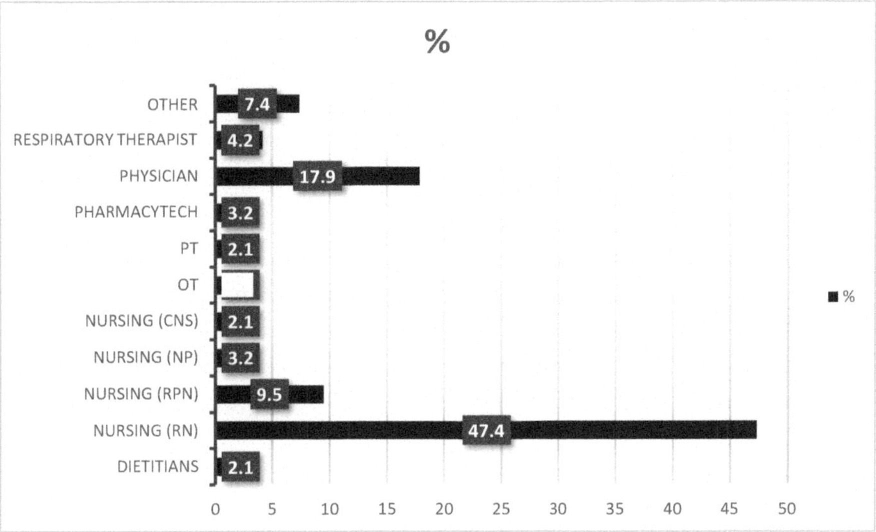

Results

Descriptive analysis of the ACLS items was carried out to assess the means and standard deviations for each of the sub-concepts and overall concept of collaborative leadership. Symbiotic relationship had a mean of 19.35 (SD = 3.190); mindfulness had a mean of 33.56 (SD = 6.06); shared assets had a mean of 26.18 (SD = 4.899); and capacity to lead had a mean of 25.41 (SD = 4.135). The overall collaborative leadership mean was 104.82 (SD = 16.747). Thus the evidence of collaborative leadership within the respondent group showed a mean item score of 3.74 which indicates some areas where collaborative leadership has some weaknesses.

Evidence for the reliability of the ACLS was carried out using Cronbach's α. The overall internal consistency of the ACLS was .96 with its subscales ranging from .85 to .92 (see Table 16.5). Thus the scale is showing good internal consistency. Only one item has a corrected item-total correlation less than .3 with the other 27 items ranging from .486 to

Table 16.5 Means, standard deviations and internal consistency for overall scale and subscales

Concept	Items	*M*	SD	Cronbach α
Symbiotic relationship	5	19.35	3.190	.868
Mindfulness	9	33.56	6.06	.920
Shared assets	7	26.18	4.899	.916
Capacity to lead	7	25.41	4.135	.853
Collaborative leadership	28	104.82	16.747	.961

.840. If the one item was removed from the scale the impact is only a .002 decrease in the scale α. While the internal consistency appears to be very good there are likely some items that are redundant and once a full EFA and CFA are carried out it is likely that removal of cross-loaded items may further enhance the reliability to closer to .90 (see Table 16.5).

Findings

The findings from the study demonstrate strong internal consistency for each of the sub-scales with an overall consistency at .96. While the recommended maximum for an instrument consistency is .90 it means that there are likely redundancies within the instrument. Once further testing is carried out and its EFA and CFA are carried out it is more likely that some items will be deleted. Further testing will provide evidence to determine whether the AICLS is a reliable and valid instrument to be used to measure collaborative leadership within interprofessional health care teams. Further testing of the AICL is needed before this instrument can be used for measuring this form of leadership.

Chapter Summary

We have provided an overview of the stages taken to theorise, to conceptualise, and to define the meaning of collaborative leadership and its attributes, antecedents, and consequences. These were then applied in the development of the Assessment of Interprofessional Collaborative Leadership and two stages of testing—content validity assessment and testing in a health care setting. Collaborative leadership is comprised of four attributes—symbiotic relationships, mindfulness, shared assets, and capacity to lead.

References

Adams, K., Greiner, A. C. & Corrigan, J. M. (Eds.). (2001). *Crossing the quality chasm.* Institute of Medicine Report of Summit. Washington, DC: National Academic Press.

Anonson, J. M. S., Ferguson, L., MacDonald, M. B., Murray, B. L., Fowler-Kerry, S., & Bally, J. M. G. (2009). The anatomy of interprofessional leadership: An investigation of leadership behaviours in team-based health care. *Journal of Leadership Studies, 3*(3), 17–25. https://doi.org/10.1002/jls.20120.

Archer, D., & Cameron, A. (2009). *Collaborative leadership: How to succeed in an interconnected world.* Woburn, MA, USA: Butterworth-Heinemann.

Avolio, B. J., & Gardner, W. L. (2005). Authentic leadership development: Getting to the root of positive forms of leadership. *The Leadership Quarterly, 16,* 315–338. https://doi.org/10.1016/j.leaqua.2005.03.001.

Baker, L., Egan-Lee, E., Martimianakis, M. A., & Reeves, S. (2011). Relationships of power: Implications for interprofessional education. *Journal of Interprofessional Care, 25,* 98–104.

Barczak, G., Lassk, F., & Mulki, J. (2010). Antecedents of team creativity: An examination of team emotional intelligence, team trust and collaborative culture. *Creativity & Innovation Management, 19*(4), 332–345. https://doi.org/10.1111/j.1467-8691.2010.00574.x.

Bethea, D. P., Holland, C. A., Jr., & Reddick, B. K. (2014). Storming the gates of interprofessional collaboration. *Nursing Management, 45*(9), 40–45.

Bleakley, A., Allard, J., & Hobbs, A. (2013). 'Achieving ensemble': Communication in orthopaedic surgical teams and the development of situation awareness—An observational study using live videotaped examples. *Advances in Health Sciences Education, 18,* 33–56. https://doi.org/10.1007/s10459-012-9351-6.

Bligh, M. C., Pearce, C. L., & Kholes, J. C. (2006). The importance of self- and shared leadership in team based knowledge work: A meso-level model

of leadership dynamics. *Journal of Managerial Psychology, 21*(4), 296–318. https://doi.org/10.1108/02689940610663105.
Bohmer, R. M. (2013). Leading clinicians and clinical leading. *New England Journal of Medicine, 268*(16), 1468–1470.
Boyle, D. K., & Kochinda, C. (2004). Enhancing collaborative communication of nurse and physician leadership in two intensive care units. *Journal of Nursing Administration, 34*(2), 60–70.
Carson, J., Tesluk, P., & Marrone, J. (2007). Shared leadership in teams: An investigation of antecedent conditions and performance. *Academy of Management Journal, 50,* 1217–1234.
Casimiro, L. M., Hall, P., Kuziemsky, C., O'Connor, M., & Varpio, L. (2015). Enhancing patient-engaged teamwork in healthcare: An observational case study. *Journal of Interprofessional Care, 29*(1), 55–61. https://doi.org/10.3109/13561820.2014.940038.
Chen, G., Kanfer, R., Kirkman, B. L., & Allen, D. (2007). A multilevel study of leadership empowerment, and performance in teams. *Journal of Applied Psychology, 92*(2), 231–346. https://doi.org/10.1037/0021-9010.02.2.331.
Chong, W. W., Aslani, P., & Chen, T. F. (2013). Shared decision-making and interprofessional collaboration in mental healthcare: A qualitative study exploring perceptions of barriers and facilitators. *Journal of Interprofessional Care, 27*(3), 223–230.
Chrislip, D. D. (2002). *The collaborative leadership fieldbook.* San Francisco, CA, USA: Jossey-Bass.
Chrislip, D. D., & Larson, C. (1994). *Collaborative leadership.* San Francisco: Jossey-Bass.
CIHC. (2010). *National interprofessional competency framework.* Vancouver, BC: CIHC. www.cihc.ca.
Costa, A. C. (2003). Work team trust and effectiveness. *Personnel Review, 32*(5), 605–622. https://doi.org/10.1108/0048310488360.
D'Amour, D., Ferrada-Videla, M., Martin-Rodriguez, L. S., & Beaulieu, M. D. (2005). The conceptual basis for interprofessional collaboration: Core concepts and theoretical frameworks. *Journal of Interprofessional Care, 19*(Supplement 1), 116–131.
D'Innocenzo, L., Mathieu, J. E., & Kukenberger, M. R. (2016). A meta-analysis of different forms of shared leadership–team performance relations. *Journal of Management, 42*(7), 1964–1991. https://doi.org/10.1177/0149206314525205.
Drath, W. H., McCauley, C. D., Palus, C. J., Van Velsor, E., O'Connor, P. M. G., & McGuire, J. B. (2008). Direction, alignment, commitment: Toward

a more integrative ontology of leadership. *The Leadership Quarterly, 19,* 635–653. https://doi.org/10.1016/j.leaqua.2008.09.003.

Drescher, M. A., Korsgaard, M. A., Welpe, I. M., Picot, A., & Wigand, R. T. (2014). The dynamics of shared leadership: Building trust and enhancing performance. *Journal of Applied Psychology, 99*(5), 771–783.

Edmonstone, J. (2009). Clinical leadership: The elephant in the room. *International Journal of Health Planning and Management, 24*(4), 290–305. https://doi.org/10.1002/hpm.959.

Ensley, M. D., Hmieleski, K. M., & Pearce, C. L. (2006). The importance of vertical and shared leadership within new venture top management teams: Implications of the performance of startups. *The Leadership Quarterly, 17,* 217–231. https://doi.org/10.1016/j.leaqua.2006.02.002.

Frenk, J., Chen, L., Bhutta, Z., Cohen, J., Crisp, N., Evans, T., ... Zurayk, H. (2010). Health professionals for a new century: Transforming education to strengthen health systems in an interdependent world. *The Lancet, 376*(9756), 1923–1958.

Frydman, B., Wilson, I., & Wyler, J.-A. (2000). *The power of collaborative leadership: Lessons for the learning organization.* Woburn, MA, USA: Butterworth Heinemann.

Gittell, J. (2002). Coordinating mechanisms in care provider groups: Relational coordination as a mediator and input uncertainty as a moderator of performance. *Management Science, 48*(11), 1408–1426.

Gittell, J. H., Godfrey, M., & Thistlethwaite, J. (2013). Interprofessional collaborative practice and relational coordination: Improving healthcare through relationships. *Journal of Interprofessional Care, 27*(3), 2010–13. https://doi.org/10.3109/13561820.2012.73056.

Henneman, E. A., Lee, J. L., & Cohen, J. I. (1995). Collaboration: A concept analysis. *Journal of Advanced Nursing, 21,* 103–109.

Hoch, J. E. (2012). Shared leadership diversity, and information sharing in teams. *Journal of Management Psychology, 29*(5), 541–564. https://doi.org/10.1108/JMP-02-2012-0053.

Houghton, J. D., Pearce, C. L., Manz, C. C., Courtright, S., & Stewart, G. L. (2015). Sharing is caring: Toward a model of proactive caring through shared leadership. *Human Resource Management Review, 25,* 313–327. https://doi.org/10.1016/j.hrmr.2014.12.001.

Hunter, D. J. (2008). *The health debate.* Bristol, UK: The Policy Press, University of Bristol.

Institute of Medicine. (2003). *Health professions education: A bridge to quality.* Washington, DC: National Academy Press.

Institute of Medicine. (2010). *The future of nursing: Leading change, advancing health*. Washington, DC: National Academy Press.

Jabbar, A. (2011). Language, power and implications for interprofessional collaboration: Reflections on a transition from social work to medicine. *Journal of Interprofessional Care, 25*(6), 447–448. https://doi.org/10.3109/13561820.2011.601822.

Klein, K. J., Ziiegert, J. C., Knight, A. P., & Xiao, Y. (2006). Dynamic delegation: Shared, hierarchical, and deindividualized leadership in extreme action teams. *Administrative Science Quarterly, 51,* 590–621. https://doi.org/10.2189/asqu.51.4.590.

Kneibel, E., & Greiner, A. C. (2003). *Health profession education: A bridge to quality*. Institutes of Medicine. Washington, DC: National Academic Press. Retrieved from http://www.nap.edu/catalog.1068.html.

Kouzes, J., & Posner, B. (2006). *Student leadership practices inventory* (2nd ed.). San Francisco, CA: Jossey-Bass.

Kouzes, J., & Posner, B. (2007). *The leadership challenge: How to make extraordinary things happen in organizations* (4th ed.). San Francisco, CA: Jossey-Bass.

Kramer, M., & Crespy, D. (2011). Communicating collaborative leadership. *The Leadership Quarterly, 22*(5), 1024–1037.

Langer, E. J. (2014). *Mindfulness* (25th Anniversary ed.). Boston, MA: Da Capo Press.

Li, S. (2004). 'Symbiotic niceness': Constructing a therapeutic relationship in psychosocial palliative care. *Social Science and Medicine, 58,* 2571–2583. https://doi.org/10.1016/j.sociscimed.2003.09.006.

Lindsay, D. R., Day, D. V., & Halpin, S. M. (2011). Shared leadership in the military: Reality, possibility, or pipedream? *Military Psychology, 23,* 528–549.

Lynn, M. R. (1986). Determination and quantification of content validity. *Nursing Research, 35,* 382–385.

Mackintosh, N., Berridge, E.-J., & Freeth, D. (2009). Supporting structures for team situation awareness and decision making: Insights from four delivery suites. *Journal of Evaluation in Clinical Practice, 15,* 46–54. https://doi.org/10.1111/k/1365-2753.2008.00953x.

Markle-Reid, M., Dykeman, C., Ploeg, J., Stradiotto, C. K., Adrews, A., Bonom, S., … Salker, N. (2017). Collaborative leadership and the implementation of community-based fall prevention initiatives: A multiple case study of public health practice within community groups. *BMC Health Services Research, 17*(1), 141. http://dx.doi.org/10.1186/s12913-017-2089-3.

McAllister, D. J. (1995). Affect and cognition based trust as foundations for interpersonal cooperation in organizations. *Academy of Management Journal, 38,* 24–59.

McCallin, A. (2007). Interdisciplinary team leadership: A revisionist approach for an old problem? *Journal of Nursing Management, 11*(6), 364–370.

Mehra, A., Smith, B. R., Dixon, A. L., & Robertson, B. (2006). Distributed leadership in teams: The network of leadership perceptions and team performance. *The Leadership Quarterly, 17,* 232–245. https://doi.org/10.1016/j.leaqua.2006.02.003.

Morgenson, F. P., DeRue, D. S., & Karam, E. P. (2010). Leadership in teams: A functional approach to understanding leadership structures and processes. *Journal of Management, 36*(1), 5–39. https://doi.org/10.1177/0149206309347376.

Morrison, M., & Arthur, L. (2013). Leadership for inter-service practice: Collaborative leadership lost in translation? An exploration. *Educational Management Administration & Leadership, 41*(2), 179–198.

Muethel, M., & Hoegl, M. (2013). Shared leadership effectiveness in independent professional teams. *European Management Journal, 31,* 423–432. https://doi.org/10.1016/j.emj.2012.11.008.

Nembhard, I. M., & Edmondson, A. C. (2006). Making it safe: The effects of leader inclusiveness and professional status on psychological safety and improvement efforts in health care teams. *Journal of Organizational Behaviour, 27,* 941–966.

Nickitas, D.M. (2012). A remedy in healthcare in 2012: Collaborative leadership. *Nursing Economics, 30*(1), 5, 37.

Nicolaides, V. C., LaPort, K. A., Chen, R. R., Tomassetti, A. J., Weis, E. J., Zaccareo, S. J., & Cortina, J.M. (2014). The shared leadership if teams: A meta-analysis of proximal, distal, and moderating relationships. *The Leadership Quarterly, 25,* 923–942. http://dx.doi.org/10.1016/j.leadqua.2014.06.006.

Northouse, P. G. (2019). *Leadership: Theory and practice* (8th ed.). Thousand Oaks, CA: Sage Publications Inc.

Orchard, C., & Rykhoff, M. (2014). Collaborative leadership within interprofessional practice. In D. Forman, M. Jones, & J. Thistlethwaite, *Leadership and collaboration: Further developments for interprofessional education* (pp. 71–94). Houndsmills, Basingstoke, and Hampshire, UK: Palgrave Macmillan.

Orchard, C., Sonibare, O., Morse, A., Collins, J., & Al-Hamad, A. (2017). Collaborative leadership, part 1: The nurse leader's role within interprofessional teams. *Nursing Leadership, 30*(2), 14–25.

Patrick, A., Laschinger, H. K. L., Wong, C., & Finegan, J. (2011). Developing and testing a new measure of staff nurse clinical leadership: The clinical leadership survey. *Journal of Nursing Management, 19,* 449–460. https://doi.org/10.1111/j.1365-2834.2011.01238.x.

Pearce, C. L. (2004). The future of leadership: Combining vertical and shared leadership to transform knowledge work. *Academy of Management Executive, 18*(1), 47–57.

Pearce, C. L., Manz, C. C., & Sims, H. P. (2014). *Share, don't take the lead.* Charlotte, NC: Information Age Publishing.

Pearce, C. L., & Sims, H. P., Jr. (2002). Vertical versus shared leadership as predictors of the effectiveness of change management teams: An examination of aversive, directive, transactional, transformational, and empowering leader behaviors. *Group Dynamics: Theory, Research & Practice, 6*(2), 172–197. https://doi.org/10.1037/1089-2699.6.2.172.

Pettigrew, T. F., & Tropp, L. R. (2008). How does intergroup contact reduce prejudice? Meta-analytic tests of three mediators. *European Journal of Social Psychology, 38,* 922–934. https://doi.org/10.1002/ejsp.504.

Posner, B. A., & Kouzes, J. M. (1993). Psychometric properties of the leadership practices inventory—Updated. *Educational and Psychological Measurement, 53,* 191–199.

Poulton, B. C., & West, M. A. (1993). The determinants of effectiveness in primary health care teams. *Journal of Interprofessional Care, 13*(1), 7–13.

Raelin, J. (2006). Does action learning promote collaborative leadership? *Academy of Management Learning & Education, 5*(2), 152–168.

Raelin, J. (2011). From leadership-as-practice to leaderful practice. *Leadership, 7*(2), 195–211. https://doi.org/10.1177/1742715010394808.

Raelin, J. A. (2017). Leadership-as-practice: Theory and application—An editor's reflection. *Leadership, 13*(2), 215–221. https://doi.org/10.1177/1742715017702273.

Rykoff, M., Orchard, C., & Wong, C. (2015). *Collaborative leadership: A concept analysis.* Unpublished manuscript, Arthur Labatt Family School of Nursing, Faculty of Health Sciences, Western University, London, Ontario, Canada.

Rykhoff, M., Orchard, C., & Wong, C. (2019). Interprofessional collaborative leadership: A concept analysis. Paper in review.

Saint, S., Kowalski, C. P., Banaszak-Holl, J., Forman, J., Damschroder, L., & Krein, S. L. (2010). The importance of leadership in preventing healthcare-associated infection: Results of a multisite qualitative study. *Infection Control and Hospital Epidemiology, 31*(9), 901–907. https://doi.org/10.1086/655459.

Salas, E., Cooke, N. J., & Rosen, M. A. (2008). On teams, teamwork and team performance: Discoveries and development. *Human Factors, 50*(3), 540–547. https://doi.org/10.1518/001892008x288457.

Sinclair, E., & Orchard, C. (2018, June 26). *Development of the Assessment of Interprofessional Collaborative Leadership Scale (AICLS).* Paper session at the Arthur Labatt Family School of Nursing Research Project session, 2018, Western University, London, Ontario, Canada.

Thompson, P. A., Navarra, M. B., & Antonson, N. (2005). Patient safety: The four domains of nursing leadership. *Nursing Economics, 23*(6), 331–333.

Turning Point National Program. (2017). *Collaborative leadership: Self-assessment questionnaires* [Measurement instrument]. Retrieved from http://www.tamarackcommunity.ca/library/collaborative-leadership-self-assessment-questionnaires.

Van Vactor, J. D. (2012). Collaborative leadership model in the management of health care. *Journal of Business Research, 65*(4), 555–561. https://doi.org/10.1016/j.buses.2011.02021.

van Schaik, S. M., O'Brien, B. C., Almeida, S. A., & Adler, S. R. (2014). Perceptions of interprofessional teamwork in low-acuity settings: A qualitative analysis. *Medical Education, 48*(6), 583–592.

Walker, L. O., & Avant, K. C. (2011). *Strategies for theory construction in nursing* (5th ed.). Upper Saddle River, NJ: Pearson/Prentice Hall.

Wang, D., Waldman, D. A., & Zhang, Z. (2014). A meta-analysis of shared leadership and team effectiveness. *Journal of Applied Psychology, 99*(2), 181–198. https://doi.org/10.1037/a0034531.

Weingardt, R. G. (1996). Partnering: Building a stronger design team. *Journal of Architectural Engineering, 2*(2), 49–54.

Weller, J. M., Barrow, M., & Gasquoine, S. (2011). Interprofessional collaboration among junior doctors and nurses in the hospital setting. *Medical Education, 45,* 478–487. https://doi.org/10.1111/j.1365-2923.2010.03919.x.

West, M., Armit, K., Loewenthal, L., Eckert, R., West, T., & Lee, A. (2015). *Leadership and leadership development in healthcare: The evidence base.* London: Faculty of Medical Leadership and Management.

World Health Organization. (2010). *Framework for action on interprofessional education and collaborative practice.* Geneva: WHO. Retrieved from http://www.who.int/hrh/resources/framework_action/en/.

17

Leadership Resilience in Collaborative Practice Projects in Mental Healthcare in Sabah, Malaysia

Wendy Diana Shoesmith, Loo Jiann Lin, and Sue Fyfe

The issue of sustainability is a problem for many people trying to lead projects, but it is particularly the case for informal leaders, who rely on influence rather than power. The following excerpt describes the experiences of one of the authors (WS) in trying to lead a collaborative practice project, which provided the impetus for writing this chapter:

> I have been running a project in a psychiatric hospital, to try to improve collaborative practice. A 'collaborative practice committee' was started, where staff, patients and carers discussed ways of improving collaboration in the hospital. Although there was initial enthusiasm and high engagement and turnout to meetings, the enthusiasm gradually reduced, both in

W. D. Shoesmith (✉) · L. J. Lin
Universiti Malaysia Sabah, Kota Kinabalu, SBH, Malaysia

S. Fyfe
School of Public Health, Faculty of Health Sciences, Curtin University, Perth, WA, Australia

W. D. Shoesmith
Faculty of Business, Curtin University, Kota Kinabalu, SBH, Malaysia

D. Forman et al. (eds.), *Sustainability and Interprofessional Collaboration*,
https://doi.org/10.1007/978-3-030-40281-5_17

> the committee and in myself. Some of the reasons for that were that decisions were made in the committee meetings and then not carried out, and people who had been initially engaged were transferred to other places. Meetings and training sessions were regularly postponed, normally due to the limited number of staff having more responsibilities than they could cope with. Some of the few initiatives that the committee implemented were reversed. Time was limited for both the leader and the committee members, and our core work and other projects started to take priority. The turnout to meetings and engagement reduced and this reduced my own motivation. However, there have been some positive outcomes from the committee and these successes have recovered motivation.

This chapter attempts to answer questions about what makes a resilient leader in collaborative projects in a low resource setting and explores leadership in three community based collaborative practice projects in mental health. The project leaders were interviewed as a part of a larger research project aiming to understand the decision making environment and design a new model of collaborative care for the mental healthcare system in Sabah, Malaysia. The projects discussed in this chapter are 'passion projects' that were initiated and managed by the leaders themselves and had not been ordered or commissioned by people above them in the hierarchy. Resources and influence had to be gained, rather than coming automatically. In this chapter we will also return to the concept of 'distributed leadership', which was discussed in the previous book (Shoesmith, Sawatan, Abdullah, & Fyfe, 2016) and consider whether the leadership seen in these projects was a function of the individuals or an emergent property of the networks of which they were part.

The Mental Healthcare System in Sabah

Sabah is one of the Malaysian states on the island of Borneo, with a population approaching 4 million. The mental healthcare system is slowly developing, but is still under severe strain, with approximately 0.5 psychiatrists per 100,000 people, which compares to 5.2 psychiatrists per 100,000 in Kuala Lumpur and approximately 10 psychiatrists per 100,000 people in Europe (Guan, Lee, Francis, & Yen, 2018). Other staff are also very limited, with around 40 trained psychiatric nurses and only one clinical psychologist working in healthcare in the state public sector. Patients coming to the psychiatric clinic will typically have only 5 minutes with a doctor who has not had formal training in mental health and whom they have not usually met before. Religious professionals, traditional healers and community leaders fill the gaps in the system and are the first contact for many patients (Shoesmith, Borhanuddin, et al., 2018).

Qualitative research was carried out in 2013 to explore collaborative practice in the mental health system (Shoesmith et al., 2017). We found that most relationships within the healthcare system were hierarchical rather than collaborative. There were six main factors that influenced collaboration in the existing system: collaborative behaviours, autonomy around decision making, motivation toward common goals and values, relatedness (caring, trusting, feeling connected to others), resources and motivation to collaborate. Barriers to collaboration in this system were a hierarchical organisational culture, a lack of persistent relationships (e.g. staff regularly getting transferred, patients seeing a different doctor each time), a lack of resources (including a lack of time to collaborate and a lack of staff trained in basic mental health skills and collaborative skills) and a lack of motivation to collaborate—in that even though many staff saw the value in collaboration they felt that it was too difficult to achieve within the existing system.

In order to try and change or influence these system features, a 'Collaborative Practice Committee' was established, as described in the box above. It aimed to use the research findings to create a model of collaborative care effective in Malaysia. Although this committee made many recommendations, it was very difficult to implement them in the context of the psychiatric hospital. However, three new collaborative projects have developed which have been more successful. These projects are described below, and the ways in which collaboration, motivation and resilience have been developed and sustained by those leaders are then explored.

Project to Reduce Alcohol Related Harm

The Intervention Group for Alcohol Misuse was started in 2009 under Mercy Malaysia (a medical NGO) by Dr. Helen Lasimbang (HL), a consultant obstetrician and gynaecologist, who was the chair of the Sabah chapter of Mercy Malaysia. This group grew into the Association for Alcohol Misuse in 2016. In Sabah, high risk drinking and alcohol related problems are prevalent among some communities (Mutalip, Kamarudin, Manickam, Abd Hamid, & Saari, 2014) and some consider drinking to be part of their culture. Projects have included training community leaders to reduce alcohol related harm in their community, through measures such as preventing the sale of alcohol to children by village shops and awareness building programs (Lasimbang et al., 2017). The group has produced a 'toolkit' of materials for village leaders to help them run activities and is now training village leaders in motivational interviewing techniques. The group collaborates with the Ministry of Health, the Church, schools, the university, NGOs and community organisations. They have secured funding from a large international NGO and have partners in Australia, Thailand and Sweden who advise and help support the work. A new conference -the Borneo Quality of Life Conference—developed from some of the collaborations with the alcohol work.

Collaboration of the Psychiatric Hospital with Traditional Healers

This project was started in 2017, led by specialist psychiatrist Dr. Chua Sze Hung (CS). In indigenous Kadasandusun communities *Bobohizan* are village elders and spiritual leaders who perform rituals at traditional ceremonies. In Sabah many people wish to rule out spiritual causes of mental health disorders by seeking help from *Bobohizan,* before seeking help from mainstream health services. Delays in seeking treatment for mental disorders negatively affect outcomes and make recovery less likely (Perkins, Gu, Boteva, & Lieberman, 2005), and traditional healers are in a good position to help reduce delays in treatment seeking. This project aims to train traditional healers to recognise mental disorders to ensure that treatment is given early, through a collaboration between the psychiatric hospital and the Kadasandusun Association.

Collaborative Practice Project on the Island of Labuan

Labuan is an island off the coast of Sabah with a population of approximately 100,000. In 2016 Dr. Boon Seng Ng (BS) set up a psychiatric service there that he has gradually built into a team of eight healthcare workers trained in the principles of working collaboratively with patients. He has used these principles from the outset, collaborating with school counsellors, village leaders, local NGOs, other specialties, other government departments and a local gym.

The leaders of these three projects were interviewed and transcripts coded to better understand the factors that had made these projects successful. All the leaders were well known by WS and she was one of the team members in the alcohol project. Two of the leaders were also members of the collaborative practice committee (BS and CS). All the leaders gave written informed consent and this project was done as part of the 'Collaborative care in psychiatry' project which had ethical approval from the Ministry of Health ethics committee. All of the leaders were sent the manuscript to approve prior to publication. The transcripts were initially open coded, using N-Vivo software by WS and SF and then discussed to consider higher level themes. A decision was taken to use the same framework that had emerged from previous research on collaboration, since the themes were very similar: (1) Collaborative behaviours (shown in Table 17.1), (2) Motivation towards goals and values, (3) Autonomy, power and influence, (4) Relatedness and personal connections, (5) Resources and (6) Motivation to collaborate with others.

Table 17.1 Collaborative behaviours seen in the leaders

1. *Asking for, accepting and valuing help from others (asking for help, referring to each other, appreciating and valuing the contribution of others)*
All three leaders regularly asked for help from others, referred to others and showed appreciation of others. HL described how asking for help required courage and sometimes led to rejection and that accepting occasional rejection was an important part of resilience
2. *Creating goals and a common vision*
All of the leaders reported that common goals and values were important for motivation. CS described how he deliberately looks for common ground with the Bobohizan:
CS: yes. I think the most important thing in approaching the traditional healer is that we are trying to find common things. There will be a lot of differences but they do agree some things. So we talk about common things first, before we talk about something else
3. *Creating and respecting boundaries and roles*
BS deliberately created a role for himself and made sure that people understood this role by making himself known across the island
BS: And of course I'm trying to market myself - I'm not sure if this is approved method - I'm trying to market myself as someone 'Dr Boon - mental health'. I am trying to familiarise people so that when they talk about Dr Boon they think about mental health. So wherever I go they will say 'ah Dr Boon - I can ask about mental health'. Then they will approach me about mental health
He also created roles for his team roles in leading projects
4. *Sharing information and learning from each other*
All three leaders described sharing knowledge and skills with the people that they are collaborating with as well as these people learning and sharing knowledge with them.
BS: during my mental health talk they actually point out and say 'this person might need some help'
5. *Sharing decision making and creating a plan (including eliciting opinions, sharing opinions, listening, giving opportunity to ask questions)*
BS described teaching his staff to do shared decision making with the patients and discussing with the village leaders about how the project should be done, finding out their ideas and expectations. HL regularly uses shared decision making in community workshops to consider ways to reduce alcohol related harm (Shoesmith, James, Lasimbang, Salumbi, & Eckermann, 2018)
6. *Sharing responsibility and accountability (e.g. proactivity and assertiveness, offering to help, following the agreed plan)*
It was clear that all three of the leaders were extremely proactive, looking for opportunities, rather than feeling afraid of accountability. This is clear from the way that they offer to help people and deliberately find out what people want and need

(continued)

Table 17.1 (continued)

7. *Sharing experiences, rewards and problems* The leaders tried to make the work rewarding for the other team members. BS described how making the environment fun to work in, for example cooking for them, was important for maintaining morale of the team. Sharing the reward of meeting a small goal was mentioned by CS
8. *Undertaking activities together and sharing resources* BS described joint activities with other medical specialties, with the welfare department and the special school department. He also described how the resources of a local gym were used to help motivate kids with behavioural problems, by giving a free session

Motivation Towards Goals/Values

All the leaders appear to have been initially motivated by values, particularly a belief in empowerment and compassion towards an underserved group. Motivation was generally high for all the leaders and a common factor was the persistence with which they worked at the projects and the number of hours of work that they invested.

> *Chua: given that we are probably 1:300,000 [number of psychiatrists per head of population] so everyone is overburdened with their own clinical work, they rarely have time to do something new. So even the Bobohizan thing that we have been doing, ... we are actually doing it over the weekend. This is something like medical volunteerism, it is passion driven.*

All of them described motivation fluctuating and being affected by factors in the external environment as well as their own thoughts and feelings. External factors which affected motivation included access to resources (see section "Resources" below), the perceived response of other people and the perceived outcome.

Effect of Values on Motivation

All project leaders were internally motivated by strong values, which was the trigger for the projects starting and what recovered them during times when things were not going so well. BS had been motivated seeing school children with mental health problems not receiving skilled care and being managed by 'disciplinary action'. CS was motivated by seeing people not seeking help for treatable mental health problems and realising that working together with traditional healers might mean that more of them get help. The reasons for HL were extremely personal, in that she had grown up in an environment with alcohol problems and described stories of violence and illness of people who were close to her.

HL… there was a personal thing, in my village. I am surrounded by people who drink. My parents don't actually drink. My father drink but not very much. My mum don't drink at all. But I am surrounded by people who drink and many of them actually become violent after they are intoxicated with alcohol. And they don't seem to have any place to go for help.

Empowerment was also mentioned as a motivator for BS and HL. As well as triggering projects, values also led to persistence with the project when things got hard.

HL: You know that it is for a good cause, so you just keep persisting and doing it.

Effect of Perceived Outcome on Motivation

The way that the leader perceived the outcomes of the project affected the motivation of the leader. BS and HL mentioned that their projects were complex, with complex outcomes which were difficult to measure. This affected motivation since they sometimes had doubt about whether their projects were making a difference.

HL: I think the main challenge is that you don't see the results. It is very hard to measure the result. Whether you are actually making a difference. Should I continue with this or not? Am I making a difference or not? We have been working on this for so long.

And sometimes you work so hard and people don't recognise -you don't see the outcome, especially in alcohol, you don't see the outcome very fast. We have been working in … for so long and you still see people drinking like crazy. So you are wondering whether you are making a difference at all. So that causes the motivation to go down.

Outcomes which increased motivation for BS included high turnout rates for events, perceived higher awareness of mental health problems and seeing people learning and skills increasing. HL described how other people telling her that the project was making a difference improved motivation. CS deliberately set small goals in order to keep the motivation of the team.

CS: I guess it is about organising meeting and getting smaller projects going, because every success in the smaller project will reinforce the passion and the energy of the people.

Effect of Other People on the Leader's Motivation

All the leaders described how the perceived motivation of other people affected their motivation in continuing with a project. Meeting someone with a similar passion was an important trigger for HL and this meeting pushed her to go to the next step. BS had been inspired by another project run by his lecturer from training and by the original collaborative practice project. Project members and collaborators with high motivation increased the motivation of the leader. Similarly, when team members appeared to disengage, for example by not coming to meetings, it made their motivation reduce.

Recognition and appreciation by other people was an important factor affecting motivation, which was also used as a way of motivating other members of the team.

HL: Of course friends, and we do have people who come to us and say that it has made changes in their life. Some of those people say – thank you so much, I appreciate it and think that our activities help them, so that also motivates ... your reading, your friends, working together and the people that you are trying to help to reduce alcohol related harm, the community.

One leader described how the misinterpretation of some of his motivations by one of the parties with whom he was trying to collaborate severely affected his motivation and nearly ended the project. The effect of others is also seen in the way that they recovered from setbacks, using their social circle as a form of support and a way of gaining courage to discuss the problem.

> *I went to one of my good friends - my support circle … and I managed to pull through. Eventually I went to see the top management … and I managed to talk to them and clear the misunderstanding. And then the collaboration started to build up again and my motivation started to build up again.*

Effect of Thoughts, Feelings and Personal Coping Style on Motivation

The way that external circumstances were perceived made a difference to the leader's motivation. BS described how he had to modify his expectations in order to not get frustrated and to stay motivated.

> *BS: Initially I was so perfectionist - initially I thought everybody is going to like this, then from time to time I was frustrated by some small thing. Then I realised I can't force everybody to collaborate. That is one of the lessons that I get.*

Reading articles and self-help books helped adjust expectations of a quick outcome and built resilience.

> *HL: Because you read a lot of articles and you can see that it is not overnight, it doesn't happen overnight, so that is what keeps you persevering and persistent with the course that you want to do.*

HL also described how persistence was part of her personality.

> *HL: Well I think that one is more like personal. There are some people that really have resilience. I mean I am not saying…I am always a person who*

don't give up easily. I think it is a little more personal, an attitude, a personality. From young I never easily give up, even in my study. So I think it goes through to the work that I do.

Autonomy, Power and Influence

In the original research project, lack of autonomy was a significant barrier to collaboration for the staff in the hospital, with many staff reporting that it was difficult to do anything new because of targets, the risk of being blamed if something goes wrong and rigid boundaries and roles. This is mentioned by CS in relationship to the original project, which had attempted to change things in the hospital.

CS: I guess it is a barrier at the top. The bureaucracy, the hierarchy, there are a lot of things that people need to go through before you can actually get things done, but that also getting things done from up to down, there are a lot of barriers as well because there are not many enthusiastic people.

This was an issue for BS in collaborating with other government workers, in that they normally needed to seek permission from people higher in the hierarchy, which led to delays.

The leaders in these projects were clearly autonomous and making decisions for themselves, although those working within the healthcare system mentioned the need to navigate the hierarchy and influence decision makers, as well as taking risks.

CS: so every service development is going to be a challenge because you are trying to do something new, there will be barriers, you will have to convince a lot of people because I believe in every organisation – everyone will try to play safe, to do things the old way and if we do things the old way. But in order for us to progress there has to be some courage to do new things, there are risks to be taken, but those risks are calculated risks, reasonable risks.

Higher autonomy was partly due to circumstances. CS described how being a professional was helpful for gaining influence.

CS: I guess it is that patriarchal thing in Malaysia. That old concept that doctors know everything. Whatever we say carries more weightage than patients.

BS mentioned that it was easier to do this kind of project on an island than in a large city. It was notable that he had a personal relationship with the hospital director and appeared to know many of the key decision makers on the island. He was also invited to budget meetings, which allowed him to ask for resources. Having access to some money was important for all of them.

Higher autonomy was also due to deliberate attempts of the leaders to increase their influence, in order to get things done. BS used his access to key decision makers and educated them about mental health problems.

BS: So I repeatedly presented this report to the administration in my hospital and I think that was the trigger … so they started to realise that yes this is something we need to take care of that we should pay attention to.

He also researched who to talk to before starting projects:

BS: I do good preparation. Before I meet someone for what I want, I do a study who to approach what to approach and I assess the financial state of the hospital.

BS and CS described using professional associations and councils to influence the people that they want to collaborate with. All the leaders used personal relationships and friendships as a way of gaining influence to get things done. BS used deliberate self-marketing as another way of gaining influence. He also ensured that people working with him would get their own goals met, for example combining the mental health screening with blood pressure and glucose screening. The frequency of contact with people and inviting people to events was also a factor, as described in the next section.

Relatedness and Personal Connections

All the leaders used personal relationships and connections as a way of getting things done. BS was new to the island and set out from the start to gain personal connections with people, using his interest in fitness.

> *BS: I have a lot of social contact I have a lot of fitness circles. The whole of Labuan is my fitness circle ... I do a lot of networking because I know this is very important. I started to find stakeholders who would help me to promote mental health in Labuan.*

He also formed close personal connections with the people that he was collaborating with, allowing them to contact him at any time:

> *BS: I allow them to contact me at any time - I receive email, I receive text messages from teachers every alternate day about how to manage.*

> *BS: One day in the hospital I can walk 10,000 steps. Because I'm frequently going to the office and to other units to invite them to our programs.*

CS described how the project was started with a personal connection and how they developed during the project. HL also described finding people to work with through friends.

Resources

Access to resources was an important factor for all the leaders and the most important resource was enthusiastic people to work with. HL described actively looking for these people, as described above in the 'decision to collaborate' section. CS described how this was an important factor in his decision to start the project.

> *CS: actually I have a lot of things going on at the same time, but this is probably something to do with the resources availability and practicability of it. Because I know that here I do have enough medical officers and staff that are quite enthusiastic when it comes to such projects.*

BS described how he created an engaged and passionate team and created passion in other hospital staff:

BS: Initially I find it hard to engage them. I was hyperactive, I am very hyperactive here. And people see me as someone who can't stop working. Because I'm frequently going to the office and to other units to invite them to our programs. I sponsor by giving a free t-shirt. I bought the unit shirt for them - for the paramedic staff. I cook for them - of course I like to cook. We are working like a family actually.

Getting new resources, for example more funding, was important in motivating them to continue with the project and gave a feeling of recognition.

H: Yes definitely, getting the money, getting the support from them really motivates you, that actually you are being recognised and they can see that you are working.

Losing resources by staff being transferred away was described as demotivating by CS.

Motivation to Collaborate

All the leaders decided to work with others, rather than trying to fulfil their objectives alone. The common factors for deciding to work collaboratively were the recognition that resources were very limited and that working with others would leverage the resources that they had and get more done. BS mentioned that his referral rates had come down as a result of collaborating, but that they had gone up initially.

BS: I get less referrals because what I did was I don't take all the referrals...Initially, in the first phase of the collaboration there was a lot of referrals. Even they referred me someone with schizophrenia ... So there is a few more schizophrenia and autism - now I think they're quite confident to refer autism, now that they have a basic knowledge about autism already.

The leaders all mentioned the rewards of working within a team, for example having fun and sharing experiences. They also mentioned the frustrations of working with others, which had an effect on motivation.

HL described the process of recognising people that she is motivated to collaborate with.

> *HL: how I find these people ... normally we ask friends, who is interested in working towards this. Looking for people with the same passion, the same drive, the same objective. Sometimes you can judge, not judge, you can kind of have an instinct whether these people are interested or not. You start talking and then you call for a meeting and they turn up. That is good enough to show that they are actually interested ... Enthusiasm from them, responsive.*

Conclusions

Interrelated personal, organisational and situational factors motivate and sustain leadership in this system. An understanding of these factors and interactions could help capacity building in this system and help new leaders emerge. Most of the 'leadership behaviours' that these leaders exhibited were also collaborative behaviours. These behaviours and examples of how these leaders show them are listed in Table 17.1. The personal, organisational and situational factors influence the occurrence of these collaborative behaviours. They also showed how they managed thoughts (for example by re-evaluating expectations) and feelings (e.g. fear and shame) so that they did not distract from goals and values.

Understanding the organisational and situational factors is also important if we wish to create systems where new leaders emerge and thrive. Some of the circumstances that allowed these leaders to thrive included adequate autonomy, financial support, mentoring, having a good support network, recognition by others, having access to people in power and getting invited to meetings where decisions are made. Being specialist doctors is also likely to have mattered in this environment in gaining the influence and resources needed to run these projects. BS said that working on an island, rather than a big city, made it much easier to run the project, indicating that working in a small, defined geographical area with clear boundaries mattered. Recreating some of the benefits of this kind of environment in a large hospital or big city may be possible, if thought is given to boundaries and ensuring people on the ground have adequate autonomy and access to people who make the decisions affecting their work. Support networks and training of healthcare staff in using them, for example through peer supervision groups, would also be helpful (Newman, Nebbergall, & Salmon, 2013). Consideration also needs to be given to structural issues, for example how to ensure that potential leaders are not blocked because they are outside a profession that typically leads.

Collaborative practice projects are inherently complex, both because of the complexity of interactions and because collaborations are normally initiated to manage a complex issue. This complexity makes it more difficult to maintain motivation, in that outcomes are difficult to appreciate. The complexity also makes it hard to convince and influence others, because the evidence is more difficult to understand and the expected quantitative evidence base is more difficult to produce and may not be the best form of outcome measure for these kind of projects (Harvey & Walshe, 2007). Measuring outcomes is important because it is one of the things that will make these projects sustainable in the end and because systems based research has been identified as a research priority in low and middle income countries (Sharan et al., 2009). This is more difficult if resources are low, in that the staff need to focus on serving and treating people which leaves little time for research, staff have less access to journals, fewer people are trained in research methods and there is less research funding. Support and collaboration between people from other settings could help with this and with supporting emerging leaders, as was seen in some of these projects.

Collaboration is a double edged sword, with benefits and costs, and sometimes the cost of collaboration is more than the benefit (Huxham & Vangen, 2004). The leaders all described the frustrations of working with others, but also the rewards. There were differences between these leaders and people interviewed in previous projects, because they had persevered with a collaborative approach despite the frustrations that it sometimes gave them. In these projects, the initial investment in collaborative relationships appears to have paid off.

We have previously discussed how an interprofessional education project started as a result of 'distributed leadership' (Shoesmith et al., 2016). This is where change in a system emerges from the interactions within the system rather than through individual action (Bennett, Wise, Woods, & Harvey, 2003; Bolden, 2011; Gronn, 2000). Although this chapter has focussed on the actions of three individual leaders, one of the most important learning points is the role of the networks of which they are part. Projects started as a result of conversations and interactions with other people, and one project nearly ended due to one of these interactions. The motivation of the leaders fluctuated based on the people that surrounded them, whether they came to meetings, appeared motivated, had similar goals and values, appeared to understand their motivations and whether they gave recognition to and valued their work. These leaders all recognised that they were part of a network and both actively used it and, in some ways, inoculated themselves against the negative effects. They surfed the waves of motivation from the network, rather than drowning in them, and created and used influence to make new waves. Leadership can be considered an emergent property of the network, but it would not have crystallised without the individual actions of the people described here.

Acknowledgements We would like to thank Dr. Helen Lasimbang, Dr. Chua Sze Hung and Dr. Boon Seng Ng for allowing us to tell their stories in this chapter. We would also like to thank the Director General of Health Malaysia for permission to publish this paper.

References

Bennett, N., Wise, C., Woods, P. A., & Harvey, J. A. (2003). Distributed leadership: A review of literature. In *National college for school leadership*. Retrieved from http://oro.open.ac.uk/8534/.

Bolden, R. (2011). Distributed leadership in organizations: A review of theory and research. *International Journal of Management Reviews, 13*(3), 251–269. https://doi.org/10.1111/j.1468-2370.2011.00306.x.
Gronn, P. (2000). Distributed properties: A new architecture for leadership. *Educational Management and Administration, 28*(3), 317–338. https://doi.org/10.1177/0263211X000283006.
Guan, N. C., Lee, T. C., Francis, B., & Yen, T. S. (2018, June). *Psychiatrists in Malaysia: The ratio and distribution.*
Harvey, G., & Walshe, K. (2007). Realist review—A new method of systematic review designed for complex policy interventions getting the most out of the findings. *Journal of Health Services Research & Policy, 10*(20), 21–34. Retrieved from https://journals.sagepub.com/doi/pdf/10.1258/1355819054308530.
Huxham, C., & Vangen, S. (2004). Doing things collaboratively: Realizing the advantage or succumbing to inertia? *Organizational Dynamics, 33*(2), 190–201. https://doi.org/10.1016/j.orgdyn.2004.01.006.
Lasimbang, H. B., Shoesmith, W., Mohd Daud, M. N., Kaur, N., Jin, M. C. P., Singh, J., … Amir, L. (2017). Private troubles to public issue: Empowering communities to reduce alcohol-related harm in Sabah, Malaysia. *Health Promotion International, 32*(1). https://doi.org/10.1093/heapro/dav090.
Mutalip, M. H. B. A., Kamarudin, R. B., Manickam, M., Abd Hamid, H. A. B., & Saari, R. B. (2014). Alcohol consumption and risky drinking patterns in Malaysia: Findings from NHMS 2011. *Alcohol and Alcoholism, 49*(5), 593–599. https://doi.org/10.1093/alcalc/agu042.
Newman, D. S., Nebbergall, A. J., & Salmon, D. (2013). Structured peer group supervision for novice consultants: Procedures, pitfalls, and potential. *Journal of Educational and Psychological Consultation, 23*(3), 200–216. https://doi.org/10.1080/10474412.2013.814305.
Perkins, D. O., Gu, H., Boteva, K., & Lieberman, J. A. (2005). Relationship between duration of untreated psychosis and outcome in first-episode schizophrenia: A critical review and meta-analysis. *American Journal of Psychiatry, 162*(10), 1785–1804. https://doi.org/10.1176/appi.ajp.162.10.1785.
Sharan, P., Gallo, C., Gureje, O., Lamberte, E., Mari, J. J., Mazzotti, G., … Saxena, S. (2009). Mental health research priorities in low- and middle-income countries of Africa, Asia, Latin America and the Caribbean. *British Journal of Psychiatry, 195*(4), 354–363. https://doi.org/10.1192/bjp.bp.108.050187.

Shoesmith, W. D., Borhanuddin, A. F. B. A., Pereira E.J., Nordin, N., Giridharan, B., Forman, D., & Fyfe, S. (2020). Barriers and enablers to collaboration in the mental health system in Sabah, Malaysia: towards a theory of collaboration. *British Journal of Psychiatry Open, 6*(1), 1–10. https://doi.org/10.1192/bjo.2019.92.

Shoesmith, W. D., Borhanuddin, A. F. B. A., Yong Pau Lin, P., Abdullah, A. F., Nordin, N., Giridharan, B., ... Fyfe, S. (2018). Reactions to symptoms of mental disorder and help seeking in Sabah, Malaysia. *International Journal of Social Psychiatry, 64*(1), 49–55. https://doi.org/10.1177/0020764017739643.

Shoesmith, W. D., James, S., Lasimbang, H. B., Salumbi, E., & Eckermann, E. (2018). Diamond dialogue: A tool to explore alcohol-related harm and strengthen community action. *Borneo Journal of Medical Sciences, 12*(2), 19–26.

Shoesmith, W. D., Sawatan, W., Abdullah, A. F., & Fyfe, S. (2016). Leadership and evaluation issues in interprofessional education in Sabah, Malaysia. In *Leading research and evaluation in interprofessional education and collaborative practice* (pp. 193–212). https://doi.org/10.1057/978-1-137-53744-7.

18

Concluding Reflections

Jill Thistlethwaite and Marion Jones

The themes of this book are sustainability and resilience within the interprofessional milieu, though they have applicability in many areas of health professional practice and education. In this final chapter we reflect on these two words, their meanings and relevance to interprofessional education and collaborative practice. We also consider the recurring language and concepts used by chapter authors to define, describe and analyse their work, and how these have resonated with ourselves.

Sustainability

The word **sustainable** is typically used these days to relate to the environment. To be sustainable for future generations, we all need to protect our planet's environment from harm by reducing carbon emissions and

J. Thistlethwaite (✉)
Faculty of Health, University of Technology Sydney, Ultimo, NSW, Australia
e-mail: jill.thistlethwaite@uts.edu.au

M. Jones
Auckland University of Technology, Auckland, New Zealand

D. Forman et al. (eds.), *Sustainability and Interprofessional Collaboration*,
https://doi.org/10.1007/978-3-030-40281-5_18

the depletion of our natural resources in order to support ecological balance in the long term. The move to sustainability requires evidence of damage to persuade the deniers of the need for change, and what will reduce or reverse this damage, as well as climate champions, large scale human behaviour change, committed leadership, appropriate legislation and global collaboration. Yes: the parallels with sustainable health care and health professional education initiatives are obvious.

In this book our chapter authors are interprofessional champions. Some describe interventions that have stood the test of time and have become embedded in their local environments. Some chapters report on more recent initiatives and steps that are being taken to ensure longevity. Some talk of the champions who have been critical for the sustainability of interprofessional development. From our experience and knowledge of the literature, factors that improve the likelihood of sustained change for interprofessional initiatives are individual and institutional motivation, interprofessional champions with a passionate desire to improve health care provision and learner experience, adequate resources including protected funding and personnel, and both top down and bottom up approaches.

It is important to remember that IPE dates back over fifty years. Interprofessional learning involving students from many health professions has been reported in Australia, the United Kingdom and the USA as well as other countries since the 1960s (Barr, 2014). IPE as a concept is therefore resilient. However, over the last 20–30 years of our personal work in this area we would describe the journey of IPE as one of peaks and troughs, with each peak slightly higher than the one before. The implementation of interprofessional approaches and activities into mainstream health professional education has taken time and we have seen many false starts and false dawns. For those with less practical experience than ourselves, the depth and breadth of IPE globally cannot be gauged solely from reading the literature, which is still dominated by English-language journals and western-facing authorship. We know from our travels and networking that there is much going on in countries under-represented in academic publications outside their own jurisdictions. Some of the projects have been included in our series of books, of which this is the fourth volume. We are also aware of projects that have not been sustained: champions have moved on, leadership has changed, accreditation standards have failed to emphasise the need for interprofessionalism, and so on.

Frequently IPE initiatives during pre-qualification begin as pilot projects or student selected placements. Logistics then become difficult if such small-scale interventions need to be scaled up for larger cohorts, which may include over 500 students from the different health professions. In our experience the logistical issues of timetables and student numbers are often cited as major barriers to reform. However, with interprofessional and interdisciplinary collaboration, these barriers can be overcome by strong leadership and collaboration across and within faculties and schools. In more recent years, when and where national accreditation standards mandate for IPE, universities and postgraduate training bodies actively seek interprofessional expertise and momentum builds. The World Health Organization's guidelines (WHO, 2013) define the transformative scaling up of health professionals' education and training as: 'the sustainable expansion and reform of health professionals' education and training to increase the quantity, quality and relevance of health professionals, and in so doing strengthen the country health systems and improve population health outcomes' (p. 11). The WHO goes on to describe the key issues that change agents need to consider: cost of changes to education and whether these can be afforded; the sources of funding; how and where to allocate money; how to ensure that funding is sustained (WHO, 2013). Alongside these issues is the all-important 'buy in' to be gained from the institutions, senior staff, educators and practitioners, who all need to work together in the development, motivation to work interprofessionally and sustainability of interprofessional learning and working.

In the pre-qualification space, we recommend that appropriately designed learning experiences should be explicitly designated in the formal curriculum as interprofessional to emphasise the importance of IPE. These can be through programmes of study including simulation, clinical placements, informal and formal learning experiences both in class as well as in practice. However, we feel that isolated interprofessional elements that are not integrated with other areas of clinical practice can leave IPL vulnerable and open to being dropped from the curriculum. We therefore advocate that, to enhance the likelihood of interprofessional sustainability, interprofessional learning is embedded with other clinical activities (Freeth, Savin-Baden, & Thistlethwaite, 2019). Examples include: mixed teams of students shadowing clinical teams and/or providing patient care under supervision; placements with agencies that work with patients whose needs are met though interprofessional or interagency collaboration; and patient-safety projects (Freeth et al., 2019).

In addition to considering the sustainability of programmes and interventions, we also need to mention the sustainability of the impact of IPE and subsequent interprofessional collaborative practice. As we know, interprofessional pioneers are still asked to provide evidence of effectiveness of interprofessional education for collaborative practice (IPECP) before widespread adoption at their institutions. In many cases such evidence is expected to include impact on patient outcomes, and indeed sustained impact in relation to improved health care. We concur with the Institute of Medicine's statement in its review of impact:

> Optimally, the business case would include evidence on the sustainability of IPE interventions; their impact on system outcomes, including organisational and practice changes and health care costs; and the resulting patient and population benefits. However, it is worth noting that complex analyses of this type typically are not being conducted for any education reform effort and that IPE should not be held to a unique standard. (Institute of Medicine, 2015, p. 42)

This all reinforces the importance of educational institutions and clinical practice areas working together to develop interprofessional capability and practice (Nisbet et al., 2018).

Resilience

The concept of **resilience** is trending in health professional education and health care practice. This has been mainly in relation to health professionals' own resilience and its possible role in preventing or recovering from stress and burnout, though this onus on the individual is not without its critics (Thistlethwaite, 2018). In terms of sustainability, while the self-care element is important, we are more interested in institutional or organisational resilience, an attribute defined in business terms as an organisation being able to adapt and evolve as global circumstances change, to respond to short-term shocks and longer-term challenges in order to survive and prosper (Australian Government, n.d.). In health care a more succinct definition has been proposed: 'a system's ability to continue to perform and meet its objectives in the face of challenges' (Barasa, Mbau, & Gilson, 2018, p. 496). The hallmarks of this type of resilience are adaptability and transformation. In the broadest terms IPE and interprofessional practice, while needing to stay within the definition of learning from, with and about, are paramount in development together. They need to adapt to local circumstances and be transformed over time as health care needs also change locally and nationally. Without such adaptation and transformation, they are unlikely to be sustained. Working together across education and practice requires the type of leadership that can build bridges, demonstrate resilience when adverse events happen for individuals and teams, and can continue to move forward.

What the Authors Are Saying: Recurring Language and Concepts

The concept of leadership, as expected, runs throughout this book, as it is the overarching theme of the series. Authors discuss different types of leadership including: collaborative, shared, distributed, transformational and the concept of servant as leader. These are not top down, hierarchical models but those that reflect the nature of the word 'interprofessional' itself. However, the engagement with the more traditional institutional type of leadership within universities is important to facilitate sustainability and, importantly, to negotiate resources.

Funding is certainly necessary but not sufficient for change, including funding for curriculum and faculty development, networks, meetings, travel, start-up costs and continuing implementation. In addition, to be truly patient and client-centred, and to include patients and communities as partners in education, payment should be given for such involvement—altruism has a real and worthwhile cost. However, when there are fewer resources, solutions tend to be more creative.

Partnerships are imperative: consensus-based, perhaps with formal constitutions, certainly with shared purposes, a clear, collective vision and commitment, as well as regular meetings, which may be virtual. The role of technology is important in keeping connected. But partnerships too need to adapt and transform. Members need to be culturally sensitive and opportunities should be equitable. There must be trust and respect. Both take time to build and both are vulnerable at times of stress.

With the acknowledgment of being patient with gains over time, interprofessional leadership development requires champions working with others to help the sustainability and development of new leaders. Interprofessional.global is a confederation which has the mission of serving as an agent of change in providing global leadership to advocate for, collaborate on, promote, develop, and research IPECP innovation. It provides the forum for interprofessional networks, special interest groups and special working groups (for example, academic and workforce) to meet through video conference and to use each other's resources to develop interprofessional learning and working globally. With regular meetings online and the ability to network for specific guidance and support, Interprofessional.global fosters interprofessional collaborative working and learning globally. In addition, there is the need for resilient leaders and organisations that move forward with interprofessional values and principles, in combination with integrity and strength during times of adversity, and realistic knowledge of risk and success (Novak, 2016; Southwick, Martini, Charney, & Southwick, 2016).

Finally, we must never forget the role of learners and students. They need to be involved from an early stage in interprofessional learning and educators need to listen to their feedback and suggestions. These are out future leaders and thinkers, those who will need to sort out the challenges of the later parts of the twenty-first century.

References

Australian Government. (n.d.). *Organisational resilience.* Available from https://www.organisationalresilience.gov.au/Pages/default.aspx. Accessed 12 Oct 2019.

Barasa, E., Mbau, R., & Gilson, L. (2018). What is resilience and how can it be nurtured? A systematic review of the empirical literature on organizational resilience. *International Journal of Health Policy and Management, 7*(6), 491–503.

Barr, H. (2014). Leading the way. In D. Forman, M. Jones, & J. E. Thistlethwaite (Eds.), *Leadership development for interprofessional education and collaborative practice* (pp. 15–25). Basingstoke: Palgrave.

Freeth, D., Savin-Baden, M., & Thistlethwaite, J. E. (2019). Interprofessional education. In T. Swanwick, B. O'Brien, & K. Forrest (Eds.), *Understanding medical education* (3rd ed., pp. 191–206). Oxford: Wiley.

Institute of Medicine. (2015). *Measuring the impact of interprofessional education on collaborative practice and patient outcomes.* Washington, DC: The National Academies Press.

Nisbet, G., Raymond, J., Batstone, A., Barclay, T., Barraclough, F., Haq, I., … Stuart-Smith, W. (2018). Building interprofessional learning sustainability: Development and evaluation of an interprofessional learning placement resource. *Health Education in Practice: Journal of Research for Professional Learning, 1*(2). https://openjournals.library.sydney.edu.au/index.php/HEP/article/view/13096.

Novak, J. C. (2016). Interdisciplinary and interprofessional collaboration: Essential for the doctoral advanced practice nurse. In H. M. Dreher & M. E. S. Glasgow (Eds.), *DNP role development for doctoral advanced nursing practice.* New York: Springer.

Southwick, F. S., Martini, B. L., Charney, D. S., & Southwick, S. M. (2016). Leadership and resilience. In J. Marques & S. Dhiman (Eds.), *Leadership today: Practices for personal and professional performance* (pp. 315–334). Cham, Switzerland: Springer.

Thistlethwaite, J. E. (2018). Be positive: resilience is all you need… *The Clinical Teacher, 15,* 359–360.

World Health Organization. (2013). *Transforming and scaling up health professionals' education and training: World Health Organization guidelines 2013.* Geneva: WHO.

Index

D. Forman et al. (eds.), *Sustainability and Interprofessional Collaboration*, https://doi.org/10.1007/978-3-030-40281-5

The manufacturer's authorised representative in the EU is Springer
Nature Customer Service Centre GmbH, Europaplatz 3, 69115 Heidelberg,
Germany. If you have any concerns regarding our products, please
contact ProductSafety@springernature.com

Printed and bound by CPI Group (UK) Ltd, Croydon, CR0 4YY
30/09/2026
02225644-0014